Competitive Advantage in Investing

Competitive Advantage in Investing

Building Winning Professional Portfolios

Steven Abrahams

Registered Office(s)

John Wiley & Sons, Inc., 111 River Street, Hoboken, NJ 07030, USA

Editorial Office

111 River Street, Hoboken, NJ 07030, USA

For details of our global editorial offices, customer services, and more information about Wiley products visit us at www.wiley.com.

Wiley also publishes its books in a variety of electronic formats and by print-on-demand. Some content that appears in standard print versions of this book may not be available in other formats.

Library of Congress Cataloging-in-Publication Data

Names: Abrahams, Steven, 1959- author.
Title: Competitive advantage in investing : building winning professional
   portfolios / Steven Abrahams.
Description: First Edition. | Hoboken : Wiley, 2020. | Includes index.
Identifiers: LCCN 2019056753 (print) | LCCN 2019056754 (ebook) | ISBN
   9781119619840 (cloth) | ISBN 9781119619857 (adobe pdf) | ISBN
   9781119619864 (epub)
Subjects: LCSH: Investments. | Portfolio management.
Classification: LCC HG4521 .A216 2020 (print) | LCC HG4521 (ebook) | DDC
   332.6—dc23
LC record available at https://lccn.loc.gov/2019056753
LC ebook record available at https://lccn.loc.gov/2019056754

Cover Design: Wiley
Cover Image: © ChubarovY/Getty Images

Set in 9.5/12.5pt STIXTwoText by SPi Global, Chennai, India

V35CB7C6D-85F4-45B9-9C8E-3DC419E13927_022820

To Maryann and Stuart,
who got me started,
and to Valerie, Ben, Margot, and Jake,
who kept me going.

Contents

Preface

Take a little time at some point to look over the public portfolios of a few larger investors. Pick a mix of mutual funds or hedge funds or banks or insurers, for example. It could include almost any professionally managed portfolio. It should start to become clear that investing takes place over a wide and diverse landscape.

Each portfolio will differ from others in ways large and small. Each manager will describe the business in different terms. Some will talk about stocks, some about bonds, some about things different altogether. Some will emphasize income, some will emphasize price. Some will talk stability, others not. Issues important to one will barely show up in the notes for another. Each portfolio will seem to run like a separate business. And that is true for the thousands of portfolios that come into the markets every day.

Similar to any other business, investment portfolios compete to make the best out of opportunities that flow through the markets daily. Similar to any other business, the most successful assess themselves and others up and down the line and create and sustain competitive advantage. Plenty of good work has challenged the ability of any investor to consistently beat the competition. But practitioners and students of finance increasingly realize some portfolios simply are better positioned than others to generate quality returns. The reasons vary, but the best investors know their relative strengths and weaknesses and try to anticipate circumstances where their strengths might capture returns unavailable to others in the market. The competitive landscape constantly evolves. Investing is a competition, but not everyone is playing the same game.

Most of the written work on investing barely reflects the diversity of portfolios and the competition between them. The daily press and most magazines, journals, and books usually offer an eclectic mix. There's the daily drama of winners and losers. There's nuts-and-bolts advice for practitioners. There are formal treatments of finance that abstract away from the institutional details of the markets. Between these islands of information is a sparse archipelago. This book tries to build a bridge from daily headlines to the actual work of most institutional port-folio managers and on to the formal literature on investing.

The formal literature does capture an important strand of institutional investing in its emphasis on balancing risk and return. This strand tends to view investing as a world of assets with particular expected risks, returns, and correlations. In the version of this world that has dominated formal finance since the 1950s, all investors see the future in just the same way and share the same expectations of asset performance. In its strongest form, the formal work in finance largely rules out the possibility of portfolios with sustainable strengths and weaknesses. This line of work has produced important insight into the best ways to trade off return against risk in both individual investments and portfolios. It has put an important spotlight on the value of diversification. And it has led to valuable tools for break-ing investor performance into the part likely due to simply taking risk and the part due to the managers' skill. At some point, practicing institutional investors do bal-ance the relative value of different assets and try to add something to portfolio performance.

Still, some of the most widely taught tenets of modern investing seem oddly distant from the concerns and activity of investors in the market every day. Some theories imply investors should largely hold portfolios of similar assets, but few do. Some theories imply little room for investors to generate performance much better than the broad market, but investors nevertheless go into the market looking for it every day. Some theories imply that investment risk, return, and correlation is all that matters, but the daily work of professional investors seems consumed by so many other things.

The formal literature on investing often assumes away the institutional con-straints that set boundaries for portfolios managing most of the world's capital. These constraints create the strengths and weaknesses that enable different portfolios to look at the same assets and see different opportunities. Only in the last decade or so have some of the best students of finance at universities and investment portfolios started to weave these constraints into explanations of asset returns and market behavior. Work that explains the origin of institutional constraints and their impact on investment and asset value offers a better theory of the markets. It explains more of investors' observed behavior.

Although the formal literature rarely deals with the institutional constraints, the literature for practitioners at times seems to deal only with these constraints. Part of the practitioners' literature lays out the definitions and conventions of securities markets. Part focuses on accounting, tax, and regulation. Part focuses on ways to finance investments. Part outlines ways to manage assets against liabilities. These are necessary and practical topics, but they do not point the way toward building a competitive investment business. Among other things, the work for practitioners rarely links back to the genuinely valuable framework that ties risk to reward and highlights the powerful implications of diversification.

Competitive advantage shapes the business of investing as much as it does any business. Some portfolios find themselves better equipped to expand into new areas or respond to investment opportunity. Some find themselves better able to leverage, deleverage, or tailor the risk and return in existing assets. Some portfolios find themselves better informed, better able to hold assets under different accounting or tax treatments, better able to navigate regulations and politics. These things and others create configurations of competitive advantage.

Portfolios that recognize strengths and weaknesses improve their chances of earning sustainable returns beyond those of broad market averages. In practice, most portfolios specialize in their strengths. This usually gets little attention in formal theory, which often relies on the simplifying assumption that all investors have the same information and investment capacities. Of course, this also implies that no investor can deliver consistent excess return and that no portfolio can sustain advantage.

Competitive advantage also figures in anticipating the plausible future states of the world, which is central to good investing. After all, future economic growth, interest rates and lending terms, hedging, information flow, taxes and accounting rules, political and regulatory changes, technology, and so on all shape investment returns. Some portfolios have comparative advantage in anticipating this kind of change. And, empirically, the time and effort spent by investors on forecasting attests to the importance of anticipating a probabilistic future.

Finally, competing portfolios shape the value of different assets all the time. Formal finance acknowledges the idiosyncrasies of preferred risk and return across investors. But once institutional constraints lead large blocks of capital to adopt similar preferences, then the idiosyncrasies of individual portfolios coalesce into systemic influences on asset value. Investors will demand compensation for these systemic influences. Among other things, the value of the US Treasury market, the agency mortgage-backed securities market, and the corporate debt market, among others, have been shaped in the last few decades by episodes of major institutional capital flow responding less to return, risk, and correlation than to policy and regulation.

This book brings together investment theory, practice, and markets to explain the differing goals of professional investment portfolios, the sources of competition between them, and the impact of competition on asset value. For theorists, it adds to the list of systemic factors that drive asset value by breaking global asset markets into local ones. For practitioners, it frames the business of investing as a competition with other portfolios operating under similar constraints. For market analysts, it details the ways that scale, leverage, funding, hedging, information, tax and accounting, and regulation and politics can suddenly shift the playing field.

The book starts with the ideas that brought investing into the modern era. Harry Markowitz revolutionized investing by changing it from an exercise in calculating present value into one of balancing risk, return, and diversification. William Sharpe and his peers then built on work by Markowitz and others to develop the capital asset pricing model, or CAPM. CAPM would offer a beautiful theory of investing but arguably one that hid as much as it revealed.

In the half-century after CAPM's debut, its critics would steadily pile up one piece of evidence after another showing shortfalls in the model's description of markets. Analysts at universities and across Wall Street would offer expanded versions of CAPM to explain the anomalies. The local capital asset pricing model, introduced here, is one such version. Local CAPM explicitly builds in competitive advantage and disadvantage across portfolios and their impact on asset value. The sources of advantage and disadvantage are specific and their impact unique.

From investment theory, the book swings into analysis of the broad investment platforms and special vehicles that dominate markets. Mutual funds and hedge funds compete to generate total returns. Banks and insurers manage asset portfolios against a series of specific liabilities. Broker/dealers stand between investors but still extract investment return and shape markets. Real estate investment trusts and sovereign wealth funds reflect the impact of mixing public policy with investment portfolios. And the potential advantages that individual investors might have in highly competitive markets get treatment here as well.

This guide is for researchers who want a better model for the observed behavior of investors. This is a guide for practicing investors who want a better, formal framework for managing the investment process and building a competitive business. This is also for students of markets who want to understand how the behavior of investors can shape the value of assets.

Kurt Lewin, the psychologist, noted that there is nothing so practical as a good theory. A good theory organizes facts and simplifies and explains an otherwise complex landscape without diminishing its most important features. The book you are about to read takes a resolute step in that direction.

Steven Abrahams
September 9, 2019

Acknowledgments

The 2008 financial crisis planted the seeds for this book. I was at Bear Stearns watching everything going on around me in the markets and covering much of it as part of Bear's fixed income research team. My job let me range across different markets and talk to different investors in the US and abroad. It had been the case throughout my Wall Street career that advantages and disadvantages mattered in investing, and the crisis made it especially clear. When Bear collapsed, I decided to try to relay some of what I had learned to a new generation.

Glenn Hubbard, dean at the Columbia Business School, and Galen Hite, who organized the adjunct faculty for him, warmed to the idea of a course that would focus on ways that different institutional portfolios dealt with markets. They gave me the chance to design and offer the course, and I took it. I've been grateful ever since.

From that first semester, the students at Columbia Business School taught me as much as I taught them. There was no precedent for the course, much less a book, so I started doing the background work and developing the materials that evolved over the years into these pages. The students contributed excellent ideas, challenged me to hone my own, and taught me that a good lecture is as much a performance as anything else. I thank them for the education.

The clients and colleagues that explained the way different portfolios work, or just showed me by analyzing the same markets in such different ways for such different reasons, also deserve thanks. My list of contacts, which I've kept carefully since my first day on the Street, runs into the thousands. They all deserve some credit. The job of analyst has always seemed an extraordinarily good place to satisfy curiosity. Morgan Stanley, Bear Stearns, Deutsche Bank, and Amherst Pierpont have given me the opportunity. I've taken full advantage.

Some friends in the business deserve specific mention for carefully reading sections of this book and offering thoughtful comments. Richard Dewey, Albert Papa, Glenn Perillo, and Robert Thompson kindly read parts of the manuscript on tight deadline. Of course, any shortfalls or errors in this book are entirely mine.

Kevin Harreld, Michael Henton, and Richard Samson at John Wiley & Sons have encouraged me throughout the drafting of this manuscript and worked with me patiently to get all the details right for publication. To my partners at Wiley, thank you.

As for my family, I thank them for the time on nights and weekends I needed to work through the book, for their support and encouragement, and for the beautiful spot by the lake in New Jersey where much of the writing took place and where all good things happen.

Steven Abrahams
September 9, 2019

Part I

Theory

1

Welcome, Harry Markowitz

In the Beginning

Imagine a simple beginning. You have some spare cash. You have covered your daily cost of living and other bills, and it's rattling around in your pocket. You start thinking about what you might do with it. Other than spend it, that is. That is the beginning. With that thought, you have become an investor.

Or imagine that you are sitting at a bank or insurance company or mutual fund. Or a hedge fund or some other place that invests professionally. In front of you is a number with the cash you have to invest. You have work to do.

You start penciling out a list. It's short at first. Maybe you think about putting the money in a drawer just because it's convenient. Perhaps you think about putting the money in a bank. Or you think about making a loan to someone or some company somewhere in the world. You think about investing as an owner of a business or several businesses. You imagine a budding international empire of businesses. The list has only started.

You could buy a bond from a government or from a company somewhere in the world. You could buy stock. You could buy an option, where someone takes a payment today and agrees to either buy or sell something at a certain price in the future. You could buy insurance or a contract that works like insurance, where someone takes a payment today and agrees to cover losses or damage in the future. You could buy gold or silver, wheat or orange juice, oil or other commodities. You could buy an apartment or an apartment building, an office building, or other commercial property. That's a lot to consider, but the list goes on.

You could buy shares in funds managed by professional investors—even if you are a professional investor yourself. The fund would invest on your behalf in any or all of the available markets. You could buy shares in funds that make loans, buy and sell private companies, buy and sell bonds or equity, own options or commodities or real estate, or any combination of these and other things. You could own funds that trade their investments all the time or almost never. The list continues.

It you printed this list out and watched the pages tick off of the printer and slide onto the floor, it would likely run longer than the longest list you have ever seen. It would fill up the room, spill into the hallway, out the front door, and down the street. It would keep going from there. You could follow it to the ocean and watch it start to fill up the deepest parts. The list would literally be endless.

Now that you have this infinite list, choose. Build your portfolio.

Choose Wisely

The challenge of investing becomes a challenge of choice and choosing wisely.

If you avoid the temptation to put the infinite list aside and do nothing, you may start to notice something common to all of these investments. Something that unifies them. Something that simplifies them. Something that enables you to compare each item on your infinite list to every other.

Start with the money in the drawer. You put the money there, and time passes. One day, you open the drawer and take the money out. You spend it.

Consider another simple investment: depositing money in a bank. You put the money in the bank, and time passes. The bank pays interest on your deposit. One day, you take the deposit and the interest out of the bank. You spend it.

Now consider another investment: a loan. You give the borrower cash. The borrower makes interest payments on a certain schedule and then returns the cash. The investment ends. You spend it.

Consider a related investment: a bond. You buy a bond with cash. The cash goes to a government or company. The government or company pays interest on a certain schedule and then repays the cash. The investment ends.

Consider buying a company or making an investment in common stock or some other form of ownership. The investor buys the stock or the ownership stake with cash. The company uses the cash to operate its business, taking in revenues and paying expenses. Whatever is left over after expenses either gets reinvested in the business or returned to investors as a dividend. The investor never gets back the original cash, although the investor can sell the stock or the ownership stake to another buyer.

Then consider options, insurance, commodities, real estate, and funds. It's a couple of lifetimes' worth of considering.

One thing unifies all of these investments: cash flow. All investing in all of its various forms starts and ends with cash flowing in and cash flowing out of an investment. The world has endless notes, articles, books, and guides to the particular ways that cash flows in and out of different kinds of investments. The investments may seem very different, but underneath the complexities and nuances of different investments is the flow of cash or value into and out of an investment over time. Look through the different names and details to the cash flow. Cash flow is investing stripped to its essentials. Cash flow is all that matters.

Different forms of investment simply entitle investors to different cash flows. The money in the drawer only generates cash in and cash out. A bank deposit generates cash and interest. A loan or bond typically gets principal and interest. Equity gets whatever cash flow is left after a business pays expenses. An option gets the chance to buy debt or equity or something else at some future date. Premiums paid for insurance get the right to recover future damages or losses.

Even when investment advice never mentions cash flow—when it focuses on buying low and selling high, or timing or not timing the market, or momentum or value investing, or the like—it still involves putting something of value in and taking something of value out. If that's not the case, then it's not an investment. It's the purchase of goods or services. Or it's a donation.

All Cash Flow Includes Risk

Both before Harry Markowitz and since, investment theory and practice has followed the thread of cash flow that runs through every item on the infinite list and has woven a broad fabric. Different investments generate cash flow over different time lines. Cash flow can come tomorrow, the next day, or years later. The frequency or circumstances of future cash flow can be easy or hard to predict. Value invested today produces expected value tomorrow. Reasonable people will disagree about the timing or magnitude of return, but the value of any investment ultimately ties back to cash in and cash out.

Think again about the list of investments. The cash in the drawer is there whenever you need it. The bank deposit is usually there, too, whenever you need it. An investor in a loan or bond usually has to wait to get interest and to have principal returned. The cash flow from a stock or other form of ownership depends on the operations of the business.

The timing of cash flows matters. Cash may not be able to buy as much in the future as it can today, so future cash may not be worth as much as cash in the pocket today. The cash in the drawer may be safe, but it may not be able to buy a loaf of bread, a dozen eggs, and a carton of milk at the same price tomorrow. For professional investors at banks or insurers or other funds, cash in a drawer may not be enough to meet future obligations to customers or partners. If prices go up, that is, if there's inflation, then the money in the drawer loses value. Or for professional investors, if customers' or partners' need for return rises, cash in a drawer may not be enough. Timing of cash flow matters because the longer it takes to get the cash, the greater the possibility that the cash loses buying power or falls short of investment expectations. In that case, time truly is money.

Timing matters, too, because borrowers compete for cash over different horizons. Borrowers offer to pay different interest rates over different horizons. The supply and demand for cash leads to a clearing rate at each horizon, often called *the real rate of interest*.

Cash flow also may not be certain. The borrower disappears or has a run of bad luck and cannot repay. Banks fail. The bond issuer fails. The company falls on hard times. Earnings rise and fall. Laws and regulations change. Taxes go up and down.

The cash flow from an investment can range from stable and predictable down to the last penny to wildly uncertain. Cash flow is dynamic. It is the fingerprint of each investment.

Investors can pack concern about the future value of cash or its uncertainty into a discount rate for each cash flow and add them all up into the discounted present value of any investment.[1] That becomes the first unifying, simplifying feature of all investments: present value. Investments with short cash flows and long cash flows, safe cash flows and uncertain or risky cash flows all get summarized in one number: present value. The infinite list of investments gets reduced to an infinite list of present values. The list of present values gets sorted from highest to lowest. Now, perhaps, choosing from the infinite list looks simple. Just pick the best.

Risk Is the Mirror to Return

It may seem that investing comes down to simply choosing the investment with the highest expected return, a single investment that for every dollar going in delivers the most dollars out. It could be the stock expected to appreciate the most or pay the

---

1 The value of cash flow over time depends on the cost to borrow money. That is the definition of a rate of interest. Various individuals and companies compete to borrow money over different horizons: a day, a week, a month, a year, 5 or 10 years and so on. Investors with disposable cash lend to borrowers. The demand for and supply of money at each horizon sets a price often called *the real rate of interest*. An investor may lend at the real rate of interest but still need compensation for inflation and other risks. The real rate, along with compensation for other risks, sets the nominal interest rate. That nominal rate becomes part of a present value calculation. Imagine a company that pays a $1 dividend each year. Over 10 years, the company would pay $10. If the real rate of interest over 10 years is 2.5% and the investor's cost of living goes up 2.5% a year, then the stream of dividends is worth only $7.72 today:
Present value = $1/(1 + 5\%)^1 + \$1/(1 + 5\%)^2 + \cdots + \$1/(1 + 5\%)^{10} = \$7.72$. If the investor worries that the company could go out of business and needs something extra to compensate, say another 2.5% a year, then the stream of dividends is worth only $6.84 today:

$$\text{Present value} = \$1/(1 + 7.5\%)^1 + \$1/(1 + 7.5\%)^2 + \cdots + \$1/(1 + 7.5\%)^{10} = \$6.84$$

highest dividend. It could be the bond that pays the highest rate of interest. It could be the piece of real estate expected to bring the highest price or produce the most income. It could be gold or silver, wheat or pork bellies, or anything expected to go up in value. Investors have developed ingenious ways to project investment cash flows and then add them up or calculate a discounted present value to compare them all. Investing may seem like a winner-take-all game.

If every investor knew the exact cash flows of every investment, then a winner-take-all hunt through the investment menu would get each investor to the right place. It would create races and anoint winners. Genius would prevail. David would beat Goliath. It would make for great television, valuable tips from one investor to another. It would venerate the hunters that find winning investments.

This is the stuff that makes up most advice on investing. The daily game of covering the markets usually focuses on winners and losers, surprises and disappointments, the new new thing. It is a rich and repeatable story. But it rarely makes for good investing.

It's 1952, and Harry Markowitz, then a graduate student at the University of Chicago, makes a simple observation about the hunt for a single best and highest rate of return: it is an unrealistic way to build a portfolio (Markowitz, 1952). Almost no portfolio ever gets built that way. An exclusive focus on expected return or even on expected discounted return rules out the possibility of holding more than one security—except for the trivial case of multiple securities that all have the highest expected return. The rational investor in a winner-take-all world of returns simply would hold the best security. Any rule that led to an undiversified portfolio with one or even a handful of securities, Markowitz argues, violates both observed investor behavior and common sense. Few things in the world are certain; most are uncertain. A winner-take-all approach to investing was silly in the best case and hubris in the worst. He rejects it.

Markowitz instead focuses on uncertainty or risk. We might like to think the world follows a determined path, but it varies in small and sometimes large ways every day. It is probabilistic. One day dawns clear, another cloudy. Traffic moves quickly one afternoon, slowly the next. Technology advances and a new business replaces an old. Earnings ebb and flow. Buyers' preferences shift.

At any point, the future state of the world is unknown. Some future states may be more likely than others, of course. As the world evolves, the probabilities of some future states rise and fall. And as possible versions of the future come in and out of view, the timing, magnitude, and certainty of investment cash flows change. The cost of living might go up or down over time, the ability of a borrower to repay may change, the prospects of a company will likely vary.

Risk can shape the estimate of expected cash flow and the calculation of present value.[2] All else equal, the higher the risk, the higher the discount rate and the lower the present value of an assumed stream of cash flow. A dividend or interest payment that an investor expects with near certainty may get discounted at one interest rate. A payment at risk from earnings or default may get discounted at a higher rate. Risk can enter the calculation of present value, but that does not address Markowitz's critique.

Whether the investor adjusts the expectations of cash flow or adjusts the discounting rate, neither approach on its own suggests any obvious metric other than judgment for choosing the cash flows or the discounting rate. And once an investor choses a set of cash flows and a set of rates, discounted expected return still points to a single best and highest rate of return. The winner is anointed.

Markowitz offers a transformative idea for building a portfolio of risky cash flows, using variance to measure risk: "There is a rate at which the investor can gain expected return by taking on variance (risk)," he writes, "or reduce variance by giving up expected return" (1952, p. 79).

In other words, risk is the behavior of cash flow from the time it starts flowing into an investment to the time it finally flows out. Some investments may produce very reliable, very predictable cash flows. The cash in the drawer has a predictable cash flow. The US Treasury bond has a predictable cash flow. The safest bank deposit does, too. An investment in a start-up company may not. The history of an investment's cash flow should reflect this, and so should expected cash flow. The safest cash flows vary only a little bit and have low variance; the riskiest vary a lot and have high variance.[3]

Investments with predictable prices or cash flows will tend to offer relatively low returns, and investments with unpredictable prices or cash flows will tend to offer relatively high returns. It's intuitive.

Imagine two companies: one that always pays a $1 dividend each year and another that flips a coin and pays $2 for heads and $0 for tails. Both produce, on

---

2 If the real rate of interest over 10 years is 2.5% and the investor's cost of living goes up 2.5% a year, then a stream of annual $1 dividends is worth only $7.72 today:
Present value = $1/(1 + 5\%)^1 + $1/(1 + 5\%)^2 + \cdots + $1/(1 + 5\%)^{10}$ = $7.72. If the investor worries that the company paying the $1 every year could go out of business, the investor might need something extra to compensate for the risk, say another 2.5% a year, then the stream of dividends is worth only $6.86 today:

Present value = $1/(1 + 7.5\%)^1 + $1/(1 + 7.5\%)^2 + \cdots + $1/(1 + 7.5\%)^{10}$ = $6.84. Alternatively, the riskier company could compensate a nervous investor by paying more than $1 a year, in fact, exactly 12.5 cents more a year:

Present value = $1.125/(1 + 7.5\%)^1 + $1.1125/(1 + 7.5\%)^2 + \cdots + $1.125/(1 + 7.5\%)^{10}$ = $7.72.

3 Variance is a measure of dispersion around an average. Variance in returns over a series of investment periods would be measured as Variance of Returns = $\sum$ (Return over period t – Average over all periods)^2/(Total number of periods – 1).

average, $1 a year. Both have expected cash flow of $1 a year. If both investments cost the same, most investors would choose the predictable $1. That would drive up the price of the predictable $1, lowering its expected return compared to the coin-flipping investment. That was Markowitz's intuition.

The simple idea of the reliability or variance of returns makes it easier to compare investment returns, including returns on investments that might otherwise seem wildly different. Almost every investment leaves a trail of returns with an average rate of return and variability around that average. An investor can measure variability by a wide set of measures: variance or standard deviation, the ratio of winning days to losing, the largest loss, and so on. They all get at a different facet of risk. A stock or a portfolio of stocks, a bond or a portfolio of bonds, options, real estate, commodities, mutual and hedge funds, and so on all leave a record. All investments leave a trail of returns as distinct as a fingerprint.

Markowitz's emphasis on risk and return encourages investors to compare investments on these two attributes. An investor could take more risk to get more return. But an investor also could compare investments with roughly the same risk and choose the one with the highest return. An investor alternatively could compare investments with similar returns and choose the one with the lowest risk. And an investor could take a view on the future risk and future return of a menu of investments. Investing suddenly becomes an exercise in trading off risk against return.

Investors trading off risk against return should transform the relative value of different assets. For assets with roughly the same risk, the one with the highest return would attract more investment. Its price would rise relative to others and its return would fall. Returns across assets in that sleeve of risk would tend to converge. For assets with roughly the same return, the one with the lowest risk would attract investment. Relative prices and returns would start to shift.

If an investor could go through all possible combinations of potential investments—all the items on our infinite list—the analysis leads to a set of portfolios that have both the highest return for a given level of risk and the lowest risk for a given level of return. These portfolios are the most efficient. Among all possible portfolios of investible assets, the efficient ones line up along a continuum or border from a point with the lowest risk and lowest return to a point with the highest risk and highest return. This becomes the efficient investment frontier (figure 1.1).

It is easy to miss the genius in Markowitz's formulation of risk and return. By bringing risk into the picture, Markowitz puts the least tangible element of investing on par with the most. Return is tangible, easy to measure and compare. It gets reported every day, every month, every year. Return can actually buy things. Risk, however, only shapes returns over time, has to be imagined in advance, and often is clear only in hindsight. Risk rarely shows up in summaries of investment performance. We tell ourselves stories of likely investment return,

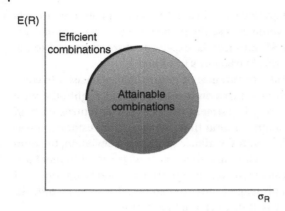

Figure 1.1 Markowitz's approach leads to a limited combination of securities that have the highest return for a given a level of risk or the lowest risk for a given level of return.

and, in an effort to convince ourselves or convince others, we tend to narrow the range of likely risk. Markowitz makes risk and return equals.

The Surprising Power of Diversification

Markowitz would have taken an important step if he had only made risk and return equals, but he has another idea that revolutionizes investing: investors can improve risk and return in a portfolio by mixing investments. In other words, investors have something valuable to gain from diversification.

To get an intuition for diversification, think again about a company that flips a coin every year and pays $2 for heads and $0 for tails. Then imagine a second company that flips a second coin and also pays $2 for heads and $0 for tails. Each company would pay $1 a year on average with a variance of $1.[4] But because the two companies flip separate coins, they don't always pay on the same schedule. Some years, both will pay and investors will get $4. Other years, both will skip payments and investors will get $0. Most years, one or the other will pay, and investors will get $2. The companies still pay their separate cash flows, but the combination over time is smoother. In other words, the combination of the two companies doesn't reduce their expected return, but it does reduce their risk.

To Markowitz, mixed investment or diversification recognizes the unmeasured aspects of an investment that might make its returns move a little differently or very differently from all the investments around it. Diversification brought humility to investing. By diversifying, the investor would have to acknowledge

---

4 For an investment that pays discrete cash flows, xi, with a certain probability, pi,
$\text{Var}(X) = \sum_{i=1}^{n} pi * (xi - \mu)^2$ where $\mu = \sum_{i=1}^{n}(pi * xi)$.

that he or she would never know the likely timing, direction, or magnitude of returns of all the items on our infinite investment list. Diversification encourages adding a wide range of investments to a portfolio to capture the widest range of possible risks and returns.

Diversification might have sounded like just another nice idea if Markowitz had not provided a powerful example of its benefits. Markowitz measured diversification by the correlation between investment returns, or how much returns on different investments move together. Investments with returns that move proportionately up and down by the same amount at the same time would have a correlation of 1 (figure 1.2). Returns that moved proportionately in opposite directions at different times would have a correlation of −1. Investments with returns that have no relationship would have a correlation of 0, such as the two companies that flipped coins. Two investments with the same risk and same return but with a correlation of less than 1, for example, could combine into an investment with the same return but less risk.[5] An investor who put the two coin-flipping companies into a portfolio would end up with an investment that returned $1 a year on average but had less than two-thirds of the risk of holding either company alone. The cash flow from the portfolio would be smoother than from either company alone. This is Markowitz's powerful insight on the benefit of diversification.

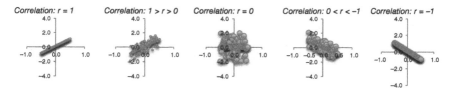

Figure 1.2 The periodic returns on different assets can vary together, with the correlation ranging from perfectly positive (1) to perfectly negative (−1) to anywhere in between.

---

5 The expected return for a simple portfolio of two securities is $E(R_p) = X_A R_A + X_B R_B$, where R_A and R_B are the expected returns on investment A and investment B and X_A and X_B are the percent of the portfolio in investment A and investment B . Markowitz assumed X_A and X_B add to 100% and the investor could not sell either investment short, in other words, that $X_i \geq 0$. The variance of a portfolio with two securities is $\sigma_P^2 = X_A^2 \sigma_A^2 + X_B^2 \sigma_B^2 + 2X_A X_B \sigma_{AB}^2$ or, more intuitively, $\sigma_P^2 = X_A^2 \sigma_A^2 + X_B^2 \sigma_B^2 + 2X_A X_B \rho_{AB} \sigma_A \sigma_B$. In the latter expression, σ_A^2 is the variance of returns on investment A, for instance, and ρ_{AB} is the correlation between returns on investments A and B. The latter expression for portfolio variance or risk shows more clearly that risk drops as the correlation between the two securities, ρ_{AB}, drops below 1 or even goes negative. This is the formal expression for the impact of diversification.

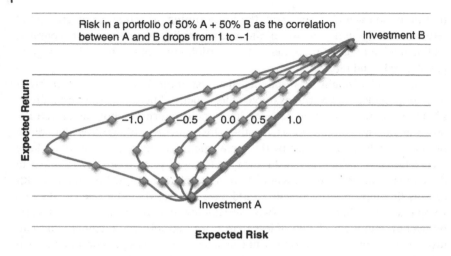

Risk in a portfolio of 50% A + 50% B as the correlation between A and B drops from 1 to −1

Investment B

Expected Return

−1.0   −0.5   0.0   0.5   1.0

Investment A

Expected Risk

Figure 1.3 Markowitz also showed that risk in a portfolio falls as the correlation between investments drops below 1.

Markowitz's insight leads to a finer appreciation for the ways investors could shape the risk and return of a portfolio by mixing different assets. The expected return from mixing assets would simply add up to the expected return from each investment, weighted, of course, by the share of the portfolio invested in each one. But the expected risk depended on the correlation between assets. Assets with a high positive correlation would simply be a weighted sum of the risk in each investment. But as the correlation fell, risk would fall, too (figure 1.3). And if an investor could add items that tended to spin off positive returns when others were spinning off negative—items with negative correlation—then risk could fall dramatically.

By showing that investors could use diversification to reduce risk without necessarily reducing return or add return without necessarily adding risk, Markowitz moved the investment discussion beyond present value and discounting rates and into modern portfolio theory. Building portfolios becomes an exercise in assembling cash flows that have the right mix of expected return, risk, and diversification.

For an investor staring at an infinite menu of choices, the challenge becomes picking the best set of choices, not just simply the single best choice. Any investment with acceptable risk and return could become part of an efficient portfolio as long as it adds diversification. Investing changed from the evaluation and pursuit of single assets into the construction of portfolios that maximized return for the portfolio of risks taken.

The Sources of Risk and Correlation

For all the insight of Markowitz's approach, he left largely unexamined the building blocks of risk and correlation. We know a good investor needs compensation for risk, and we know that correlation provides the glue that joins the elements of an efficient portfolio, but we do not know how risk and correlation arise. They simply seem to exist, and Markowitz arrived on the scene to tell us how to use them.

To better understand risk and correlation, the idea of companies in different coin-flipping businesses is a good way to start. The coin that each company flips stands for the risk that each company takes to earn a return. One company can flip the same coin as another or a different coin. Another company can earn returns by flipping multiple coins, and those coins may overlap partially or completely with the coins flipped by yet another company. And the payoff or sensitivity to the outcomes from those coins may differ across companies as well.

In the real world, companies do not flip coins to earn returns but they do take risks. Companies can take the same or different risks, those risks can overlap partially or wholly, and the sensitivity to those risks can vary as well. Some companies buy bricks and mortar and lumber, for instance, and turn them into buildings. Some companies own airplanes, trains, trucks, or automobiles and move materials around to different buyers. Some companies buy and sell buildings. Some companies take computer chips and software and make computers. Some companies buy meats and vegetables and make restaurant meals. Some companies do nearly the same thing but in different places. This list of things that companies do is as endless as is the list of companies itself. Sometimes the risks provide good return; sometimes they do not, just like a coin can come up heads or tails.

This idea of flipping coins and taking risks extends beyond companies to all investments. The value of the cash in the drawer depends on inflation, so the owner with the key to the drawer has flipped an inflation coin. The value of a loan or bond depends on interest rates, so those investments flip the interest rate coin. The value of an oil company depends on the supply-and-demand-for-oil coins.

Once it becomes clear that companies or investments flip different risk coins, then building a diversified portfolio becomes a hunt in part for investments that flip different coins and take different risks. Some risks are truly independent, but some are related. Companies in very different businesses, very different locations, or both may show returns that look relatively independent. Companies in the same or similar business may show returns that look related or correlated.

In practice, companies and investments usually take multiple dimensions of risk. And each investment's performance may show different sensitivity to each dimension of risk.[6] Items on a menu of investments could show sensitivity to interest rates or corporate profits or the weather or new technologies, and a given investment may be more sensitive to one risk than to another.

Instead of thinking of a menu of investments as a list of instruments or companies or funds, it is better to think of the risk dimensions packed into a given investment—the list of risk coins being flipped or the risks embedded in each item on the menu. Some investments involve the same or similar risks; other investments involve very different risks. Some involve concentrated risks; others involve a broad set of risks. Some risks actually offset others. By looking through the individual items on the infinite list of investments to the underlying risk dimensions, the actual number of choices that an investor has to make goes down dramatically. Even a few risk dimensions can be combined in different amounts to create an infinite list of investments. But the underlying risk dimensions are much smaller, and the investor's challenge much more manageable.

Because each item on the investment menu involves a different set of risks and different sensitivity to each risk, an investor can shape the return, risk, and correlation among elements of a portfolio by combining different items from the menu. The investor can choose which risks to take and which risks to avoid. And as different dimensions of risk come in and out of a portfolio, then performance

---

6 This idea, too, can have a formal representation for a set of assets, A, B, and C, and a set of risk factors, N, M, and P:

Assets with sensitivity to different risks

Asset	Risk factor		
	N	M	P
A	$\beta_{A,N}$		
B	$\beta_{B,N}$	$\beta_{B,M}$	
C	$\beta_{C,N}$	$\beta_{C,M}$	$\beta_{C,P}$

The return on each asset depends on a common risk factor N, the return on assets B and C depend on factor M, and the return of asset C only depends on factor P. And each asset has a different sensitivity to its underlying risk factors.

Any asset is a combination of exposures to a wide range of underlying risks. In other words, an asset itself is already a portfolio—a portfolio of risk exposures. And those risk exposures can change over time. The variance of any asset at any point in time depends on both the sensitivity to each underlying risk and the variance in each underlying risk. For an asset sensitive to two latent factors:

$$\sigma_A^2 = \beta_n^2 \sigma_n^2 + \beta_m^2 \beta_m^2 + 2\beta_n \beta_m \sigma_{mn}^2$$

where

σ_A^2 is the variance of return on the asset

σ_n^2 is the variance of factor n

σ_m^2 is the variance of factor m

σ_{mn}^2 is the covariance between factors n and m

of the portfolio changes. Rather than choosing from a menu with an infinite set of discrete investments, an investor builds a portfolio from an underlying set of broader risks.

Markowitz's Open Questions

Markowitz also left open an essential aspect of his approach: the best way to determine expected return, risk, and diversification:

> To use the E-V (*expected return and variance*) rule in the selection of securities we must have procedures for finding reasonable (expected returns and variances). These procedures, I believe, should combine statistical techniques and the judgment of practical men. My feeling is that the statistical computations should be used to arrive at a tentative set of (returns and variances). Judgment should then be used in increasing or decreasing some of these (returns and variances) on the basis of factors or nuances not taken into account by the formal computations. (Markowitz, 1952, p. 91)

The correlation between assets depends on shared risk dimensions, correlated risk dimensions, and sensitivity to the underlying risks. For a pair of assets, A and B, that both depend on the influence of two risk dimensions, N and M, their returns look as follows:

$$R_A = \beta_1 N + \beta_2 M + \epsilon_A$$
$$R_B = \lambda_1 N + \lambda_2 M + \epsilon_B$$

It is easy to show that

$$\sigma_{A,B}^2 = \beta_1 \lambda_1 \sigma_N^2 + \beta_2 \lambda_2 \sigma_M^2 + \beta_1 \lambda_2 \sigma_{M,N}^2 + \beta_2 \lambda_1 \sigma_{M,N}^2$$

This means that the covariance between A and B depends on their respective sensitivity to the underlying risk dimensions. If the investor changes that sensitivity through hedging, for instance, the covariance between the assets will change. Consequently, the diversifying effect of the assets in a mean-variance portfolio also will change.

Changing asset exposure to underlying risk dimensions means that investors can manage the correlation between two assets. The ability to hedge or offset some or all dimensions of risk embedded in an asset allows an investor to choose the amount of variance and correlation in and between assets. Take the example where an investor takes a long position in A and a short position in B:

$$R_A - R_B = \beta_1 N + \beta_2 M + \epsilon_A - \rho_1 N - \rho_2 M - \epsilon_B$$
$$R_A - R_B = (\beta_1 - \rho_1) N + (\beta_2 - \rho_2) M + \epsilon_A - \epsilon_B$$

The resulting risk combination differs from both A and B. The new combination will have a unique correlation to A, B, and to other assets.

Once an investor breaks an asset down into underlying exposures, applying Markowitz's framework involves even more judgment about expected return, variance, and correlation. Portfolios that include hedges or short positions further open the possibility of competitive advantage because investors can exclude risks where they might have disadvantage and emphasize ones where they have advantage.

Despite the investors' essential job of combining risk, return, and correlation into portfolio performance, Markowitz still left open the best way to predict these things. If use of time is a good signal, then performance depends on expectations about asset cash flow and plausible changes in the relevant risk factors. A large block of investors' time goes to anticipating asset cash flow, whether it is earnings or dividends in the case of equity securities or coupons, option exercise, prepayments, or defaults in the case of fixed income securities. Another block goes to anticipating the path of events that might re-price securities such as changes in monetary or fiscal policy, politics, the economy, interest rates or option prices, science or technology, or other factors. These effectively are the risk exposures embedded in available securities. The intersection between probable scenarios and the value of specific security cash flows is the daily work of portfolio construction.

In a Markowitz world, investors may end up with competitive advantage. Some investors may simply have more or different or better information than others. Some may be able to run faster or better analysis. Some investors may be able to consistently anticipate the return, risk, and correlation of assets more accurately than others. Some may be able to consistently build portfolios that perform better than others'. Markowitz would expect a return to investing in research and analysis.

But most individuals or organizations will lack the resources to develop comparative advantage along every underlying risk factor. When an investor has no clear advantage or disadvantage, diversification improves returns to risk-taking by washing out idiosyncratic risk. Diversification protects an investor from his or her own blind spots.

Arguably the greatest value in Markowitz's framework is to emphasize the importance of trading off risk and return. Each investor operates in a multidimensional return-risk space and constantly faces choices not just about the best combination of securities to hold but also the combination of risk dimensions along which to optimize. If investors can identify their universe of securities and the underlying risk dimensions, Markowitz provided a starting road map for making those choices. Each investment ultimately reduces to risk, return, and correlation. That reduces the infinite menu of investments to a smaller and more manageable set.

What Markowitz did not do, however, is provide a specific recommendation about how to build a portfolio. He led us to the efficient frontier but does not tell us where to settle. For that, the world had to wait for William Sharpe and the capital asset pricing model (1969 Sharpe, 1964; Lintner, 1965).

2

A Sharpe Line

Finding a Place on the Efficient Frontier

Although Markowitz in 1952 drew the map of the efficient frontier, he still left it up to each investor to find the best place to settle. Some places along the frontier offered low risk and low reward, some high risk and high reward, and some a Goldilocks combination. To each, his or her own.

Markowitz's only advice was to ask for more return with each extra measure of risk taken. Investors should not take risk for free. An investor might put money in a drawer and get just enough return to protect against inflation. But as risk goes up, so should the required return. The amount of additional return might differ for each investor. The adventurous might require a little, the cautious a lot. Markowitz does not prescribe the trade-off.

Markowitz does describe investors as risk averse, meaning not that investors avoid risk but only that investors need more return to compensate for more risk. As risk rises, so does required return. The trade-off that each investor makes between risk and return creates a map of the investor's preferences. A line on that map might start at the point of no risk and return and slope gently or sharply upwards, or it might curve up like an airplane lifting off a runway. For the same level of risk, of course, the investor would take the highest return. That moves the line or the curve up to a higher starting point.

An investor's map of preferred investment risk and return can help the investor or the investor's advisor find a place along the efficient frontier. One line in that map should intersect with the combinations of risk and return that are available along the efficient frontier (figure 2.1). Preference meets reality. At that intersection, Markowitz advised, invest.

Markowitz's advice still left investors with a lot of work to do. Each investor had to figure out risk, return, and correlation of each investment on the infinite list. That led to each investor's own efficient frontier. And the investor still had to

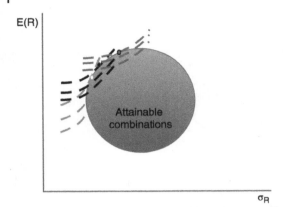

E(R)

Attainable combinations

σ_R

Figure 2.1 In Markowitz's world, every risk-averse investor would make a different trade-off between extra risk and extra return and choose a different portfolio.

figure out the map of risk and return preferences and where those might line up with the investor's own efficient frontier.

Markowitz had changed the state of the investment art, but a simple guide to using it would have to wait at least another 10 years.

Traveling Along the Capital Market Line

William Sharpe at Stanford and later John Lintner at Harvard separately came along more than a decade later and built on Markowitz's approach (Sharpe, 1964; Lintner, 1965). They developed a method that not only had something to say about the best way to combine all the items on the infinite investment list and choose a single best portfolio but also had something to say about how much each investment was worth. Known today as the capital asset pricing model, or CAPM, it probably has become the most broadly taught framework for building a portfolio and for valuing the assets that go into it. It has also led to important tools for measuring the important costs of running a company and for gauging the performance of asset managers. And, like all good theories, it was beautifully simple. Perhaps too beautiful.

To Markowitz's framework, Sharpe added the assumption that all investors agree on the most important features of asset returns over a given investment horizon: their likely mean, variance, and correlation. Investors see the same security cash flows, the same risk attributes driving those cash flows, and the same future path for those risks. All investors see the same world of possible investments. Most important, all investors see the same efficient frontier. He might have argued that investors can all have different opinions about given investments, but they can't have their own facts. Common facts prevail.

Sharpe also saw that investors often held cash, and cash did not fit readily into the world of risky assets that Markowitz outlined. Cash might sit in a drawer or a bank account or a Treasury bill and offer an unvarying return over an investor's time horizon, a return uncorrelated with returns from riskier assets. He also saw that investors could borrow cash and invest in risky assets. Cash and similar riskless assets had a special role to play.

Sharpe adapted an idea originally described by James Tobin at Yale and assumed that all investors could borrow or lend money at a single, common riskless rate (Tobin, 1958). Individuals, corporations, and even the US Treasury would pay the same rate of interest. This is not as unrealistic as it might sound at first. Once individuals or corporations put up valuable property or other collateral to secure a loan, interest rates can vary by only a small amount at least over short periods.

Sharpe knew he would be challenged. "These are highly restrictive and undoubtedly unrealistic assumptions," he noted. But he argued that the implications of his approach fit beautifully with some of the key predictions of classical finance. Beauty in theory would win over beauty in practice.

The immediate implication of holding cash or lending at a common riskless rate along with a common view of risky assets would be that an investor could hold a mix of cash and risky assets. If the investor held only cash, the portfolio would spin off a riskless return. If the investor held only efficient risky assets, the portfolio would spin off a return somewhere along the efficient frontier. If the investor held a mix of cash and risky assets, returns would fall somewhere along a line between a riskless return and a single point on the efficient frontier.

If the investor then went a step further and borrowed money to buy an efficient portfolio of risky assets, the line would extend beyond the efficient frontier. This was a striking idea. If an investor borrowed enough to double the size of the investment in the efficient portfolio of risky assets, the resulting leveraged portfolio would have a multiple of the expected return and risk. The line would start at the riskless asset, touch a portfolio on the efficient frontier, and keep going from there (figure 2.2). This was Sharpe's transformational idea of the capital market line. This line represents all combinations of the riskless asset and a risky portfolio. The investor could hold only the riskless asset, only the risky portfolio, or all combinations in between. If the investor borrowed money and used it to buy more of the risky portfolio, then investors would hold more than one times their money in the risky portfolio and the capital market line would keep on going.

Sharpe's capital market line had a remarkable feature: for any level of risk, it offered an equal or higher expected return than any point along the efficient frontier. And for any level of return, the capital market line offered equal or lower risk than the efficient frontier. Sharpe had found a solution to choosing from the infinite investment list that was better and simpler than Markowitz. Rather than settling along the efficient frontier, an investor instead should buy the risky

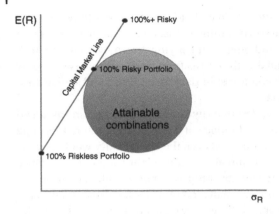

E(R)

100%+ Risky

Capital Market Line

100% Risky Portfolio

Attainable combinations

100% Riskless Portfolio

σ_R

Figure 2.2 Borrowing and lending at the riskless rate allows any investor to hold a combination of a riskless and risky asset, which Sharpe dubbed the capital market line.

portfolio when the capital market line touches the efficient frontier and then combine that portfolio with borrowing or lending at the riskless rate. Portfolios along the capital market line offer a better result than anything the investor could find along the efficient frontier.

Sharpe's capital market line reduced the complexity of Markowitz's approach. With a common view of asset performance, investors all should buy the same market portfolio of risky assets and individually either blend it with a relatively riskless investment or borrow and buy more of the portfolio to suit preferences for risk and return.

The complexity of the infinite investment menu had moved from the search for the single best investment through Markowitz to the efficient frontier and now through Sharpe to the capital market line. Investing had been reduced to a simple decision about the best mix of cash, borrowing, and a single efficient risk portfolio.

Putting a Price on Assets Along the Capital Market Line

Sharpe's approach also led to another powerful conclusion about the value of available investable assets, a conclusion that ever since has broadly set the terms for evaluating assets and investment managers.

Sharpe noted that if every investor decided to invest at least partially in the same risky portfolio, then the assets included in that portfolio would rise in value. A higher price would mean a decline in potential return compared to assets outside the initial portfolio. The assets outside the initial portfolio would become more attractive, and investors would look for portfolios that included the previously excluded assets. The value of those assets would rise until they aligned with the value of the initial portfolio, and investors' search for the next margin of excluded assets would continue. The value of included and excluded assets would continue to change until all assets had a place in at least one portfolio that lay along the capital market line—portfolios that promised a constant extra measure of return for each extra measure of risk (figure 2.3). Not all portfolios would have to include the same assets, but all portfolios would offer a combination of risk and return that matched at least one possibility along the line. And all portfolios along the capital market line would produce returns perfectly correlated with one another.

Sharpe then made the case that the value of any investment depends *only* on the amount of risk the asset shares with portfolios along the capital market line. Think of that as the risk of overall economic growth or decline. The remaining risk in an asset was unique or idiosyncratic. It could reflect the unpredictable effects of personnel or reputation or local markets or other factors. By combining investments, a portfolio could balance bad luck on one investment with good luck on another, just like the effect of flipping multiple coins can balance out into a smooth set of outcomes. But the core, systematic risk in an investment an investor cannot diversify away. And if the investor cannot eliminate the risk, then the investor needs fair compensation.

The expected return on any specific asset, according to Sharpe, reflects the expected return on the riskless asset, the expected return on the market portfolio of risky assets, and the proportion of risk that the specific asset shares with the market portfolio. In the world of CAPM, the expected return on a specific asset becomes $E(R_i)$. The expected return on the riskless asset becomes $E(R_R)$. The return on the market portfolio becomes $E(R_M)$, and the excess return on the market portfolio above the riskless return becomes $E[R_M] - E[R_R]$. Finally, the excess return on the market portfolio is multiplied by a number, β_{iM}, or beta,

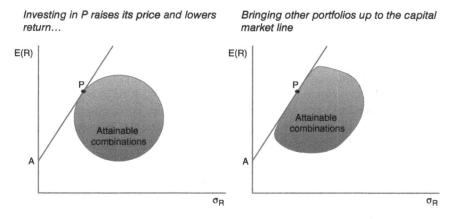

Figure 2.3   Steady investment in portfolios along the capital market line raises their price and lowers return, flattening the population of attainable investments against the line.

which indicates whether the specific asset is more or less risky than the market portfolio overall.[1] If the asset is more risky, beta is greater than 1; if it is less risky, beta is smaller than 1. All of these pieces fit together in a simple equation that revolutionized finance in the same way that Einstein's equation revolutionized physics:

$$E(R_{Asset}) = E(R_{Riskless}) + [E(R_{Market}) - E(R_{Riskless})]\beta_{Asset,Market}$$

An asset's expected return depends on the riskless rate and a multiple, $\beta_{Asset,Market}$, of the excess return on the market portfolio. The return on the complete market portfolio of investable assets has to reflect the broad return to the overall economy. Returns to some assets in that portfolio will rise and fall faster than the overall economy, and returns to others will rise and fall more slowly. Returns on a government bond, for instance, might only rise and fall modestly with changes in the economy. Returns on a corporate bond, however, might rise and fall more as the issuer's profits and prospects change. Returns on corporate equity might vary even more, with the equity of a large, established company varying more than the equity of a new entrant.

In CAPM, the multiplier, $\beta_{Asset,Market}$, measures the proportion of risk a specific investment shares with the market portfolio. Assets with returns more stable than the overall market will have a value of $\beta_{Asset,Market}$ less than one, assets with return more volatile will have a $\beta_{Asset,Market}$ greater than one, and assets with no shared risk at all will have a $\beta_{Asset,Market}$ of zero. A $\beta_{Asset,Market}$ of zero is the definition of a riskless asset!

The assumption of riskless lending and borrowing for all investors in the Sharpe and Linter framework immediately came under scrutiny, but Fischer Black in 1972, then at the University of Chicago, showed that the general relationship between $\beta_{Asset,Market}$ and expected return holds even without a riskless asset (Black, 1972). Black substituted a limitless ability to sell any asset short and still found that an asset's expected return depends on $\beta_{Asset,Market}$ scaled by an asset's return premium over a more general asset uncorrelated with the market. An asset uncorrelated with the market echoes the idea of a riskless investment, but Black's model does not require this asset to return a riskless rate. Black only requires that the expected return on an uncorrelated asset is less than the expected return on the market portfolio. In other words, $\beta_{Asset,Market}$ must be positive.

CAPM has provided much of the intellectual foundation for arguments that investors should hold positions along the capital market line because that is the only risk for which investors get compensated. The portfolio manager's job simply becomes deciding how to leverage or deleverage the exposure to the market basket.

---

1 $\beta_{iM} = \sigma(R_i, R_M)/\sigma^2(R_M)$

CAPM also obviously implies a fair value for an asset's expected return. That value should line up with its beta. An asset with a beta of one should have the same return as the market basket, and an asset with a beta of two, for instance, should have twice the return. This is also the same framework for estimating the cost of equity capital. Once an analyst has calculated a beta or $\beta_{Asset,Market}$ for a company, the return on equity required by CAPM immediately falls out.

CAPM has encouraged the use of market indices in evaluating the performance of asset managers. A manager who holds a portfolio along the capital market line will show excess returns—returns beyond the riskless rate—with a beta that reflects the portfolio's risk position. If the manager holds only the riskless asset, for example, the excess return and the beta would be zero. If the manager holds only the risky asset, the beta would be 1. If the manager borrows at the riskless rate and invests the funds in the risky asset, the beta will be greater than 1. Investors that put \$1 of their own money in the risky asset and then borrow \$1 to buy more of the risky asset, for example, would show a beta of 2 because a 1% gain or loss on the risky asset would create a 2% gain or loss on the original invested money. A simple regression of the manager's periodic excess returns on the excess returns from the risky asset would produce estimates of beta. After adjusting for the manager's beta, a portfolio that sat somewhere along the capital market line would show no excess return over the market basket. In a regression, it would show no alpha.

CAPM has framed investment performance on individual investments and funds in terms of alpha and beta. Because a range of cash and derivative instruments such as index funds, exchange-traded funds, futures, and swaps has made it relatively easy to get exposure to the market basket, the value of simple beta exposure is low. Almost any individual or institution can get beta exposure at low cost and with great liquidity. Managers instead try to produce alpha or excess return beyond the level in an index portfolio. This is valuable because the aggregate market alpha is zero. Managers should get paid well for delivering alpha. This sets a high bar for manager performance. As investment analysts Richard Grinold and Ronald Kahn note (1999), one implication of CAPM is that "investors that don't think they have superior information should hold the market portfolio. If you are a 'greater fool' and you know it, you can protect yourself by not playing" (p. 17).

The Power of Leverage, the Price of Equity, the Value of a Good Manager

Sharpe's case for the best way for an individual or manager to construct a portfolio and for the best way to value an asset or an asset manager would have a powerful impact over the following decades, ultimately leading to a Nobel Prize in 1990—a prize shared with Harry Markowitz and option theorist Merton Miller. Among other things, Sharpe's approach implied important things about financial leverage, or borrowing money to make risky investments. It implied important things about the fair rate of return for providing investment capital. And it also implied important things about the ability of an asset manager to beat the market.

Sharpe's approach underscored the importance of financial leverage. The ability of investors to borrow money and reinvest in riskier assets plays a critical role in making markets efficient. When investors can borrow and reinvest easily, the riskiest investments have to compete against returns available from a leveraged position in a safer portfolio of assets. When investors cannot borrow and reinvest easily, the riskiest investments can get away with providing returns below a fair rate. Investors who need an above-average rate of return have to invest in assets that provide less-than-fair compensation. That might hurt the individuals, banks, insurers, pension funds, and others that might need high rates of return to cover some of their greatest expected future expenses. This belies the common perception that financial leverage only adds risk to an investment portfolio without adding sufficient return. In Sharpe's world, it is just the opposite. A portfolio unable to use leverage or borrow to invest will likely buy risky assets nevertheless but get underpaid for taking the risk.

Sharpe also gave the market a yardstick for measuring the fair price of an equity investment in a company. The fair price of equity had always been elusive. Investors hand over their money and then wait for dividends, a rise in the value of their equity stake, or both. By making the case that the value of an investment depended on its expected performance compared to the market, investors had a way of setting fair price. Equity investments with roughly the same risk as the overall equity market—in other words, investments with a beta of 1—should provide the same rate of return as the overall market. If the market had an expected excess return of 8%, for example, equity with a beta of 1 should also provide a combination of dividends and price appreciation of 8%. Similarly, equity with a beta of 0.5, or half the risk of the overall market, should provide returns of 4%. And equity with a beta of 1.5 should provide returns of 12%. The cost of equity depended on risk relative to the market overall. That gave investors and companies a way to measure and compare the cost of debt and equity.

Sharpe also put the performance of asset managers in a spotlight, one that left many a little pale. Investors who entrusted their capital to an asset manager could now compare periodic returns in their portfolio to periodic returns in the market overall. If the manager invested in equity, the investor could compare the manager's equity returns to an equity market index such as the S&P 500. If the manager invested in bonds, the investor could compare returns to a bond market index. If a manager invested in real estate, the investor could compare returns to a real estate index. The comparison provided an alpha, beta, and a measure of idiosyncratic risk in the manager's portfolio. This simple approach has transformed asset management.

One thing investors quickly realized is that an asset manager could deliver an above-market return simply by taking on above-market risk, or deliver a below-market return by taking below-market risk. Absolute return alone didn't indicate either a good or bad job. It could all depend on beta. Once the investor measured a manager's beta, it became clearer whether the manager was adding any value beyond the portfolio's level of market risk.

The measure of value showed up in the manager's alpha, and one revolutionary implication of Sharpe's approach was that investment managers may not have any sustainable competitive advantage in creating alpha. Alpha for a portfolio that just invested in the market basket of assets would simply be the average riskless rate over the investment period. If a manager showed an alpha higher than this average riskless rate, the manager had added value above and beyond the simple returns from beta or systematic market risk. If the manager's alpha came in below, then the manager had destroyed value. Across the entire market, however, the average manager would neither add nor destroy value. The average alpha across the market always had to equal the average riskless rate. This challenged the very value of asset management itself. Not long after Sharpe published, Burton Malkiel, an economist at Princeton, wrote *A Random Walk Down Wall Street,* arguing that few if any managers can consistently beat the market (Malkiel, 1973). And decades of research since Sharpe first published have tended to show that few asset managers consistently deliver alpha across long periods after subtracting their fees. In Sharpe's world, no manager can beat the market. No manager can get a sustainable competitive advantage.

A Theory that Changed Investing

Sharpe's powerful simplification of investing into the capital market line and the yardsticks of alpha and beta changed investing. By the end of the 1970s, John Vogel had launched the first passive equity market index fund at Vanguard to enable investors to have an easy way to own the market portfolio. The evaluation of managers by alpha, beta, and other measures had begun.

As research into the implications of Sharpe's framework blossomed, however, a few odd results started turning up. Some of the predictions about asset returns made by CAPM did not seem to fit actual data. This is the essence of any scientific approach: theory may be beautiful, intuitive, or appealing, but it must explain the real world. Theory without confirmation in data risks becoming fiction. Ultimately, one professor at the University of Chicago and one at Dartmouth would make a decades-long project of unveiling considerable flaws in Sharpe's beautiful theory.

3

The Counsel of Critics

Putting Theory to the Test

The capital asset pricing model comes along and creates a new paradigm in investing. It comes with simplicity, rigor, and direct application to practical matters. It simplifies investing into a choice between cash or other riskless assets and the market portfolio. The infinite menu of investments becomes manageable. It helps measure the performance of Wall Street's investment managers. The model even helps companies set the cost of equity capital by scaling the return on the market portfolio up or down depending on the beta of a company's stock. It quickly becomes the orthodoxy of pure finance and, over time, the most if not the only model of portfolio investing taught in business schools. But over time, the model also proves to be flawed.

All good theory needs testing in the real world, and the best tests take predictions made by theory and look for evidence in data. Theory proves itself through prediction and confirmation in observable results. The testing of CAPM started almost immediately, and the results immediately signaled that something was amiss.

A Problem with Alpha

To start, CAPM predicted that the return on any asset begins with the riskless return and then adds a multiple of the excess return on the market portfolio of risky assets:

$$E(R_{Asset}) = E(R_{Riskless}) + [E(R_{Market}) - E(R_{Riskless})]\beta_{Asset,Market}$$

Michael Jensen (1967), then at the Harvard Business School, noted that if investors stripped out the riskless rate from the periodic return on each asset, then CAPM predicted the only thing left would be the multiple of the excess return on the market portfolio:

$$E(R_{Asset}) - E(R_{Riskless}) = [E(R_{Market}) - E(R_{Riskless})]\beta_{Asset,Market}, \text{ or}$$

$$E(R_{Asset}) - E(R_{Riskless}) = 0 + [E(R_{Market}) - E(R_{Riskless})]\beta_{Asset,Market}$$

In other words, the return on any investment above and beyond the riskless rate was simply the excess return of the market portfolio scaled up or down by a multiplier, $\beta_{Asset,Market}$. That pointed to a CAPM prediction that investors could test directly:

$$R_{Asset} - R_{Riskless} = \alpha_{Asset} + [R_{Market} - R_{Riskless}]\beta_{Asset,Market} + \epsilon_{Asset}$$

In this test, if CAPM described the world well, the value of α_i should be zero. That was one place where analysts could test CAPM theory against actual investment results. A number of analysts did exactly that (Douglas, 1968; Black, Jensen, and Scholes,1972; Miller and Scholes,1972; Blume and Friend, 1973; Fama and MacBeth, 1973; Fama and French, 1992).

When investors followed Jensen's lead and tested CAPM they found that not only did α_i have a value other than zero but also it followed a surprising but reliable pattern: α_i had a positive value when $\beta_{Asset,Market}$ is low and a negative value when $\beta_{Asset,Market}$ is high. In other words, more stable assets had a better return than predicted by CAPM and more volatile assets had a worse return. The capital markets line in the real world was flatter than predicted by theory.

As recently as 2004, Eugene Fama at the University of Chicago and Kenneth French at Dartmouth again ran the numbers on portfolios of stocks built to be either high or low beta (Fama and French, 2004). Assembling these portfolios at the beginning of each year, they looked at performance over the year that followed. CAPM would predict that the safest portfolio of stocks would return only slightly more than the riskless rate for the year. As portfolios became riskier, their return simply would be the excess return of the market portfolio that year multiplied by each portfolio beta. Testing from 1928 through 2003, they compared actual returns on these portfolios to returns predicted by CAPM. They found that low beta stocks had returns higher than predicted, and high beta stocks had returns lower than predicted (figure 3.1). Again, the line was too flat.

Higher beta investments still showed higher returns, but the flatness of the observed capital markets line suggested that CAPM alone might not explain it. The theory had a mysterious flaw.

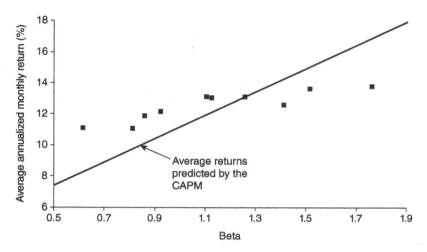

Figure 3.1 On stock portfolios that vary in their beta, realized returns are too flat compared to the predictions of CAPM.

Note: Average annualized monthly return versus beta for value-weight portfolios formed on prior beta, 1928–2003.

Source: From Fama and French (2004).

Performance Turns on More Than Beta

CAPM also predicted that investment returns depend only on an asset's expected return premium over the riskless rate, or $[E(R_{Market}) - E(R_{Riskless})]\beta_{Asset,Market}$. This ensures that the market portfolio sits somewhere on Markowitz's efficient frontier. If other factors influence asset returns, then the simplest and most elegant version of CAPM falls apart.

Starting in the late 1970s, studies of investment returns started making the case that factors other than expected return premium explained asset returns. A study by Sanjay Basu showed that earnings-to-price ratios added to the ability of CAPM to predict stock returns, with high earnings-to-price equities outperforming low (Basu, 1977). A study by Rolf Banz a few years later showed that market capitalization helped, too, with smaller market capitalizations performing better than predicted by CAPM (Banz, 1981). Laxmi Bhandari followed this lead and by the end of the 1980s found that debt-to-equity ratios helped CAPM explain returns, with high debt-to-equity performing better than predicted by beta alone (Bhandari, 1988). And other researchers found that high book-to-market equities also performed better than predicted by beta (Stattman, 1980; Rosenberg, Reid, and Lanstein, 1985).

Eugene Fama and Kenneth French later incorporated influences beyond beta into a proposed model of asset returns (Fama and French, 1993, 1996). In their view of the investment world, the expected excess return on any specific asset at a point in time, $E(R_{Asset,t}) - E(R_{Riskless,t})$, again depends on the excess return on the market portfolio multiplied by the CAPM's familiar beta, $[E(R_{Asset,t}) - E(R_{Riskless,t})]\beta_{Asset,Market}$. But unlike CAPM, Fama and French also argue that returns depend on the difference between small and big stocks, or $E(SMB_t)$, and on the difference between stocks with a high ratio of book value to market value and stocks with a low ratio, or $E(HML_t)$. These factors represent elements of asset returns separate from broad exposure to the economy and, more important, elements that investors cannot diversify away. Investors consequently need compensation for those risks.

Fama and French fit the elements of their approach together in a single statement:

$$E(R_{Asset,t}) - E(R_{Riskless,t}) = [E(R_{Mkt,t}) - E(R_{Riskless,t})]\beta_{Asset,Mkt}$$
$$+ E(SMB_t)\beta_{Asset,SMB} + E(HML_t)\beta_{Asset,HML}$$

Fama and French point out that the average annual excess return of the market portfolio over the riskless rate from 1927 to 2003 was 8.3%. The average difference in return between small and large stocks, however, was 3.6%, and the average difference between high and low book-to-market stocks was 5.0%. They also put their approach to the same test that Jensen applied to CAPM:

$$R_{Asset} - R_{Riskless} = \alpha_{Asset} + [R_{Mkt} - R_{Riskless}]\beta_{Asset,Mkt} + SMB_t\beta_{Asset,SMB}$$
$$+ HML_t\beta_{Asset,HML} + \epsilon_{Asset}$$

In this test, if Fama and French's model described the world well, the value of α_i also should be zero. Fama and French have broadly found that this approach does leave a value of α_i about zero. Work by other researchers has found similar results (see, for example, Loughran and Ritter, 1995; Mitchell and Stafford, 2000). Studies of performance in mutual funds have also found that Fama and French's factors explain performance better than a simple CAPM approach (Carhart, 1997). Beyond the academic, investment firms such as Dimensional Advisors and AQR have built substantial businesses on Fama and French's observation, running portfolios that use these factors to try to outperform broad market benchmarks.

In addition to Fama and French, other work has found more factors that seem to sway asset returns. Jegadeesh and Titman have found that returns seem to depend on a sort of momentum (Jegadeesh and Titman, 1993). Stocks that do better than the market over the most recent three or 12 months tend to continue doing well over the next few months, and stocks that do poorly continue doing poorly. Performance seems to persist and shape returns beyond even the factors that Fama and French describe. The list of influences on asset return grows.

Significant elements of investment performance seem to rely on things beyond CAPM's simple multiple of excess market performance. CAPM again falls short.

Seeds of New Approaches

At the same time that both theorists and practitioners embraced CAPM and began to see its shortcomings, intriguing explanations and steps in new directions began to emerge.

Both the flatness of returns relative to Sharpe's CAPM predictions and the influence on returns of factors beyond beta have led other analysts to argue that structural aspects of markets—not addressed by CAPM—lead to these results. In fact, Fischer Black, who spent years immersed in theory at the University of Chicago and years immersed in markets at Goldman Sachs, notes this possibility (Black, 1993):

> Another reason for a flatter line is restricted borrowing. Margin requirements, borrowing rates that are higher than lending rates, and limited deductibility of interest costs all tend to make the line flatter. Those who can't borrow at good rates bid up the prices of high-beta stocks instead.

> Yet another reason for a flatter line, I believe, is investor psychology, in particular "reluctance to borrow," even when the rules allow it and the rates are good. Many people seem to dislike the idea of borrowing or the trading needed to adjust borrowing amounts to the values of their securities portfolios. (p. 38)

Andrea Frazzini and Lasse Pedersen also argue that limits to investors' ability to leverage or deleverage positions in the market basket explain some of the flatness in realized returns (Frazzini and Pedersen, 2012):

> For instance, individual investors and pension funds may not be able to use any leverage, banks face regulatory capital constraints, and hedge funds must satisfy their margin requirements. However, an investor can gain substantial market exposure without using outright leverage by buying options, leveraged ETFs, or other securities that embed the leverage. In fact, many of these securities are designed precisely to provide embedded leverage. (p. 1)

Because of these limits to leverage, Frazzini and Pedersen echo Black's assumption that investors pay a premium to buy assets with embedded leverage. That leverage can come from a high beta to an underlying index or assets. They show that a series of assets with high betas, such as short-dated, out-of-the-money options on single equities or equity indices, produce consistently lower returns than similar assets with low betas, such as long-dated, in-the-money options on single equities or equity indices. They find the same result when comparing exchange-traded funds without embedded leverage, such as a simple exchange-traded fund that might track the S&P 500, against a fund that tracks some multiple of the daily return on the same S&P 500. Adjusted for exposure to the referenced asset, the leveraged fund produces consistently lower returns. Limits to leverage may be only one limit that explains the shortfall of CAPM.

Cliff Asness and Tobias Moskowitz have joined Lasse Pedersen, all affiliated at some point in their careers with the University of Chicago and the asset manager AQR, to extend the search for factors that influence value on a wide range of assets (Asness, Moskowitz, and Pedersen, 2013). They find evidence for a value factor, such as book-to-market for equities and similar measures for other assets, and evidence for a momentum factor, linking recent and future performance. And they find evidence for value and momentum in a wide range of settings: in the US, UK, European, and Japanese equity markets; in equity index futures, government bonds, currencies, and commodity futures. The search across markets enables Asness and his colleagues to look at the correlations among these strategies in otherwise unrelated markets, and they find returns on value strategies positively correlated with value strategies across markets, momentum strategies similarly correlated across markets, and value and momentum negatively correlated within and across markets. That raises the issue of a potential common cause. They find modest links to macroeconomic variables such as business cycle, consumption, and default. They find more evidence of a common link through liquidity, particularly the availability and cost of funding, although it only explains a small part of the return premium.

The work that finds factors other than beta that help explain asset performance draws criticism from theorists who argue that the factors only represent ad hoc ways to capture historical patterns of return, and that the factors do not represent separate, systemic, and undiversifiable sources of risk. But Fama and French (2004) argue that additional factors still challenge CAPM if they are well diversified and capture aspects of performance that the market portfolio alone misses. This is less of a concern for practitioners.

Theorists also argue that CAPM has not been properly tested and maybe never will because no one has looked at performance against a complete portfolio of market assets. That complete portfolio might not include just traded equity and debt; it might also include real estate, insurance, earnings, and other things that accrue from human capital. The factors highlighted by Fama and French and Jegadeesh and Titman might simply be measuring the extra return from these excluded factors. Including these factors might properly steepen the line between beta and

The tendency for constrained investors to overinvest in high beta assets raises the price for these assets and lowers their expected return. Underinvestment in low beta assets lowers their price and raises their expected return. This distortion, Frazzini and Pedersen argue, leads to the flat capital markets line—stronger returns in lower risk assets, weaker returns in higher risk assets.

To test their theory, Frazzini and Pedersen build a series of portfolios that buy assets with a low beta and sell short assets with a higher beta.[1] The portfolios balance their holdings so if markets go up or down, portfolio value should hold steady. Betting-against-beta becomes less about taking market risk and more about buying undervalued assets and selling overvalued assets. If constrained investors shape asset performance by underinvesting in low beta and overinvesting in high beta assets, Frazzini and Pedersen's betting-against-beta portfolios will produce excess returns that get stronger as limits to leverage become more binding. There is an exception to the rule, however. If limits to leverage become so binding that every investor becomes constrained, then leveraged investors get forced to deleverage and betting-against-beta unravels.

Frazzini and Pedersen first show that splitting up assets into portfolios with low beta and high beta produces the predicted result: as portfolio beta runs from low to high, portfolio alpha steadily declines. The list of markets where this pattern holds is impressive: US equities, international equities, Treasury debt, corporate debt, commodities, foreign exchange, indexes for equities, corporate debt, and credit default swaps.

Frazzini and Pedersen then build betting-against-beta portfolios in each market starting with US equities. Using returns from January 1926 to March 2012, their analysis shows that betting-against-beta delivers average monthly excess returns of 0.70%. They further test their strategy by comparing it to the performance of the US equity market basket and find that average excess return rises to 0.73%. They compare it to the performance of a portfolio built on the factors that Fama and French highlight—the market, company size, and book value—and still find excess return of 0.73%. And when they add strategies built on momentum and liquidity, excess return drops to 0.55% but still stands well above the returns predicted by CAPM.

In international equities, betting-against-beta adds average monthly excess return of 0.64%, beats the international equity market basket by 0.64%, exceeds returns on the Fama and French factors by 0.65%, and outperforms more elaborate models by 0.28% to 0.30%. The results suggest limits to leverage in equity markets worldwide.

---

1 The return on a betting-against-beta or BAB portfolio is

$$R_{BAB,t+1} = \left(\frac{1}{\beta_{Low,t}} \right)\left(R_{Low,t+1} - R_{Riskless,t} \right) - \left(\frac{1}{\beta_{High,t}} \right)\left(R_{High,t+1} - R_{Riskless,t} \right) \text{ where } \beta_{Low,t} < \beta_{High,t}.$$

The US Treasury market might seem to offer the most efficient pricing in the world because of its relatively simple cash flows, the general uniformity of the debt, average daily trading of hundreds of billions of dollars, a global audience of investors, and ready financing, but predictions made by betting-against-beta show up in Treasury debt, too. Investors targeting a particular yield may find it easier to buy 10-year or longer debt than to buy one-year or shorter debt and leverage their position. In Treasury debt, measuring asset beta against a market index is equivalent to measuring asset maturity or duration, a measure of interest rate sensitivity. Building portfolios of low and high beta debt still shows alphas that decline steadily with portfolio beta. Sharpe ratios decline steadily from short- to long-maturity bonds. And betting-against-beta from 1952 to 2012 delivers average monthly excess returns of 0.17%.

In markets for corporate bonds, in credit default swaps, and across indexes for equity, the bonds of different countries, foreign exchange, and commodities, betting-against-beta has delivered excess return. Limits to leverage seem to shape returns across a broad range of assets.

Finally, Frazzini and Pedersen look for evidence of limits to leverage in the investment portfolios of a sample of individuals, mutual funds, private equity funds, and in the portfolio of Berkshire Hathaway, the company famously run by investor Warren Buffett (Frazzini, Kabiller, and Pedersen, 2018). Individuals face clear regulatory limits to borrowing against stocks, and the Investment Company Act of 1940, which sets the guidelines for mutual funds, sets clear limits to leverage, too. Mutual funds also often have to hold cash to pay out investors redeeming their shares, which also limits their leverage. Private equity funds, however, often issue debt in the capital markets to buy target companies, and Berkshire Hathaway, which operates as an insurance company, borrows by taking in insurance premiums from its clients. Betting-against-beta predicts individuals and mutual funds would hold high beta portfolios, and private equity and insurers would hold low beta portfolios. Frazzini and Pedersen, in fact, find that individuals and mutual funds from 1980 to 2012 held stock portfolios with betas significantly higher than the market basket beta of 1.0, and private equity and Berkshire Hathaway held portfolios with betas significantly lower than 1.0.

More Betting-Against-Beta

J. Benson Durham at the Federal Reserve Bank of New York noticed Frazzini and Pedersen's surprising results with betting-against-beta in the US Treasury market and decided to repeat the test and extend the analysis to 10 other global government bond markets (Durham, 2015). In the US Treasury market, widely assumed to be one of the most efficient in the world, Durham found betting-against-beta from 1962 through 2013 delivered better returns—more return for each measure of risk—than either the overall Treasury market itself or even the overall US equity markets. He tried the same test in the government bond markets for Germany, France, the Netherlands, Belgium, Italy, Spain, Japan, the UK, Canada, and Switzerland. Betting-against-beta only delivered better returns than the overall bond market in Italy, but it beat the equity markets in all countries. The results for government bonds beyond the US Treasury market could reflect a relatively smaller proportion of investors who are limited by leverage in those markets. In the US, a larger share of investment coming from individuals, mutual funds, and foreign portfolios averse to leverage may explain the good results from betting-against-beta in the US Treasury market.

A Natural Experiment

Finally, the market over time has run through a natural experiment that puts Frazzini and Pedersen's thinking to the test, thanks to the Federal Reserve. The Securities Exchange Act of 1934 gives the Fed the right under Regulation T to set a minimum amount of equity, or margin, and, consequently, the maximum amount of debt an individual can use to buy common stock on credit on a US exchange. From October 1934 to January 1974, the Fed changed the minimum margin requirement 22 times, allowing it to range from 40% of the market value of stock purchased to 100%. Each change in required margin shifted the limits on leverage across the entire US stock market. Each change put Frazzini and Pedersen to the test.

In Espoo, Finland, on the Baltic Sea, Petri Jylhä, a professor at the Aalto University School of Business, noticed the Fed's natural experiment as a way to test Frazzini and Pedersen. As the Fed's margin requirement moved higher, Jylhä recognized, the capital market line should get progressively flatter. If that happened, it would give further support to the case for betting-against-beta.

Jylhä started by showing that the Fed typically changed margin requirements in response to a surge or drop in credit, raising margin requirements after a steady rise in the amount of stock bought on credit and lowering margin requirements after a steady drop (Jylhä, 2018). After the Fed raised margin requirements, the amount of credit would fall over the next year by an average of 15%. And after the Fed lowered margin requirements, credit would rise over the next year by an average of 17%. Jylhä also found the Fed raised the margin after a steady run-up in stock prices and lowered the margin after a steady drop. Congress had given the Fed responsibility for managing leverage available to investors and smoothing the ups and downs in stocks, and the Fed was doing its job.

Jylhä then went on to see if a change in margin also changed important elements of the market or the economy, elements that might also change the performance of low or high beta stocks. Changes in margin had no impact on market returns, trading activity, inflation, the money supply, or industrial production. That lined up nicely with comments from Fed chairs and press reports about the time of policy changes that the market and economy took the changes in stride.

Finally, Jylhä turned to a direct test of Frazzini and Pedersen. Betting-against-beta would predict that rising margin would steadily raise the returns on low beta assets and lower the returns on high beta assets, flattening the capital markets line. Jylhä found a striking result. At high levels of required margin, expected returns from low to high beta not only ran flat, they actually fell. When the ability to borrow vanished, expected returns in high beta stocks fell well below the likely outcomes in low beta stocks. As Frazzini and Pedersen had predicted, CAPM had unraveled.

Limits on More Than Leverage

The line of thinking first kindled by Fisher Black and fueled by Andrea Frazzini and Lasse Pedersen leads directly to considering all limits that shape investor behavior and asset value. Differences in access to leverage, for instance, create incentive for some investors to hold assets that inefficiently deliver risk and return. Those constrained investors reach for high beta stocks, and pricing of high beta stocks becomes dominated by inefficient capital flows. Limited leverage is not the only investor constraint, however. The cost of funds, the ability to hedge or offset risk, the quality of information, tax law, accounting rules, and legal and political constraints have heavy influence on individual and institutional portfolios. To the extent that constraints divide investors and their capital into groups and groups dominate different parts of the investment market, constraints shape asset value. Asset value changes systematically not just with the broad influences captured by market beta but also with the changing constraints on groups of investors.

In a market with constrained investors, each investor has to find a portfolio that efficiently considers the risk and return of the broad market, the current and future constraints the investor faces, and the current and future constraints of other investors. These all are risks that investors cannot diversify away and that require compensation. Robert Merton (1973a) long ago sketched the outlines of a market where investors considered not just the market basket of investments but also their ability to actually use the returns from their investment portfolios or reinvest those returns. Managing an efficient portfolio requires looking out into possible future investment opportunities and the constraints that shape both the investor and competing portfolios. That is the direction where theory goes next.

5

The Local Capital Asset Pricing Model

Shopping in the Neighborhood

Portfolios operating under limits have to find assets that accommodate those limits. And as the limits vary, so should the set of assets. Constrained portfolios will still focus on assembling the best combinations of risk and return within limits, but the investable set of assets falls back from a global to a local market. This model of portfolio construction and asset pricing takes an important step toward bringing investment theory and practice much closer together.

Black and Frazzini and Pedersen take important steps by modeling a market shaped and even segmented by leverage. But a model that allows segmentation by a wider set of constraints offers a richer set of possibilities. An enriched model predicts a market line of investment returns flatter than traditional CAPM. It predicts that factors other than traditional market beta can help explain performance. It predicts an observed market basket of securities that no longer sits along a global efficient frontier, and it predicts that global CAPM pricing no longer applies identically to all assets. It predicts, too, that investors will go to extraordinary lengths to diversify the risks and returns of their holdings all in an attempt to create and sustain competitive advantage in investing. A model of investing constrained from multiple directions begins to reflect the actual market of highly differentiated groups of investors competing within each group to extract returns from a limited set of assets. This model can start to bridge the divide between portfolio theory and practice.

Local Markets for Investing

Investors can have different practical access to assets for a wide range of reasons, dividing the global investment set into local sets. Access to leverage, for instance, can clearly divide investors into haves and have-nots. Those with access extract returns more efficiently from some assets than those without, creating preferred asset sets for each group. Investors can also have different sources or terms of asset funding, different access to or ability to hedge investment exposures, different asset information or investment expertise, different legal or regulatory limits on investing, or even different sources of investments. These differences separate investment portfolios as effectively as borders, oceans, or distances that once separated investors in different countries.

A range of work focuses on groups of investors and their preferred assets. Stefania D'Amico and Thomas King, analysts at the Federal Reserve Board, for instance, find evidence of segmentation even in the deep and liquid market for US Treasury debt (D'Amico and King, 2012). In 2009 the Fed bought $300 billion of Treasury securities to help ease financial conditions, and the purchases had the biggest impact on the specific securities bought and the nearest substitutes, with limited impact on the rest of the Treasury market. Investors did not simply sell their holdings to the Fed and move on to any other security but apparently stayed in the neighborhood. Arvind Krishnamurthy and Annette Vissing-Jorgensen, then at Northwestern University, found that Fed purchases of mortgage-backed securities helped lower mortgage rates, but Fed purchases of Treasury debt did not (Krishnamurthy and Vissing-Jorgensen, 2011; see also Krishnamurthy and Vissing-Jorgensen, 2007). Mortgage-backed securities and Treasury securities have distinct audiences where changing circumstances in one market do not send capital, unimpeded, into the other.

Federal Reserve chairman Ben Bernanke in 2012 spoke to the importance of these segmented markets in the Fed's approach to the 2008 financial crisis and its aftermath (Bernanke, 2012). The Fed decided to buy US Treasury securities and agency debt and mortgage-backed securities to lower the cost of debt in specific sectors of the US economy.

> The key premise underlying this (portfolio) channel is that, for a variety of reasons, different classes of financial assets are not perfect substitutes in investors' portfolios. For example, some institutional investors face regulatory restrictions on the types of securities they can hold, retail investors may be reluctant to hold certain types of assets because of high transactions or information costs, and some assets have risk characteristics that are difficult or costly to hedge.
>
> Imperfect substitutability of assets implies that changes in the supplies of various assets available to private investors may affect the prices and yields of those assets. (Bernanke, 2012)

The seminal work on financial intermediation by Douglas Diamond, at the University of Chicago, and Philip Dybvig, at Washington University, rests on the assumption that intermediaries exist only because of their competitive advantage in holding different kinds of assets and in monitoring and enforcing the contracts implicitly or explicitly embedded in those contracts (Diamond and Dybvig, 1983; Diamond, 1984). Even with comparable physical access to assets, the constraints that bind different portfolios can limit their ability to realize potential asset returns.

The idea of markets segmented by information appears in a different guise to work on the ways producers, consumers, and investors form expectations about prices (see, for example, Grossman, 1981, p. 545). "An individual producer will in general have more information about the demand of his own customers and the productivity of his own land than he has about those of other producers," wrote Sanford Grossman years ago at the University of Chicago. "Thus information is likely to be distributed throughout the economy." For investors, there's a cost to gathering information, but the cost is worth it if the investor can buy or sell ahead of shifting demand or supply. But constrained investors may not be able to take advantage of all information equally. Constraints create incentives to focus only on assets that accommodate those constraints, so investors' information and views on risk and return across assets will differ. Unlike the market described by global CAPM, where all investors see the complete set of investment opportunities in exactly the same way, segmented markets create different groups of investors who see the same investment opportunities in different ways.

Investors commonly have different views of likely asset returns, their variability, and their correlation with other assets. These differences can come from different views of plausible future states of the world or from different views of security cash flows in those states. Investors can have different views on the direction of interest rates or oil prices, for instance, which shape the value of holding debt or equity in automakers and oil producers.

To generalize, if the return on Asset A depends on changes in underlying risk attributes, N and M, and on the asset's sensitivity to those changes, β_1 and β_2, then

$$R_A = \beta_1 N + \beta_2 M + \epsilon_A.$$

Differences in the expected value of N or M become equivalent to differences in expected future states of the world. If Asset A is the stock of an oil producer, for instance, N might be the supply of oil, and M the average winter temperature in the markets serviced. If discovery of a new oil field suddenly sends up the local supply of oil, the value of the company's current oil fields might drop and with them the value of the stock. However, if average annual temperatures drop, then demand for winter heating might rise and with it the price of oil and the value of the company's stock. Producers, consumers, and investors are always trying to anticipate future states of the world.

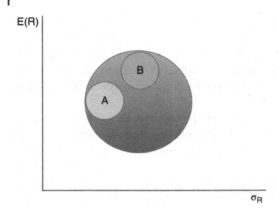

E(R)

σ_R

Figure 5.1 Investors can operate, and assets can trade, in separate local markets.

Even with identical views of N and M, differences in β_1 or β_2 effectively create different securities. Investors looking at the same securities can see very different things. Different securities in turn can combine into different portfolios. This creates distinct sets of securities and portfolios with overlap only where investors have identical expectations of future states of the world and identical expectations of asset cash flows. That overlap is likely very small.

Anecdotally, the significant amount of time and money spent researching and debating macroeconomic issues, industry developments, and potential security performance attests to the wide range of opinion on plausible future states of the world and security performance in those states.

Whether from one or a set of constraints, sets of investors can end up operating in separate markets where each market constitutes a subset of the universe of feasible assets. Assets in a hypothetical market A can exist distinct from assets in a hypothetical market B—asset markets figuratively and occasionally are literally separated by an uncrossable ocean (figure 5.1). This has significant implications for portfolio construction and asset pricing.

Implications of Local Markets

Investor behavior and asset value changes when markets go from global to local.

Local Pricing

In a segregated market, the traditional CAPM should apply within separate segments. Assets within each segment would compete against each other, creating separate efficient frontiers, separate market portfolios, and separate capital market lines. If each market had a comparable riskless asset, the difference in market

Figure 5.2 Local investors hold the market portfolio along local capital market lines.

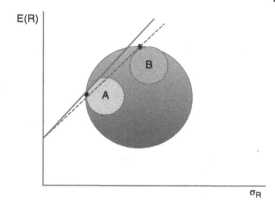

line would imply a different beta and risk premium in each segment for asset pricing:

$$E(R_{i,j}) = E(R_{ZM}) + [E(R_{M,j}) - E(R_{ZM})]\beta_{iM,j}$$

where

$E(R_{i,j})$ is the expected return on Asset i in market segment j,
$E(R_{M,j})$ is the expected return of the market portfolio in market segment j,
$\beta_{iM,j} = cov(R_{i,j}, R_{M,j})/\sigma^2(R_{M,j})$

Investors operating in a market segment would hold a portfolio somewhere along the local capital market line (figure 5.2). No investor will hold the global market portfolio. Because no one can actually see the local capital market line or the local market portfolio, the best benchmark would be the aggregate portfolio of assets held by investors operating under similar constraints. Assets held by banks might define one local market, for instance, where the aggregate bank portfolio would define the market basket and set the point on the local efficient frontier for the capital market line. Assets held by insurance companies might define a second local market, and so on.

Assets trading exclusively within a local segment should price based on the local beta and risk premium and not on global measures. In other words, in a market where assets and investors are segregated, assets price against others in the same segment or against cash and nothing else.

An Inefficient Aggregate Market Portfolio

Because investors in each market segment will invest along the local capital market line, and because the local capital market lines differ from the potential global capital market line, the aggregate portfolio in a segmented market will be global

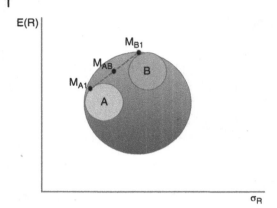

CAPM inefficient. That is, a combination of portfolios from each segment is not equal to the optimal portfolio under traditional CAPM.

The aggregate portfolio of investor holdings will be a linear combination of local market portfolios weighted by the amount of capital operating within each segment. Put another way, the aggregate portfolio will be a simple sum of securities weighted by their market capitalization. In a simple case of two local markets where investors in each hold the local market basket, M_{A1} and M_{B1}, the aggregate portfolio will simply be a weighted mix of the two portfolios, M_{AB} (figure 5.3).

The aggregate portfolio, M_{AB}, nevertheless will not match the optimal CAPM portfolio, which would take into account the correlation between the local portfolios. Consequently, in any market where investors have constraints that prevent investing at the single CAPM efficient point on the frontier, the weighted average portfolio of those investors, which is the effective market portfolio, will be inefficient. As proven formally in the appendix to this chapter, investment portfolios will be locally efficient but globally inefficient.

Weighted Pricing of Overlapping Assets

For assets that somehow trade at the same time in more than one local market, more than one capital market line determines their prices. Put differently, more than one factor or more than one beta will explain asset returns, just as Fama and French and others have found. Some assets may be able to travel across the figurative uncrossable ocean. Examples could be oil, grain, or some other commodity. The share of asset performance due to each separate capital market line depends on the amount of capital invested in the relevant market segments. That is,

$$E(R_{i,}) = \sum_{j=1}^{n} w_j E(Ri, j)$$

where w_j is the share of total capital invested in the overlapping market segments.

Incentives to Diversify

In a segregated market, some investors may be able to diversify freely across different segments. These investors consequently have the ability to operate along the global capital market line. Their portfolio performance should reflect several important features:

- Their portfolio will be globally efficient, meaning expected returns adjusted for risk should be higher than any other local portfolios available in the market (see the appendix to this chapter for a formal proof).
- Their portfolios, when measured against the performance of other investors in any other market segment, will produce alpha relative to any local capital market line. This in turn has several implications:
  - Investors have significant alpha incentives to move outside of limited market segments to capture alpha not available to other constrained portfolios.
  - Investors have significant incentives to create barriers to other portfolios trying to move outside of limited market segments; if all investors follow the first movers, the first movers' alpha advantage goes away.
  - The correct benchmark for portfolio performance is either the local capital market line or the performance of similarly constrained portfolios, not the global capital market line.
- Investors who can operate freely across segments create an additional influence on the price of all assets. Those investors introduce the influence of the global market basket of securities:

$$E(R_{i,}) = \sum_{j=1}^{n-1} w_j E(Ri, j) + w_M E(R_{i,M})$$

where w_j is the share of total capital invested in the asset across different market segments and w_M is the share in the global market basket. (See figure 5.4.)

Figure 5.4 Investors free to diversify outside local markets move along the global capital market line.

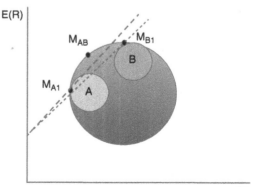

A Flatter Capital Market Line than Global CAPM

In a segregated market with assets largely priced along local capital market lines, modeled asset returns more closely approximate observed returns. Because the aggregate capital market line is a weighted average of local capital market lines, it accommodates patterns of return consistent with observations by Fama and French and others that asset returns look "flatter" than those predicted by traditional global CAPM (Fama and French, 2004). Specifically, because the global CAPM market line is optimal, it is steeper than all others and implies a higher rate of return per unit of risk (figure 5.5). As proven formally in the appendix to this chapter, all local CAPM market lines are flatter than the global CAPM line.

Although local CAPM predicts a flatter capital market line, it does not, on its own, predict that assets with a low beta against the global capital market line will produce returns higher than predicted by the Sharpe-Lintner CAPM. Local CAPM predicts that all assets will underperform the predictions of Sharpe-Lintner CAPM, including both low and high beta assets. This prediction of local CAPM, however, may nevertheless be correct.

Studies that find values for a traditional CAPM alpha well above the risk-free rate may have a methodological issue that contributes to a flat estimated line: the riskless rate used to estimate equity returns may not be the right one (see, for example, Jensen, 1967). Instead of subtracting a short riskless rate, such as the rate on Treasury bills or short Treasury notes, from equity returns, tests of CAPM should instead subtract a longer riskless rate that better reflects the longer cash flows or duration of equity. Because long riskless rates tend to be higher than short riskless rates, that is, the Treasury yield curve tends to slope upward, the longer rates would reduce the estimates of alpha. A lower estimate of alpha and the flat capital market line predicted by local CAPM would fit the literature on observed returns quite well.

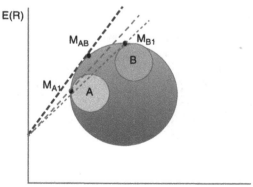

Figure 5.5 The global capital market line is always steeper than local capital market lines.

6

Creating Competitive Advantage

Constrained Optimization

Local CAPM emphasizes that almost all investors work under some kind of internal or external constraints that create advantages and disadvantages relative to other portfolios investing in the same assets. Each constraint affects an investor's ability to hold and extract return from available assets. Each constraint also adds or subtracts from an investor's ability to create new configurations of risk, return, and correlation. Because these constraints create different feasible sets of risk and return, each investor or type of investor operates in its own local market. When investors operate in local markets, local CAPM holds. Almost anything could be a source of advantage or disadvantage, but the most prevalent sources of competitive advantage fall in a limited range of categories:

- Scale, cost, and compensation
- Leverage
- Funding terms
- Hedging
- Quality and cost of capital
- Information
- Access to assets
- Tax and accounting rules
- Political and regulatory environment

Capacity and flexibility along these dimensions largely determine a portfolio's ability to compete effectively in its own local market.

Scale, Cost, and Compensation

Scale and marginal cost may be the simplest and most fundamental source of comparative advantage in investing or any other business. Scale helps reduce cost, and the provider with the lowest cost often wins. Many investors make their investments through intermediaries such as banks, insurers, pension funds, mutual funds, and others for exactly this reason. This applies both for individuals and for the fiduciary agents of smaller institutions such as banks, insurers, or pensions. These investors could invest directly, but most do not.

Diamond (1984, 1996) has offered an elegant explanation of financial intermediation, one that argues that intermediaries help investors lower the cost of sourcing, monitoring, and managing investments, among other services. Monitoring goes beyond just the size of staff and the marginal cost of overseeing a new investment. It also encompasses the increasing specialization often allowed by size, which not only lowers cost but improves quality of information. As long as the net returns from the funds managed by the intermediary exceed the returns that the individual investor could get—net of the individual's cost to source, monitor, and manage directly—the investor will keep putting money in. The issuers of securities benefit from intermediaries' services as well, mainly because the intermediaries reduce the cost of finding investors. The intermediaries in turn will compete to lower relevant costs and develop other comparative advantages.

Within the framework of local CAPM, lower costs raise the expected return from any potential investment. Returns for the entire set of feasible assets shift up from the level that the individual or smaller fiduciary might realize. This creates tremendous incentives to scale any investment portfolio. Other competitive advantages allow the intermediary to develop combinations of return and risk otherwise not available to the underlying client.

Compensation, or more precisely, the flexibility to structure compensation, creates potential competitive advantage by more closely aligning the incentives of the investment management team with the provider of capital. Platforms with tighter alignment should produce better results.

Leverage

Differences in allowable leverage may be the most powerful source of competitive advantage in investing. It's no surprise that leverage plays a central role both in traditional CAPM and in the critique of CAPM. Leverage can come classically from the ratio of debt to equity used to finance an investment. Leverage can reshape portfolio return, risk, and correlation, giving the investor asset profiles that other portfolios cannot attain. That effectively changes the feasible set of investments from one investor to another.

A simple example illustrates the effect. Imagine a market where three portfolios want to buy different amounts of a bond at a price of $100 that pays 3% interest annually for 10 years and then matures, returning the original $100 (table 6.1). Each portfolio has $1,000 in equity. One portfolio uses the $1,000 in equity to buy

Table 6.1 Examples of portfolios with different amounts and types of leverage

Portfolio #1		Portfolio #2		Portfolio #3	
Asset/Long	Liab./Short	Asset/Long	Liab./Short	Asset/Long	Liab./Short
$1,000 10Y Bond at 3.00%	$1,000 Equity	$10,000 10Y Bond at 3.0%	$1,000 Equity	$10,000 10Y Bond at 3.00%	$1,000 Equity
			$9,000 Cash at 1.00%		$9,000 10Y Bond at 2.00%

Source: Author.

$1,000 of the bond. A second portfolio buys $10,000 of the bond using $1,000 in equity and $9,000 in cash borrowed at an interest rate that gets reset every night. And a third buys $10,000 of the bond using $1,000 in equity and $9,000 in debt with a 2% annual interest rate that is fixed to maturity in 10 years. In the case of the last portfolio, its stronger credit allows borrowing at an interest rate lower than the rate on the bond. That leads to distinct portfolio positions.

The first portfolio has no leverage because the ratio of the asset-to-equity is $1,000-to-$1,000 or 1. The second and third portfolios, however, have substantial leverage because the ratio of asset-to-equity is $10,000-to-$1,000 or 10.

If interest rates do not change over the next year, then the impact of leverage is immediately clear (table 6.2). The first portfolio with a $1,000 bond pays the investor $30 or 3% on the $1,000 in equity. The second portfolio with a $10,000 bond pays $300, but the investor spends $90 to borrow cash for a net amount of $210 or 21% on the $1,000 in equity. The third portfolio with a $10,000 bond pays $300, but the investor spends $180 to service the bond for a net amount of $120 or 12% on the $1,000 in equity.

If interest rates move and the prices of the bonds change, then things become even more interesting. Assume the expected states of the world a year later involve three equally likely scenarios: interest rates unchanged, up 100 basis points, and down 100 basis points. Each portfolio would have the stylized properties shown in table 6.2.

Take the case of a 100 basis point or 1% drop in interest rates. Nothing changes in the cash flows of the three portfolios, but the prices of the bonds definitely change. A bond paying 3% becomes more valuable in a market where a similar new bond might pay only 2%. Based on reasonable assumptions, the price of the bond would rise from $100 to about $109. The first portfolio gets $30 in cash flow and a $90 gain in price for a total return of $120 or 12% on the $1,000 in equity. The second portfolio gets $210 in net cash flow and a $900 gain in price for a total return of $1,110 or 111% on the $1,000 in equity. And the third portfolio gets $120 in net

Table 6.2 The impact of shifting rates depends on leverage

Scenarios (Probability)	Return on Equity Portfolio #1	Return on Equity Portfolio #2	Return on Equity Portfolio #3
Rates + 100 bp (33.33%)	(6%)	(69%)	3%
Rates unchanged (33.33%)	3%	21%	12%
Rates − 100 bp (33.33%)	12%	111%	21%
Expected ROE	3%	21%	12%
Standard deviation of ROE	9%	90%	9%

Note: these calculations make the stylized assumptions of a flat yield curve, a nine-year duration for both 10-year bonds, no effect of convexity on price, and no change in yield spread between the 10-year bonds. In practice, a positively sloped yield curve would mean that both bonds would price at a premium to the nine-year part of the curve after one year, the 2% and 3% bonds would have slightly different durations, convexity would affect the price of both bonds if rates moved, and yield spreads could easily change and affect repricing. A negatively sloped yield curve would price both bonds at a discount to the nine-year part of the curve after one year. Source: Author.

cash flow, a $900 gain on the bond, and an $810 loss on its 10-year debt for a total return of $210 or 21% on the $1,000 in equity. What difference leverage makes!

If interest rates go up and bond prices go down, of course, the results look very different again.

Although those portfolios would have perfect correlation across the interest rate scenarios, they involve distinctly different mixes of expected return and risk. The portfolio funded only with equity offers relatively low expected return and low risk; average return on equity across the three scenarios is 3% with a standard deviation of 9%. The portfolio funded with equity and 10-year debt involves higher expected return and low risk; average return is 12% with a standard deviation of 9%. And the portfolio funded with equity and borrowed cash offers the highest expected return and highest risk; average return is 21% with a standard deviation of 90%. The portfolio funded with equity and debt clearly dominates the position funded with equity alone, offering a much higher average return with equal risk.

In general, leverage multiplies the portfolio return on equity, or ROE[1]:

$$ROE = (\text{Asset Return} - \text{Liability Return}) \times \text{Leverage} + \text{Liability Return}$$

---

1 This follows from the following: $ROE = (r_A A - r_L L)/E$, where r_A is the percentage return on the asset, A is the dollar amount of the asset, r_L is the percentage return on the liability, L is the dollar amount of the liability, and E is the dollar amount of equity. Because $A = L + E$, then $ROE = (r_A[L + E] - r_L L)/E = (r_A L + r_A E - r_L L)/E = (r_A - r_L)L/E + r_A$. Because $r_A = (r_A - r_L)E/E + r_L$, then $ROE = (r_A - r_L)(L + E)/E + r_L = (r_A - r_L)\text{Leverage} + r_L$.

Leverage also affects the variability of ROE, although the impact depends not just on the amount of leverage but also on the form, or, more precisely, on the covariance between the performance on the asset and performance on the instrument used to leverage the position. In the sample portfolios, the position funded with equity and cash showed the highest variability because the asset and the funding have a covariance of zero. The price of the asset, a bond, moves up and down with interest rates while the price of cash is always a constant $100. The covariance of a variable and a constant is always zero. The position funded with equity and 10-year debt, however, had the same variability as the unleveraged position because the asset and the funding had almost perfectly offsetting covariance. Gains on the bond offset losses on the debt and vice versa. In general:

$$\sigma^2_{\text{ROE}} = (\text{Leverage})^2_A \sigma^2_A + (1 - \text{Leverage})^2_L \sigma^2_L + 2(\text{Leverage})(1 - \text{Leverage})\sigma^2_{AL}$$

Investors could use derivatives to set up a return-and-risk profile that matched the one from combining equity with bonds or equity with cash or equity with other instruments. An investor who funded with equity and cash and then entered into a pay-fixed swap transaction, for instance, would have the same position as an investor who funded with equity and debt having the same maturity as the swap.

Leverage can also come from derivatives such as forward contracts, futures, swaps, and options that give the investor economic exposure to larger positions than affordable with equity alone. A forward or futures contract, for instance, can allow an investor to buy an asset at some future date while putting up only a few dollars of the purchase today. An investor might agree to buy a Treasury bond in a year for $100 while putting up only $10 today. If the price of the bond a year later is $109, the investor still buys it at the agreed price of $100 and can sell for an immediate profit, producing a leveraged return on the original $10.[2]

Differences in investors' ability to access or use leverage create differences in the range of return-and-risk profiles that portfolios can entertain. Those differences in ability can arise from differences in regulation, the creditworthiness of the investor, the creditworthiness of the investments or the portfolio, or the covenants governing investment behavior. Regulations limit the amount of leverage that US banks and insurers can use, for instance, while leaving hedge funds potentially unconstrained. Mutual funds have their leverage limited by provisions in the Investment Company Act of 1940 or by their investment covenants. Individuals often get very limited leverage at best. All of these differences in leverage create competitive advantage or disadvantage in investing by creating differences in the available configurations of return and risk.

---

2 Because the pricing of forwards and futures also takes into account the difference between the interest paid on a bond and the cost of borrowing cash, the returns would be identical to a leveraged position in the bond.

Funding Terms

Beyond the amount of funding available to finance an investment, the terms of funding create competitive differences, too. One set of investors may get funds on terms that other investors do not—funds at a lower cost or with different lengths or maturities. Another set may get funds with different options built in, such as the ability to repay or to extend the funding—or the obligation to repay or extend at the discretion of the lender. All of these different terms have potential to change the expected return, risk, and correlation on the funded investment. Just as the amount of funding or leverage effectively changes the feasible set of investments from one investor to another, so do funding terms.

One way to see the impact of funding terms is to return to the relationship between return and leverage:

$$\text{ROE} = (\text{Asset Return} - \text{Liability Return}) \times \text{Leverage} + \text{Liability Return}$$

All else equal, return improves as the return or cost on the liability goes down and suffers as cost goes up. Borrowing cash at 1% clearly has a better return than borrowing at 2%.

The impact of funding terms also shows up in the relationship between return and funding risk:

$$\sigma^2_{\text{ROE}} = (\text{Leverage})^2_A \sigma^2_A + (1 - \text{Leverage})^2_L \sigma^2_L + 2(\text{Leverage})(1 - \text{Leverage})\sigma^2_{\text{AL}}$$

All else equal, the variability of funding costs, σ^2_L, and its covariance with returns on the investment asset, σ^2_{AL}, changes the variability of returns on the combined funded investment position, σ^2_{ROE}. Both the variability and covariance will change with the maturity of the funding and with any embedded options. A position funded with cash, for instance, has a σ^2_L of zero and a σ^2_{AL} of zero as well. That leaves the risk of the funded position solely dependent on the risk of the funded asset, σ^2_A, and leverage. A bond funded with debt having identical maturity has similar σ^2_A and σ^2_L, largely offsetting σ^2_{AL}.

Differences in funding terms show up clearly across portfolios. Banks differ from other investors in their access to deposits, and one bank will differ from another in the cost and length of their deposits. Insurers differ from other investors in their access to funding through insurance premiums and from one insurer to another in the costs and options embedded in policy premiums. The US Federal Home Loan Bank system, for instance, nearly stands alone in the cost and flexibility of available funding, having developed a funding curve with maturities that run from cash to beyond 10 years and with a wide range of embedded options. The list of examples is almost as long as the list of distinct investors.

From differences in funding terms arise differences in portfolio return, risk, and correlation and, consequently, competitive advantage relative to peers.

Hedging

An investor's ability or willingness to hedge carries some of the same potential as leverage or funding terms. Hedging transforms important attributes of a portfolio. It can work through either the financing that supports an asset or directly on the asset itself. For example, a hedge can allow the investor to borrow under one set of funding terms and then transform the funds into another set of terms. A hedge can allow the investor to choose the asset risks worth bearing and the asset risks worth shedding. A hedge can also disaggregate an asset into the set of net risks best suited to the investor's particular competitive advantage.

The ability of a portfolio to use hedging to transform funding terms is best illustrated by the previous example of funding a portfolio with equity, with equity and cash, or with equity and a bond (table 6.3).

An investor who funded with equity and cash runs the risk that the cost of cash changes over time, raising returns as the cost of cash falls but lowering it if the cost rises. That risk is hedgeable. The investor could pay the fixed rate on a 10-year interest rate swap and receive the floating rate in return. Receiving the floating rate, barring default by the swap counterparty, would ensure that the investor could always cover the changing cost of holding cash. Paying the fixed leg, barring default on the bond, would ensure a stable spread between asset return and liability cost. This puts the investor in the same position as the portfolio that funded with equity and a 10-year bond.

On the asset side, hedging or offsetting some or all dimensions of risk embedded in an asset enables an investor to transform the risks that the portfolio ultimately

Table 6.3 Candidates for hedging

Portfolio #1		Portfolio #2		Portfolio #3	
Asset/Long	Liab./Short	Asset/Long	Liab./Short	Asset/Long	Liab./Short
$1,000 10Y Bond at 3.00%	$1,000 Equity	$10,000 10Y Bond at 3.0%	$1,000 Equity	$10,000 10Y Bond at 3.00%	$1,000 Equity
			$9,000 Cash at 1.00%		$9,000 10Y Bond at 2.00%

Source: Author.

Table 6.4 Assets with sensitivity to different risks

| Asset | Risk factor | | |
	N	M	P
A	$\beta_{A,N}$		
B	$\beta_{B,N}$	$\beta_{B,M}$	
C	$\beta_{C,N}$	$\beta_{C,M}$	$\beta_{C,P}$

Source: Author.

bears. Most assets represent a bundle of risks. Assets can differ in the number of risk exposures, in the sensitivity to those exposures, or in both (table 6.4).

Take again the example where an investor takes a long position in Asset A and a short position in Asset B:

$$R_A - R_B = \beta_{A,N}N + \epsilon_A - \beta_{B,N}N - \beta_{B,M}M - \epsilon_B$$
$$R_A - R_B = (\beta_{A,N} - \beta_{B,N})\ N - \beta_{B,M}M + \epsilon_A - \epsilon_B$$

The investor can choose a short position in Asset B sufficient to offset the common exposure to Risk N. But because of the Risk M embedded in Asset B, the portfolio will end up short this exposure. A short position in Risk M may play to the portfolio's competitive advantage. And, as noted in previous chapters, the resulting risk combination differs from both A and B. The new combination will have a unique correlation to A, B, and to other assets. As an investor's flexibility to hedge improves, the available combinations of return, risk, and correlation expand.

Quality and Cost of Capital

The quality and cost of capital also can set one portfolio apart from another by shaping the plausible set of investable assets. Capital with different performance horizons or return and risk preferences will have competitive advantage in holding one set of assets rather than another.

Performance horizon can dictate the structure of portfolio funding and the liquidity of portfolio assets. Horizon can vary from overnight to permanent. In the case of mutual funds, where shareholders can buy and sell daily, the horizon is overnight, although inertia can lead to longer effective horizons for large portions of a mutual fund. In the case of banks, insurers, real estate investment trusts (REITs), or other institutions that sell public equity shares, the capital is permanent. The horizons of hedge funds, private equity funds, or other privately held institutions vary depending on provisions that govern shareholder ability to withdraw equity. In general, portfolios with short performance horizons need shorter funding and more liquid assets to meet the potential need to return capital. Longer horizons allow broader funding terms and less liquid assets.

Return and risk preferences also create competitive advantage. Some capital may accommodate high risk in exchange for high return; some may not. Portfolios will try to only hold assets that match those preferences.

Information

Investors also have access to different information, and those differences can create advantage often equal to or greater than advantage drawn from other sources. Differences in information lead to differences in expected return, risk, and correlation. Investors effectively see different sets of feasible assets. But information advantages may be the most difficult to sustain.

In the simplest cases, one investor simply knows something that other investors do not. That information could come from company insiders, suppliers, clients, competitors, regulators, or other sources. It could come from collecting information from enough sources to piece together a picture of likely return and risk more complete or more realistic than available to investors who did not do the work. It could come from collecting the same information as other investors but having better judgment or more expertise in weighing conflicting implications. Some sources of information raise clear issues of unfair or improper advantage, whereas others do not.

Information advantage can also come from speed. That could involve using technology or other means to transmit information faster or simply from talking to good sources before anyone else. Or advantage can come from analyzing information faster. That could require expertise broad and diverse enough to analyze changing market circumstances or the evolving prospects for security performance. It could involve aspects of organization or investment process that speeds review. It also could involve developing technology that organizes or weights incoming information faster than competing investors.

A long, formal literature focuses on the costs and advantages of collecting information and argues that scale advantages in collecting information and investing on it lead naturally to professional investment advisors (Grossman and Stiglitz, 1980; Admati and Pfleiderer, 1988; Ross, 2005; Garcia and Vanden, 2009; Garleanu and Pedersen, 2015).

In evaluating the probability of future states of the world and the prospects for security performance in those future states, information advantage will distinguish one investor's return-and-risk expectations from another's. The likely correlation between assets' returns changes, too. That shifts the set of feasible investments and puts the investors in a local market with advantages over the competition.

Access to Assets

Getting access to assets unavailable to other local investors also creates advantage. Diversifying assets creates alpha relative to the local market line. Investors in one country, for instance, may have better access to their own domestic loans and securities than investors in another country. A bank may have better access to investments in its own deposit footprint than to investments outside that footprint. Insurers may be able to source investments from their current client base more easily than sourcing investments from new clients. Portfolios with a facility for evaluating rare or novel investments or evaluating them faster may end up seeing a broader or steadier flow of those investments. And regulations or investment covenants may explicitly prevent a portfolio from investing in certain assets, ceding those investments to others. In these various ways, access to assets varies across portfolios and creates different feasible sets of investments. Each portfolio consequently operates in a slightly or even a significantly different investment market.

Tax and Accounting Rules

Tax and accounting regimes change investment behavior, too. They can allow one portfolio to hold assets under more favorable conditions than another portfolio, and they can change the true economic value of assets.

Accounting, for instance, can influence a portfolio's ability to hold different assets by reporting some elements of performance through income while leaving others out. Banks and insurers prefer securities that pay high yields to those that deliver the same performance through price appreciation because US generally accepted accounting principles allow the entity to report yield as income while the price appreciation shows up on the balance sheet as stockholder equity. Banks also prefer to buy callable securities, such as mortgage-backed securities, relatively close to par because changes in call risk will have only modest impact on reported security yields and limited risk to reported earnings. Accounting can allow a portfolio to hold assets with high yield and high price volatility because only part of performance gets reported in the most widely followed measure of enterprise value.

Tax changes the true economic value of assets. Portfolios operating in places with high marginal tax rates should value tax-free bonds more highly than portfolios in places with low marginal rates. Individuals who pay income tax on a bond's full coupon should prefer tax-free bonds more than leveraged institutional portfolios that may only pay tax on the yield spread between the bond coupon and the cost of funds.

Where tax or accounting rules create advantages to holding an asset, investors advantaged by the rules will pay more for the asset than investors at a competitive disadvantage. Tax and accounting rules can change the profile of particular feasible assets or the set of feasible assets altogether.

Political and Regulatory Environment

The political and regulatory environment can also change investor behavior by changing allowable leverage, shifting the terms of funding, ruling out certain assets altogether, or by raising the cost of holding an asset through additional reporting requirements or other means. Politics and regulation set the social rules that define allowable portfolio behavior.

Common rules for the amount of capital that banks and insurers need to hold against their investments changes the allowable amount of marginal leverage. A US bank needs to hold 4.0% capital against a mortgage loan today, for instance, but only 1.60% capital against a mortgage-backed security guaranteed by Fannie Mae or Freddie Mac and 0% against a security guaranteed by Ginnie Mae, which backs its guarantee with the full faith and credit of the US government. Depending on the amount of capital that a bank has available to support its investments, the relative appeal of one investment over another can differ substantially.

Guarantees on bank deposits from the Federal Deposit Insurance Corporation (FDIC) provide access to funding at a cost that many banks might not otherwise have. The FDIC currently guarantees deposits of up to $250,000, allowing individuals to feel safe depositing up to that limit without worrying about the creditworthiness of the bank. For insurers, the regulatory oversight of state insurance commissions allows access to premium streams that the insurers might not otherwise be able to access. For Fannie Mae, Freddie Mac, or members of the Federal Home Loan Bank System, the government charters that authorize these institutions have allowed them to access funds at a cost and with terms that similar private entities might be able to enjoy. In the aftermath of the financial crisis of 2008, institutions judged too big to fail—systemically important financial institutions—and implicitly backed by their government might be able to access funds at a cost or with terms not available to other portfolios.

Politics or regulation can also rule out investing in certain assets altogether. Governments regularly enact laws or regulations preventing local portfolios from investing in certain foreign countries or their enterprises. The charters of Fannie Mae and Freddie Mac forbid investing in any assets other than mortgages or mortgage-backed securities, except for limited circumstances. The rules required by the US Dodd-Frank legislation will define qualified mortgages and qualified residential mortgages and will set up clear incentives to invest in one type of loan or security rather than another.

Away from the bright lines drawn by politics and regulation, softer lines create risks for investing in enterprises or activities likely to attract public backlash.

Investing in tobacco companies has been politically unpopular at times, as has investing in businesses that sell alcohol, pollute, operate in certain countries, or conduct other politically unpopular activities. Depending on the range of issues that a portfolio might have before political bodies or regulators—or depending on the power of those bodies over those issues—a portfolio might decide to steer clear of otherwise economically attractive investments.

* * *

All of these factors create advantage and disadvantage that shapes the feasible investments available to a particular portfolio. Each portfolio or type of portfolio consequently invests in its own local market where performance relative to the broad market or relative to competition in the local market will vary.

The portfolio best positioned to respond to market opportunity usually has taken strong positions on each dimension. The portfolio has sufficient leverage but only uses it prudently. It uses futures and forwards, swaps and options to take leveraged positions or to take on or lay off risk. It has a flexible base of funding at the lowest possible cost. It has proprietary sources of assets and information. Equity capital is stable and comes at low cost. Accounting treatment evens out market volatility. Investment returns get favorable tax treatment. And the political and regulatory environment give the portfolio flexibility. But few portfolios hit the mark on all of these targets.

7

Building a Portfolio on Competitive Advantage

Navigating Future States of the World

Within a portfolio's local market, the investment team has to set return and risk targets. Of course, return horizons can range from days to decades even within a single portfolio. And investors consequently have to imagine future states of the world ranging from the almost certainly knowable to the almost certainly unknowable. From the local feasible investments, the investor has to choose a set with the best chance to deliver targeted return and risk over the anticipated states of the world.

Return and Risk Goals

Most finance theory, including Markowitz, traditional CAPM, and even local CAPM, assumes that investors try to build the most absolute wealth subject to acceptable risk. This is a reasonable starting point but says little about how investors might actually strike the balance. In practice, investment return is almost always linked to investors' implicit or explicit expectations of how the future wealth will be used.

Acceptable return and risk invariably gets set implicitly or explicitly against future liabilities. One portfolio might set a minimum return goal, and this goal becomes the liability that the portfolio works against. Another might set a goal relative to competing portfolios or relative to performance in a broad asset class, and the performance of competition or the broad asset class becomes the liability. A third portfolio might have scheduled or conditional expenses that it needs to cover, and so on. Liabilities and the stream of returns needed to cover them can vary in timing and magnitude. Return goals can be absolute or relative but rarely get made independent of the likely use of investment proceeds.

The use of investment proceeds, the potential gains from exceeding expectations, and the consequences of falling short end up shaping preferred risk. Daniel Kahneman and Amos Tversky, psychologists, or, as they might be called today, behavioral economists (Kahneman and Tversky, 1979), emphasize that people often value unexpected gains less than they fear unexpected losses. Gains might give investors an extra measure of return after expenses or a wider margin of performance against competition or a market benchmark, but shortfalls could mean that expenses or other commitments do not get covered.

A portfolio also has to decide how to best realize its performance goals. Returns on any asset come from either the cash flows generated by the asset, reinvestment of cash flows, or the repricing of the asset in the market, and a portfolio can realize return and risk targets based on any combination of these. The components are subtly different, and preference for one over another shapes asset choice.

Security cash flows and reinvestment often are the most stable components of any asset return. Interest or dividends, scheduled or unscheduled return of principal, or returns from reinvestment often come much more reliably and with much less risk than returns generated through repricing.

US Treasury debt, for instance, pays interest and principal on dates specified at issuance with the only risk coming from the US Treasury's ability to pay. Most corporate debt similarly has defined payment schedules at risk only from the issuer's ability to pay. Debt with coupons that float or reset adds some risk to security cash flows. Debt where principal amortizes or prepays or is callable or extendable adds risk to the timing of principal return. This risk gets priced into the interest rate or other terms on the debt. For equity holdings, dividends provide the cash flow. Those vary depending on the net income and dividend policy of the company.

The pricing of portfolio assets can vary much more significantly than the asset cash flow largely because pricing depends on both cash flow and other factors—changes in the rates used to discount the cash flow, changes in the risk of default, shifts in liquidity, supply and demand for the asset, and so on. With factors beyond cash flow influencing price, it shows more variability. That makes price a riskier component of asset return.

Portfolios that want stable returns will often set return and risk targets in terms of asset cash flow. US government money market funds, for instance, try to produce all of their returns through cash flow and none through repricing so clients can deposit or withdraw $1 in the funds at any time. Banks and insurers put heavy emphasis on portfolio income rather than repricing because of particular accounting rules. Banks and insurers can classify assets into accounting categories that allow the institution to include portfolio income in quarterly earnings and but not any changes in asset price. If an asset pays $1 in interest, the institution can report $1 in income. If the price on the asset instead rises by $1, the repricing has no impact on income, although it does add to the overall equity value of the firm.

The rules that allow income to become an important part of earnings encourage banks and insurers to emphasize steady asset cash flow. These portfolios consequently tend to select assets that produce steady income even though the selected assets may not have the best chances of producing the highest total return.

Portfolios that may not need regular cash flow have more freedom to invest in assets that produce return through price appreciation. Life insurers, for instance, usually have a very low probability of paying out claims for years after writing a new insurance policy. Life insurers might be more inclined to set portfolio return and risk targets in terms of both cash flow and repricing. These portfolios may be able to afford to go for quite a long time without cash flow, giving them competitive advantage in buying zero-coupon bonds, for instance, or equities that pay no dividends.

A portfolio can define return and risk in terms of naturally occurring cash flow, reinvestment, and repricing, or the portfolio can value some of these components more than others. The band of income or total return and risk targeted by a particular portfolio will depend in part on its ability and inclination to reposition and the weight assigned to different components of return.

Competitive advantages and disadvantages can have a significant effect on return and risk targets. For a given set of liabilities, all the tools of competitive advantage—cost, leverage, funding and hedging, capital, information and access to assets, tax and accounting rules, and political and regulatory environment—can all differentiate portfolios' abilities to generate return. A portfolio with low operating costs can generate higher returns across all assets and, consequently, set higher return targets than a portfolio with high operating costs. A portfolio with better access to leverage might choose to generate return by leveraging safe assets rather than investing without leverage in riskier assets. Leveraged portfolios with low cost of funds can generate better returns across all assets than leveraged portfolios with high costs of funds. The possibilities continue, and this is just focusing on local assets.

Portfolios also have different abilities to set return and risk goals based on the cost and flexibility of liabilities. Low-cost liabilities allow a portfolio to set lower return targets; high-cost liabilities, just the opposite. Flexible liabilities allow the portfolio to adjust expenses or other liabilities to suit available investment opportunities. Inflexible liabilities in markets without sufficient returns to cover them can leave a portfolio in a very risky position.

Anticipating Future States of the World

Except for the rare riskless asset, portfolio performance depends on the events or future states of the world that unfold over a given horizon. This creates tremendous incentives for portfolios to develop and sustain a flow of information about potential future states. Some of those states will affect the expected performance of existing positions. Others will affect the performance of prospective positions. One of the central responsibilities of any portfolio manager is to try to anticipate events or future states and position accordingly, either increasing or decreasing exposure to those events or states to align asset performance with targeted goals.

Future events or states of the world occur with probability. An investor consequently needs to assign to each potential state, S_1 through S_n, a probability, P_1 through P_n, reflecting the investor's judgment that the particular state occurs. There are various methods for defining future states and various methods for assigning probability.

Future states must be defined based on the risk dimensions embedded in existing or prospective assets. These risk dimensions are the only ones relevant for portfolio performance; everything else is a distraction. If a portfolio holds assets where cash flows or repricing depend on interest rates, asset spreads and volatility, for instance, then future states need to be defined by combinations of these risk dimensions. If asset performance depends instead on changes in law or regulation, then future states need to be defined by combinations of those risk dimensions. If performance depends on a unique combination of risks independent of any others, then that combination can stand as a future state on its own. Risks can change along a continuum or in discrete steps. They can be correlated or uncorrelated. More generally, for a portfolio where performance shows sensitivity, β_1 to β_n, to underlying risk dimensions, R_1 to R_n,

$$P = \beta_1 R_1 + \ldots + \beta_n R_n,$$

future states will be defined by different values or levels, $\lambda_{n,m}$, of each risk dimension, R_1 to R_n (table 7.1).

A portfolio sensitive to the yield on the 10-year US Treasury notes, the spread on 10-year corporate debt, the implied volatility in one-year options on 10-year debt,

Table 7.1 The level of a risk can take on a different value in each future state

Risks	Future states			
	S_1	S_2		S_m
R_1	$\lambda_{1,1}$	$\lambda_{1,2}$	$\ldots$	$\lambda_{1,m}$
R_2	$\lambda_{2,1}$	$\lambda_{2,2}$		
$\ldots$	$\ldots$			
R_n	$\lambda_{n,1}$			$\lambda_{n,m}$

Source: Author.

Table 7.2 Examples of risk levels in hypothetical future states

Risks	Future states		
	S_1	S_2	S_3
10Y Treasury yield	2.00%	2.50%	3.00%
10Y corporate spread	70 bp	80 bp	90 bp
1Y10Y implied volatility	50 bp	70 bp	90 bp
Legislation passes	1	0	1

Source: Author.

and the passage of a piece of legislation, for example, might define future states as shown in table 7.2.

The range of values within a risk dimension will reflect the expected variability of that risk over a given horizon, and the combination of values across dimensions will reflect expected correlation. Variability and correlation will differ continuously, although material differences in asset performance often depend on a limited number of discrete possibilities.

For some risks, investors can infer future value, variability, and correlation from current asset prices. A large body of literature deals with ways to infer future interest rates, their variability and correlation based on current levels of interest rates, and the pricing of interest rate options (Black, Derman, and Toy, 1990; Heath, Jarrow, and Morton, 1990). The literature on pricing equity options also implies the future level and volatility of equity prices (Black and Scholes, 1973; Merton, 1973b). Markets that provide investors with discrete payoffs if specific events occur also allow inferences about the expected level and variability of events (predictit.org).

The same models that imply future value, variability, and correlation also imply the probability of certain ranges of outcomes. Even though these models imply individual combinations of values that have equal probability, the values tend to form distributions that have familiar means, standard deviations, and other moments. Investors can use these models as guides to assign probabilities to future states or to ranges of future states.

Models that allow an investor to infer future value, variability, correlation, probability, and other aspects of future states often mark a starting place for anticipating those states. Under the assumptions embedded in those models, the market has priced in those projected future states of the world. If the investor accepts those projected states, then at least the assets used to calibrate the models are fairly valued. Other assets may not be.

Investors clearly can reject the future states implied by market models and configure alternatives and assign probabilities based entirely on their own information, analysis, and judgment. A large component of investment research arguably is devoted to exactly these issues and to identifying configurations and probabilities that differ from market expectations. The value of business information and the laws against using inside information and other unfair informational advantages attests to the value of anticipating future states of the world. To the extent that investors have different information or analyze it differently, expectations about future states of the world will differ, too. Investors might imagine different risk factors, different levels and combinations of risk, or assign different probabilities to configurations of risk. This is the primary way that competitive advantages or disadvantages in information translate into differences in portfolio performance.

Choosing Among Feasible Investments

Given a view of the future states of the world, an investor has to choose a set of securities that deliver an expected combination of return and risk.[1] Not all investors will have equal access to all assets. Some investors will have better access through location, knowledge of new assets, or relationships with brokers bringing new assets to market. Others will have better ability to configure new assets by changing leverage, developing new liabilities, or using new hedges. Others will have access limited by the quality or cost of capital or by political, regulatory, tax, or accounting barriers.

Even among investors with equal access to the same assets, not all will have the same expectations for asset performance in a given future state. Not all portfolios taking credit risk will have the same expectations about issuers' abilities to pay in all future states of the world. Not all portfolios taking prepayment or call risk will have the same expectations about the exercise of those options. Not all portfolios will have the same expectations about changes in the supply and demand for securities. Portfolios that develop material advantage in anticipating security performance can take out excess return without adding commensurate risk or can reduce risk without giving up commensurate return. Differences in access and performance expectation will contribute to differences in portfolio performance.

Portfolios also differ in their ability to freely liquidate and replace existing positions to keep expected performance aligned with targeted return and risk. In some

---

1 Securities that produce unique cash flow under specific circumstances are often called contingent claims, pure securities, or Arrow/Debreu securities. These securities typically produce a $1 payoff when a particular event happens, and their spot price indicates the probability of the event as well as the cost of money over a given investment horizon.

circumstances, existing positions will no longer perform as well as alternatives. A portfolio that needs a targeted duration or interest rate sensitivity, for instance, will need to sell and replace positions over time as duration shortens. In other circumstances, return and risk goals change, and the portfolio will need to reposition accordingly. A portfolio that decided to increase duration, for instance, would have to reposition accordingly.

In practice, portfolios often have limited ability or inclination to reposition, forcing the portfolios to adjust goals only on the margin. High transactions costs, for instance, allow repositioning only if performance can recoup the costs and add incremental return over the portfolio investment horizon. Taxes can affect decisions to rebalance, especially if tax rates vary across different investment holding periods. If taxes on realized gains fall as the holding period lengthens, then investors will hold positions longer. Accounting can affect repositioning if realized gains or losses get reported in portfolio income and potentially add income volatility. These constraints and others often encourage portfolios to set goals based on marginal new investments rather than wholesale repositioning.

Putting the Pieces Together

Investing becomes an iterative process of setting performance goals, anticipating changing states of the world over an investment horizon, and choosing portfolio positions that get to the goals most efficiently. The goals, the plausible future states, and the best positioning can change continually as new information arrives. The process can take place informally or in structured steps. However, there is limited literature if any on the links between investment process and outcome, although this line of work would seem to have significant promise.

Portfolios that do want to formalize the investment process can take some straightforward steps:

- *Goals.* Agree on one or more investment horizons. Agree on targeted return relative either to funding or other liabilities, relative to competing portfolios, or relative to other investment benchmarks. Agree on the allowable amount of risk or deviation from targeted returns, defined either as variability, maximum underperformance, or some other metric.
- *Future states.* Develop a regular process for defining and updating potential future states of the world and assigning probabilities. Define the risk dimensions relevant to those states. Identify potential independent events. Develop sources of information and analysis. Determine the plausible range of risk configurations. Identify the degree to which each configuration differs from market expectation. Assign probabilities. Focus on states with risk configurations that differ significantly from market expectations or that occur with

a probability significantly different from market expectations. States that differ from consensus in configuration, weighting, or both are most likely to differentiate one portfolio's performance from another's.

- *Securities.* Identify positions or combinations of positions that deliver targeted performance efficiently. If possible, project position performance over the full set of future states of the world. Weight position performance in each state by the probability of each state to get expected return, risk, and correlation. Focus on maximizing portfolio performance in states where risk configuration or probability differs from market expectations. Focus also on securities where expected state performance differs from market expectations.

Not all portfolios will have strong views on all elements of portfolio goals, future states, or securities. The potential amount of information needed to develop views across a broad asset base can overwhelm the capacity of most investment teams. Works by Black and Litterman (1991) and others (He and Litterman, 1999; Idzorek, 2005) outline a quantitative framework that investors can use to combine market models of future states and future security performance with proprietary views that differ from the markets'. When a portfolio has competitive advantage in identifying a likely future state or in anticipating security performance in one or more future states, the portfolio can disproportionately raise or lower exposure and try to create excess return. Everywhere else, the portfolio can hold positions equivalent to broad market averages.

From Theory to Application

The tendency of investors to operate in local markets, the tremendous incentives to create competitive advantage, and the effort to monetize advantage through portfolio construction is the core of investing. A general description of these principles can take an investor's understanding so far. The rest of the way will depend on the specific application of these principles to different investment platforms. The leap into application comes in the remaining chapters.

Part II

Practice

8

Investing for Total Return: Mutual Funds

Mutual fund investing might seem to come closest to the approach outlined by Sharpe or Black in traditional CAPM. Portfolios would try to maximize absolute total return subject to acceptable risk, and the average CAPM fund manager would hold a market basket of securities. But US mutual funds operate under guidelines that limit asset allocation, leverage, liquidity, and other aspects of investing. Although mutual funds as a group still have certain competitive advantages over other institutional investors, the constraints imposed on mutual funds limit the advantage one fund can gain over another. The limits create a local market that focuses competition between mutual funds on a handful of grounds where one fund might distinguish itself from others. The sharpest competition comes around operating cost, the ability to successfully diversify away from a performance benchmark, and the cost and quality of investment capital. It becomes clear that the primary competitive goal of any mutual fund is to efficiently create an investment exposure that its shareholders cannot create on their own. Most efforts seem focused on this end.

To understand the sources of advantage for mutual funds, it helps to first outline the structure of the industry, the details of the Investment Company Act of 1940 that created it, and the most important features of the benchmarks used to measure fund performance.

The Structure of Mutual Fund Investing

Mutual funds have grown much faster than the overall market for US debt and equity over the last few decades, suggesting a strong case for their value as a financial intermediary. As of the end of 2018, according to the Federal Reserve, mutual funds held nearly $14.7 trillion in total assets (figure 8.1).

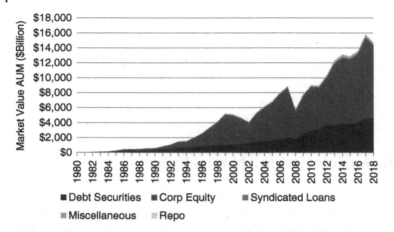

Figure 8.1 The market value of mutual funds since 1980 has grown at an annual compounded rate of 15.1% and outpaced growth in outstanding debt and equity. *Source:* Federal Reserve Financial Accounts of the United States (March 2019).

The value of US mutual fund fixed income holdings since the end of 1980 had grown at a compounded annual rate of 15.9% and total US debt outstanding had grown at only 7.4%. Similarly for equity, the value of equity under management at mutual funds had grown at a compounded annual rate of 14.8%, whereas broad measures of market capitalization, such as the Wilshire 5000 Index, had grown at 10.6%.

The industry has become more concentrated as it has grown, highlighting potential returns from greater scale and lower marginal cost. By the end of 2012, according to the US Treasury's Office of Financial Research, the top five mutual fund groups held 49% of US mutual fund assets, including 48% of equity funds and 53% of fixed income funds. The top 25 mutual fund groups held 74% of US mutual fund assets (figure 8.2). The steady rise in concentration of mutual fund assets from 1999 through 2017 coincided with a swing toward passive management, where the 10 largest passive fund managers since 2004 have held about 90% of passive fund assets (Anadu, Kruttli, McCabe, Osambela, and Shin, 2018). Mutual fund concentration and growth of passive management suggests increasing returns to scale. Nevertheless, a long list of funds continues to survive, suggesting that many managers have found sustainable advantages beyond marginal cost alone.

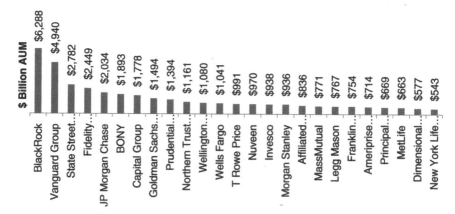

Figure 8.2 Independents and bank and insurer affiliates make up the 25 largest US asset managers.

Note: AUM includes mutual funds, separate accounts, alternative investments, and other vehicles.

Source: WillisTowersWatson (2018).

Constraints on Mutual Funds

In contrast to the idealized investors in CAPM, mutual funds and similar vehicles operate within bounds set by the Investment Company Act of 1940 and its amendments. The act imposes a number of limits (Kramer Levin Naftalis & Frankel, 2013). Among the more important are the following:

- *Diversification.* A mutual fund has to have at least 75% of its assets in positions where no more than 5% of fund value is in the securities of any one issuer and no position represents more than 10% of the voting shares of the issuer. A fund could meet this requirement, for example, by investing 5% of fund value in the securities of 15 issuers. The fund also can meet this requirement by investing in other registered investment companies, such as mutual funds or exchange-traded funds, government securities, or registered private securities, or the fund can hold cash or its equivalents. A fund can declare itself nondiversified and meet the diversification requirement against 50% of asset value.

- *Concentration.* A mutual fund may not put more than 25% of its market value in the securities of issuers from any one industry unless the fund discloses that approach; in that case, the fund always has to hold more than 25% of its value in that industry. A diversified fund could meet the concentration requirement by investing 25% of fund value in one issuer or issuers from a single industry, and a nondiversified fund could invest 25% in one issuer or single industry and another 25% in another issuer or industry.

- *Leverage.* A fund cannot issue debt but can borrow from a bank up to a maximum ratio of debt-to-assets of 1-to-3, limiting leverage to 1.5:1. This does not apply, however, to the underlying assets or funds or ETFs in the borrower's portfolio, which can have embedded leverage.
- *Derivatives.* A fund can use swaps, futures, and other derivatives with some restrictions, namely, that it has sufficient cash or equivalents set aside against its potential liability and that it limits exposure to broker/dealer counterparties.
- *Short selling.* A mutual fund can sell short if it has a tri-party collateral agreement sufficient to cover its liability.
- *Commodities.* A mutual fund must get 90% of its income through passive investment, and commodities do not quality. But investing in ETFs that hold commodities is allowed.
- *Daily redemption.* Mutual funds have to provide daily net asset value and allow daily redemptions payable within seven days, which often forces funds to keep some cash on hand.
- *Illiquid assets.* Because of the need for daily liquidity, mutual funds have to limit illiquid assets to 15% of holdings. The act defines as illiquid any asset that cannot be sold at fair market value in the normal course of business within seven days. Closed end funds, however, have no limit on illiquid assets.
- *Compensation.* Mutual funds can charge a fixed fee on assets under management without having to qualify the investors, but charging any kind of performance fee requires investors to have minimum income or net worth.

Beyond the limits imposed by the Investment Company Act of 1940, most mutual funds also operate against performance benchmarks and within limits set by investment covenants that further detail allowable investment strategy. Benchmarks and covenants arise out of the need for investors and their fund managers to agree on an investable target mix of return and risk, to decide whether any limits apply in getting the job done, and to measure results. Performance relative to a benchmark and within the limits set by the investment covenant consequently becomes a central element of total return investment management. Both the index and the covenant establish the boundaries for comparative advantage and deserve some further attention.

Role of Performance Benchmarks

A performance benchmark effectively establishes a local market of investable assets, and the investment covenant determines how far outside that market the fund manager can operate, at least within the bounds set by the Investment Company Act of 1940. The benchmark can be a broadly published index of all securities outstanding in particular markets, or it can be a list customized to meet the particular return-and-risk preferences of an individual mutual fund client. Any good index will have some minimal attributes:

- *Transparency*. The names and weightings of included securities will be clearly defined.
- *Investablity*. Included securities can be purchased or replicated in the open market.
- *Frequent pricing*. Included securities will be priced with sufficient frequency.
- *Manageable turnover*. The composition of included securities will change at a manageable pace.
- *Specification in advance*. The investor and manager can define the benchmark before investing starts.
- *Published risk statistics*. The investor and manager can see the differences in risk between the managed and the passive portfolio.

A good benchmark makes clear to both the investor and manager that the mandate involves targeting at least the return and risk embedded in the benchmark assets.

The Bloomberg Barclays US Aggregate Bond Index, for example, is a widely used benchmark for US bond mutual fund performance. It determines the securities in the index with a set of rules (see table 8.1).

As of April 2019, the index included $21.5 trillion in debt and 10,374 issues of US government and agency debt, corporate debt, agency mortgage–backed securities, asset-backed securities, and commercial mortgage–backed securities. The mix of securities has changed over time as outstanding balances in different securities have changed. The benchmark's rules occasionally have changed, too, to allow securities to enter or exit the benchmark.

A performance benchmark helps measure several explicit and implicit features of portfolio returns. A benchmark explicitly shows the separate contributions of cash flow, reinvestment, and market pricing. It also shows the relative contribution of each asset or asset class in a diversified portfolio. Implicitly it shows the impact of asset turnover, repositioning, and manager fees. Because a passive benchmark typically assumes none of these, the costs of active management show up as a reduction in benchmark returns. All investment managers start off behind in the race to beat their performance benchmark.

The manager's contribution to portfolio performance typically gets measured against the passive benchmark. This can take different forms, but the most common looks at portfolio performance as follows:

$$R_{Fund,t} - R_{TBills,t} = \alpha_{Fund,t} + (R_{Benchmark,t} - R_{TBills,t})\beta_{Fund,t} + \epsilon_{Fund,t}$$

where

$R_{Fund,t}$ is the return to the fund in period t,

$R_{TBills,t}$ is the return to Treasury bills in period t,

$R_{Benchmark,t}$ is the return to the benchmark in period t,

$\propto_{Fund,t}$ is the manager's average contribution in period t,

$\beta_{Fund,t}$ reflects the sensitivity of the fund's returns to those on the benchmark,

$\epsilon_{Fund,t}$ is a measure of residual risk, and

$\propto_{Fund,t}/\epsilon_{Fund,t}$ is the information ratio.

This is simply a regression of periodic portfolio excess returns on those of the benchmark, but it produces a couple of valuable pieces of information.

The alpha, $\propto_{Fund,t}$, indicates whether the manager is reliably providing returns different from the passive benchmark. This is often the most important measure of manager value. The alpha can be positive or negative. By definition, the average alpha across all possible combinations of outstanding assets in the benchmark is zero, leaving the alpha on individual funds distributed above and below that

Table 8.1   Rules for including securities in the Bloomberg Barclays US Aggregate Bond Index

Inclusion Rules	Key Features
Outstanding/Issue Size	• $300MM minimum par outstanding for Treasury, government-related and corporate securities; <u>SOMA Treasury holdings deducted</u> • $1B minimum aggregate pool for MBS pass-throughs • $500MM minimum deal size and $25MM tranche size for ABS • $500MM minimum deal size with $300MM minimum outstanding, and $25MM minimum tranche size for CMBS Quality
Quality	Investment-grade or higher using median of Moody's, S&P, and Fitch, or the lower if only two agencies rate the issue
Maturity	At least one year to maturity or conversion to floating-rate or comparable WAL
Seniority	Senior and subordinated issues included
Taxability	Only fully taxable, including taxable municipal securities
Coupon	Fixed rate or coupons that change according to a predetermined schedule
Currency	USD
Market	Any SEC-registered or exempt security or securities with registration rights

Source: Bloomberg (Feb. 8, 2017).

mark.[1] A manager who reliably delivers alpha after the investor pays management fees is valuable.

The beta, $\beta_{Fund,t}$, reflects the covariance between returns to the fund and returns to the benchmark. Beta indicates whether the manager is taking more or less systematic risk than average. A beta of 1.0 marks average risk, a beta of less than 1.0 marks below-average risk and a beta of more than 1.0 marks above-average risk. Because returns in theory should rise and fall with beta, this helps identify the return-and-risk profile of different managers. Returns for some funds may trail the benchmark simply because the manager takes below-average risk. Others may show above-average return for taking above-average risk. There is no magic to simply moving portfolio risk up or down. If portfolio returns simply come from dialing broad market risk up or down, then the manager may deserve something for turning the dial but not for anything else.

The residual risk, $\epsilon_{Fund,t}$, shows the past distribution of performance caused by factors other than manager contribution or market returns. In classic CAPM, this is all the diversifiable risk left over after accounting for the systemic risk in the benchmark. In practice, it reflects all of the influences on performance outside of the benchmark, including the impact of the manager and other assets.

Perhaps most important, the information ratio, $\alpha_{Fund,t}/\epsilon_{Fund,t}$, helps measure the probability that the manager's alpha will deviate by a given amount from its average in any period. The manager's contribution after subtracting covariance with the benchmark becomes $\alpha_{Fund,t} + \epsilon_{Fund,t}$, creating a distribution around alpha. The information ratio translates alpha into the number of standard deviations above or below the average market alpha of zero. An information ratio of 1.0, for instance, means the manager's contribution is one standard deviation above zero. According to Grinold and Kahn (1999), the distribution of information ratios across manager performance is roughly as shown in table 8.2.

If better asset managers still have an information ratio of 1.0 and if the residual error follows the normal distribution, then there's still a 34% chance in any given period that even those managers will fail to beat a passive benchmark.

Grinold and Kahn (1999) also argue that the information ratio indicates the potential incremental return that a portfolio might generate by taking more risk. That suggests that the ratio measures return per unit risk. That implicitly assumes that the portfolio's comparative advantages are linearly scalable. That seems intuitively unlikely. Comparative advantage likely has diminishing marginal returns, and even hard limits. Funding terms tighten as demand increases. The availability of appropriate assets can cap an information advantage.

---

1 All possible combinations of assets averages to the market basket, which is the benchmark. In that case, $r_f(t) = 0 + 1.0 \times r_B(t) + 0$.

Table 8.2 Grinold and Kahn's estimate of information ratios across managers

Information Ratio	Percentile of Performance
1.0	90
0.5	75
0.0	50
−0.5	25
−1.0	10

Source: Grinold and Kahn (1999).

Benchmarking ultimately suggests that not all performance is equal. Alpha is much more valuable than beta, and reliable alpha more than unreliable alpha. That implies that managers who deliver reliable alpha get rewarded the most and likely have the easiest time attracting more assets. That also implies that the mutual fund total return business model is actually two-in-one: one model that uses all plausible means to generate alpha net of expenses and a second that focuses on scale and costs to most efficiently deliver beta.

Role of the Investment Covenant

The investment covenant defines the benchmark that the investor and manager will use and outlines any investment limits. Local CAPM predicts that both the benchmark and limits are important because investing in diversifying assets beyond the constraints of either one is a likely route to alpha, or excess returns over the benchmark.

The covenant outlines how far the manager can deviate from the benchmark holdings. The covenant may require the manager to abide by certain minimum or maximum exposures to the benchmark's components. It may limit deviations from key benchmark risks such as duration or convexity. It may enable the manager to leverage some portion of the portfolio through borrowing, repurchase agreements, securities lending, or the use of forward contracts, swaps, options, or other derivatives. It may enable the manager to take short positions in benchmark securities. It alternatively may enable the manager to invest in assets outside the benchmark altogether and may specify the allowable range of outside assets. The more the manager is enabled to deviate from the benchmark, the greater the ability to enlarge the investable set of return, risk, and correlation. A broader investable set improves the odds of showing local alpha.

To the extent that different mutual funds operate against different benchmarks and have different abilities under the governing investment covenant, performance potentially will differ, too. Even with a sector that would seem to match the assumptions of the CAPM, these become the bases of comparative advantage. Funds with more flexible covenants have the best chances to outperform.

Mutual Fund as Intermediary

Almost every pooled investment platform creates value through diversification, and some do so through helping contributing shareholders manage liquidity. Mutual funds create diversification much more efficiently than each contributing shareholder might separately. Funds can attract professional managers, do investment research, collect market information, monitor investments, and trade more efficiently. And funds absorb and manage the liquidity risk that individual investors might otherwise bear on their own. A shareholder can get in and out of a fund daily whereas an individual investor would struggle to build, liquidate, and rebuild a portfolio as easily. The broad value of mutual funds is clear, but that leaves mutual funds competing vigorously with each other and with other vehicles that would manage capital.

Sources of Comparative Advantage

Given the local market set by the Investment Company Act of 1940, the fund's investment benchmark, and the guidelines laid out in the covenant, mutual funds potentially develop comparative advantage from the factors available to any asset portfolio:

- Scale, cost, and compensation
- Leverage
- Funding terms
- Hedging
- Quality and cost of capital
- Information
- Access to assets
- Tax and accounting rules
- Political and regulatory environment

Scale, Cost, and Compensation

Cost is a critical source of advantage for mutual funds or any financial intermediary. It involves not just operating expense but the human capital and expertise needed to assemble and manage a portfolio. Lower cost means more net return for the investor, and that advantage compounds over time.

Investors in mutual funds, whether individuals or institutions, could invest directly in the underlying assets but most do not. Diamond (1984, 1996) offers an elegant explanation of financial intermediation, arguing that mutual funds and other intermediaries help investors lower the cost of sourcing, monitoring, and managing investments, among other services. As long as the net returns from the funds exceed the returns that clients could get on their own—net of the clients' cost to source, monitor, and manage directly—the clients will keep capturing value and putting money in.

Issuers of securities also benefit from mutual funds' services if the funds reduce the cost of finding investors. Issuers should be willing to share some of the savings from lower search costs with the fund itself in the form of a lower dollar price, a higher interest rate, or other features. Concessions from issuers improve fund returns.

Scale is one obvious way to lower marginal costs in any business. But rising size and scale in investing also raises the possibility that marginal returns to any strategy start to decline as more capital drives up the price of assets. Jonathan Berk and Richard Green (2004) propose that the flow of capital into funds with the strongest performance reduces and ultimately eliminates the odds of beating a benchmark. Lubos Pastor, Robert Stambaugh, and Lucian Taylor (2015) counter that the tendency for excess return to fall with scale is clouded by overall growth in active management during the periods studied, claiming that overall industry capital rather than a single fund's scale has driven down returns. Beyond the impact on performance, scale also potentially increases complexity and the risk that the cost to manage the complexity starts to offset some or all of the benefits of scale. In an investment business, scaling depends on an investment decision process that can reliably and efficiently accommodate more clients and cover more assets. If a fund can manage impact on performance, complexity, and risk, scale clearly improves profitability.

Compensation structure also can create comparative advantage by aligning the fund manager with fund investors, but there is limited room for this under the Investment Company Act of 1940. Mutual funds usually charge a fixed percentage of asset value.[2] That makes the mutual fund a co-investor in an amount equal

---

2 Mutual funds can charge a performance or fulcrum fee in which the annual fee rises if fund returns exceed a benchmark. However, performance fees require the mutual fund investors to meet requirements for income and minimum net worth.

to the annual fee. The fee provides a stream of income to the fund manager, and that stream rises or falls depending on the value of the managed assets. However, a fund manager can get the same fee either by attracting another dollar of investment or by adding another dollar of return. And increasing portfolio size through marketing is often easier or more reliable than increasing it through return.

Leverage, Funding Terms, and Hedging

Mutual funds can borrow and use hedges or derivatives only within the bounds of the Investment Company Act of 1940. These tools still allow funds to create return-and-risk profiles that differ from their performance benchmark, improving their chances of showing alpha. Despite these limits, leverage, funding, and hedging can still give funds comparative advantage over investors who cannot use these tools or cannot use them to the same extent. That gives mutual funds clear advantage over most individual investors, although most institutions have varying access to these tools.

The Quality and Cost of Capital

The more predictable the length or term of the capital and the lower the cost, the easier it should be for the mutual fund to keep cash balances in the fund low and the capital fully invested. Stable, patient capital improves the ability of a portfolio both to stay fully invested and to invest in illiquid assets. Capital inclined to withdraw at any moment forces the manager to underinvest and keep cash or liquid assets on hand to service redemptions, often a significant drag on performance. Returns on the fund benchmark usually set the cost of capital for a mutual fund, but fund investors can differ in sensitivity to performance. Investors highly sensitive to performance could withdraw if relative performance lags. The more permanent the shareholders' investment and the lower the cost of capital, the wider the range of assets that a manager can use.

Because the Investment Company Act of 1940 requires mutual funds to provide daily redemption, funds have to watch their capital carefully. Managers have to anticipate the need for liquidity over time, under different market circumstance, and across different types of investors. Holidays and tax deadlines, for instance, likely raise the need for cash. Volatile markets may trigger withdrawals. Some investors may be quick to withdraw and others much slower.

Unlike bank depositors that expect to withdraw $1 for every $1 deposited, however, mutual fund shareholders bear the risk of the fund assets. The fund redeems shares at the daily net asset value. That lowers risk for the fund but does not eliminate it. A surge in withdrawals could run through available cash and force liquidation of securities. A fund that wants to capture the returns in relatively illiquid assets often needs to compensate by holding enough cash or liquid securities to buffer potential withdrawals.

Because of the need to manage liquidity, different segments of shareholders can have different value to a fund. Shareholders quick to withdraw and sensitive to returns put the most pressure on fund liquidity, and those slow to withdraw and relatively insensitive to return put the least. The latter provide the most stable, least expensive capital and potentially allow the fund to hold the least cash and capture the biggest illiquidity premia.

Information and Access to Assets

Quality of information and access to assets generally improve with mutual fund size. Larger funds can afford larger staffs, more specialization, wider sources of information, and better systems for organizing and analyzing information. Larger funds also tend to have a wider base of contacts with broker/dealers or other sources of information and assets, or can use larger trade flows to get earlier or better allocations of scarce assets. A number of analysts (see, for example, Grossman and Stiglitz,1980, and Garleanu and Pedersen, 2015) persuasively argue that acquiring information efficiently is one of the most important functions of any asset manager.

Despite these advantages, the diversification and concentration requirements for mutual funds limit the impact of these advantages, as do limits to leverage, use of derivatives, and short sales. Information is only as valuable as an investor's ability to position with it. Requirements to diversify prevent mutual funds from building highly concentrated positions. Limits to leverage constrain potential return to finding undervalued assets. Bounds on derivatives limit mutual funds' ability to isolate undervalued risks within assets. And limits to short sales constrain potential return to finding overvalued assets. All of these factors limit mutual funds' incentives and ability to exploit informational advantage.

Tax and Accounting, Politics, and Regulation

Tax and accounting rules and the political and regulatory environment might help mutual funds build competitive advantage over other institutional investors, but there's limited room for funds to build advantage over one another on these grounds. Tax authorities, accountants, policymakers, and regulators historically have preferred a consistent approach to all investment companies, limiting room for differentiation within the industry. Compared to other investment platforms, however, mutual funds in recent years have done well by the relatively stable requirements of the Investment Company Act of 1940. One clear exception has been money market funds, which almost saw the equivalent of a run on the bank in 2008. The Securities and Exchange Commission has put a spotlight on these funds and imposed new requirements for daily net asset value, allowed fees, and gates for managing liquidity risk and added requirements for diversification, disclosure, and stress testing. These requirements have triggered an exodus of hundreds of billions of dollars from funds most constrained by the new requirements.

Predictions of Local CAPM

Local CAPM predicts that a business measured by its ability to produce reliable alpha would pursue strategies designed to capitalize on a range of potential comparative advantages, including the ability to invest outside of benchmark assets. In particular, the business would have a few major incentives:

- *To relentlessly pursue scale.* This lowers funds' marginal operating costs and likely improves access to assets, liquidity, and information, as long as organizational complexity and costs to coordinate do not offset the benefits.
- *To narrow the definition of the benchmark as much as possible.* This makes the local market as small as possible and increases the manager's chance of creating local alpha by investing or creating risk-and-return profiles outside of the benchmark.
- *To expand allowable assets and investment strategies beyond those in the benchmark as much as possible.* This would include broadening the list of eligible assets beyond the benchmark, broadening exposure limits, allowing various forms of leverage, and allowing short positions, among other things. This allows the manager to create return and risk configurations well beyond those in the benchmark, increasing the odds of local alpha.
- *To pursue relative value and other strategies within and across benchmark and other allowable assets that capitalize on the manager's comparative advantages.* This generates alpha by capitalizing on a manager's differential access to benchmark assets, differential access to liquidity, advantages in information and analysis, and so on.
- *To improve the quality and lower the cost of capital.* Because mutual fund capital basically is the money provided by investors, mutual funds have incentive to find capital willing to take lower net rates of return, limit demands for liquidity, and take other services—such as customer service, reporting, or access to fund staff—in lieu of alpha. This enables the manager to hold onto the stream of fees despite average performance. Limited demands for liquidity will enable the manager to invest in illiquid assets, a possible source of alpha.

Evidence on whether mutual managers take these approaches is largely anecdotal, as is evidence on whether these approaches deliver targeted alpha. Nevertheless, the evidence is worth noting.

Pursuit of Scale

Whether mutual fund managers pursue scale or whether capital is attracted to scale regardless of managers' intent, the mutual fund industry and the broader asset management industry has become more concentrated over time. US mutual funds show high and rising levels of concentration (Office of Financial Research, 2013; Anadu, Kruttli, McCabe, Osambela, and Shin, 2018). A significant part of the concentration has come from the swing toward passive management, where funds compete on fees and where scale and marginal costs matter the most. In the broader global asset management industry, the share of assets managed by the 20 largest operators has also become more concentrated, running from 38.3% in 2008 to 43.3% in 2017 (WillisTowersWatson, 2018).

Narrower and Broader Benchmarks

The more narrow the benchmark, the greater the potential for a fund manager to add excess return simply by diversifying into return and correlation positions outside of the benchmark. Managers should want performance benchmarked against a narrow index with an investment covenant that enables investing in a broader set of assets or latitude to reshape return and risk. Investors, however, should prefer the broader benchmark.

Sensoy (2009) offers the most extensive analysis of misspecification of benchmarks and finds evidence for nearly a third of the funds studied. He reviewed 1,815 US equity mutual funds benchmarked, at the funds' own designation, against one of several broad market indexes. He compared the sensitivity of each fund's returns to the market capitalization and book value factors that Fama and French (1993) showed added to portfolio returns. The analysis finds 31.2% of funds mismatched. They tend to hold more small companies and more companies with high book-to-market value than the benchmark. These holdings tend to outperform their benchmark. Sensoy showed further that beating a benchmark helps bring in new investors, creating compelling economic incentives for a self-designated mismatch.

It is straightforward to show the gains from holding assets outside of a broad index. The Barclay's Aggregate US Bond Market Index includes multiple subindices, which exemplify the more narrow benchmarks that a fund manager

Table 8.3 The Bloomberg Barclays Aggregate US Credit Index is a subset of the Bloomberg Barclays Aggregate Bond Market Index

Index	Market Value	No. of Issues	Major Sectors
Barclay's US Aggregate Bond Market Index	$21.5 trillion	10,374	US Treasury, Government-related, Corporate, Agency MBS, Consumer ABS, CMBS
Barclay's Aggregate US Credit Index	$5.3 trillion	5,898	Investment-grade corporate and non-corporate debt

Source: Analysis of Bloomberg Barclays Aggregate US Credit Index (April 21, 2019) via Bloomberg L.P.

might prefer. The Barclay's Aggregate US Credit Index, for instance, includes just the taxable investment grade debt issued by US corporations, municipalities, and other entities (table 8.3).

Because the Bond Market Index represents the market portfolio for a larger set of assets than the Credit Index, the more diversified Bond Market Index should show alpha relative to the more local Credit Index. In fact, regressing daily returns on the Bond Market against returns for the Credit Index from 1995 through 2013 shows significant alpha for the broader index (table 8.4).

Major benchmarks commonly leave out elements of asset return that managers can use to produce local alpha. For instance, Barclay's and other indices leave out the returns from special financing that is available occasionally for securities in the index. But US Treasury securities and agency mortgage–backed securities, or

Table 8.4 Regressing a more diversified index such as the Bloomberg Barclays US Aggregate Bond Market Index against a less diversified index such as the Bloomberg Barclays Credit Market Index shows the alpha common from diversification

Statistic	Value	t Stat	P-value
Annualized alpha (%)	0.84	3.13	0.002
Beta	0.69	205.56	0.000
R-squared	0.89	42,255.64	0.000
Number of observations			5,006

Note: Analysis uses daily returns from April 22, 1999, through April 18, 2019.
Source: Analysis of daily returns on the Bloomberg Barclays US Aggregate Bond Market Index and the Bloomberg Barclays Credit Market Index from April 22, 1999, to April 18, 2019, via Bloomberg L.P.; author's calculations.

MBS, often finance for various reasons at special rates well below the standard rate paid to finance other assets. Sometimes the special rates can be hundreds of basis points below the average market rate. When that happens, the fund manager can borrow $1 in cash against Treasuries or MBS at the special rate and lend it out at the market rate, capturing the difference and adding it to the portfolio's return. Funds that use leverage this way or find other ways to profit by borrowing against fund assets can earn returns that show up as alpha against a benchmark.

Major benchmarks also leave out small or illiquid issues that might get in the way of providing regular pricing. For any manager trying to show alpha, illiquidity can be valuable. Infrequent trading or stale pricing alone creates alpha even if the securities provide returns over time that match the benchmark identically. Merton (2008) provides an ingenious example of this. He describes an exercise in which he creates a hypothetical fund, S&P 500 Private, where he holds only the S&P 500. Although he reports a weekly fund value to his shareholders, he prices the actual portfolio only every two weeks. That simulates stale pricing, and the value of the fund changes only every two weeks. The interesting results start when he benchmarks the fund's weekly returns against the S&P 500. He knows that the true alpha for the fund is zero and the true beta is 1.0 because its only asset is the S&P 500. By repricing infrequently, however, he has reduced the correlation between the fund and the benchmark. That affects the estimate of beta as follows:

$$\beta_f = \rho_{Fund,Benchmark} \times (\sigma_{Fund}/\sigma_{Benchmark})$$

The lower correlation reduces beta. The lower beta makes a big difference in the estimate of alpha. After all, alpha is just the difference between a fund's actual returns and the returns estimated from beta and the benchmark:

$$\alpha_f = r_f(t) - \beta_f \times r_B(t)$$

When Merton ran this exercise using S&P 500 returns from 1995 to 2000, a period where excess returns on the S&P ran about 20%, the estimate of beta came out at around 0.5 and alpha at about 10%—not a bad lift for alpha from simulated illiquidity!

Investing Outside of Benchmarks

Broadening the list of eligible fund assets, broadening exposure limits, allowing various forms of leverage, and allowing short positions, among other things, help the manager create return and risk configurations well beyond those in the benchmark. This increases the odds of local alpha.

Seminal work by Cremers and Petajisto (2009) argues that mutual funds have to actively differ from their benchmark to generate excess return. A portfolio holding the same assets in the same proportion as its benchmark obviously differs not at all. But as the portfolio goes overweight in one investment and underweight in another, it begins to differ or show a higher active portfolio share. The more aggressively the fund differs from the benchmark, the higher the excess return. Smaller funds tend to do this more often than larger funds. The tendency to differ from the fund benchmark often creates excess return that persists over time. And even though funds that aggressively differ from the benchmark tend to charge higher fees than pure index funds, the excess return delivered by the differentiated funds is usually enough to give them an advantage in net performance, too. This and subsequent work on mutual funds (Petajisto, 2013) and their active share offer empirical support for the prediction from local CAPM that investors will try to create return-and-risk profiles outside the confines of their local investment set.

The work on active share suggests that analysis of mutual fund performance based on indicators of comparative advantage might be a better test of the ability of mutual funds to deliver measurable excess return. Investing in assets outside of the performance benchmark, using leverage and derivatives, taking short positions, owning illiquid assets, developing unique access to assets, or informational advantage could all contribute to returns above benchmark levels. Outside of the work on active share, the literature has not tried to measure these aspects of fund strategy and their impact on excess return.

A cursory look at asset allocation and alpha in the largest US fixed income mutual funds echoes results from the work on active share. As of April 2019, for instance, funds with asset allocation that differed the most from their benchmark tended to show the most alpha over the trailing year. The Bloomberg Barclays Aggregate US Bond Market Index in April 2019 held approximately 44% of its market value in government debt, 28% in mortgage debt, 27% in corporate debt, and less than 1% in municipal debt. Comparing the asset allocation of the 28 mutual funds available through Bloomberg that listed the aggregate index as the primary benchmark and held more than $10 billion in assets shows a number of differences (figure 8.3):

- Only two of 28, both marketed as index funds, mirrored the asset mix of the index.
- All of the 28 held out-of-index exposures in cash, 15 showed some equity, and 14 showed some exposure to preferred stock.
- Seven showed some net short position used to leverage total assets.

Of the 28 funds, 19 produced positive alpha before fees over the prior 52 weeks of returns; the rest produced no alpha or negative alpha (figure 8.4).

The alpha produced by the 19 funds correlated with the difference between the fund's and the benchmark's asset allocation. That difference, D, can be calculated

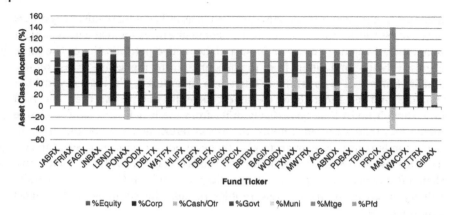

Figure 8.3 Diverse asset allocation in the largest US fixed income mutual funds.

Note: US mutual funds using the Bloomberg Barclays Aggregate US Bond Market Index as a primary benchmark and with assets of $10 billion or more as of April 2019. The index is shown with the fund ticker AGG.

Source: Mutual fund asset allocation as of March 2019 via Bloomberg L.P. (April 19, 2019).

across all of the reported asset classes, j, using the share in each class held in the fund, F_j, and the share held in the benchmark, I_j:

$$D = (\Sigma(F_j - I_j)^2)^{1/2}$$

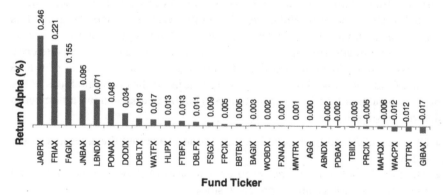

Figure 8.4 Alpha generated by the largest mutual funds benchmarked against the Barclay's US Aggregate Bond Fund.

Note: Based on weekly returns for 52 weeks ending April 19, 2019.

Source: Bloomberg alpha estimated from regression of 52 weekly returns from each fund on weekly returns from the Bloomberg Barclays Aggregate US Bond Market Index via Bloomberg L.P. (April 19, 2019).

That difference will range between a maximum of 100% for a fund that holds 100% of its assets outside of the benchmark and a minimum of 0% for a fund that holds exactly the benchmark allocation. In this small sample, funds positioned a greater distance from the benchmark tended to show a larger weekly alpha over the preceding year (figure 8.5).

These funds took different routes to alpha. The funds with the largest weekly alpha all had significant positions in equity or corporate debt. Equity might seem an unusual asset for a fund benchmarked to a fixed income index, but investment covenants can be very flexible. Equity generally has a lower correlation to fixed income than one part of fixed income has to another, and the lower correlation creates valuable diversification and lift to alpha relative to a fixed income benchmark. Funds without equity tended to show heavy weightings to mortgages and to corporate and preferred debt and low weightings to Treasury debt.

Although these data suggest differences in risk configuration between the funds and the benchmark, they do not show it directly in any way other than asset mix. The broad asset categories also show nothing about whether any fund holdings within a category still fall outside the index or whether the funds had strong overweight or underweight positions within asset categories. Funds could also create leverage through interest rate or other derivatives, which also might not show up in broad disclosures. Consequently, the difference between fund and benchmark risk profiles may be substantially different than a quick review suggests.

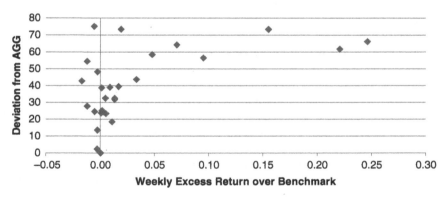

Figure 8.5 Relationship between alpha and the deviation of fund asset allocation from benchmark weightings.

Note: Alpha based on weekly returns for 52 weeks ending April 19, 2019. Asset allocations based on fund disclosures as of April 19, 2019, and categorized by Bloomberg. Deviation calculated as the Euclidian distance between the fund and the benchmark asset allocation along all listed asset class dimensions.

Source: Data via Bloomberg L.P. (April 19, 2019).

Relative Value Investing

A large part of manager effort goes into finding securities or strategies that make a portfolio more efficient, adding return without proportionately adding risk or reducing risk without proportionately reducing return. In practice, this is extremely difficult. Any two securities almost always differ along at least one risk dimension. For fixed income securities, the difference could come along key rate durations, spread duration, volatility, prepayment or call risk, liquidity, or some other dimension. One security that purports to substitute for another almost always involves some different or incremental risk. The new security will still offer good value if the manager believes that the probability of realizing above-market returns is greater than the probability of realizing below-market returns. But the manager has to have some clear comparative advantage to gauge that probability distribution credibly.

Assuming a manager has identified a return distribution that promises excess return with sufficient confidence, the menu of possible relative value positions is as large as the possible combinations of securities. But a couple of categories tend to get regular attention by fixed income managers:

Asset allocation. Fund managers have to decide whether their mix of assets will match the benchmark. If the fund manager believes that circumstances favor one asset category over another—Treasury over agency debt, MBS over other securitized products, corporate over other debt, for instance—allocation to the favored category should go up. The rationale could reflect an expected change in states of the world. An expected rise in volatility, for instance, would tend to favor Treasury debt over MBS with a fall in volatility favoring the opposite. A weakening economy might favor Treasury debt over corporate, with a strengthening economy favoring the opposite. Without an expected change in future states, asset allocation could reflect expected changes in security performance. Legal or regulatory changes could change the ability or willingness of corporations to repay debt, for instance, or the ability of mortgage borrowers to refinance. In these cases, the cash flows of the securities themselves would shift, changing their value.

Yield curve trades. Fixed income fund managers also have to decide whether their exposure to change in the yield curve will match the benchmark. Prices on some securities show more sensitivity to change in two-year rates, for instance, and others to change in 5-, 10-, or even 30-year rates. If the manager believes that one or more rates will move more than others, and more than implied by current market rates, then the portfolio can reposition. Changes in the yield curve almost always reflect changes in the expected future state of the world. That could follow changes in monetary policy, economic growth, inflation, or other factors.

Spread trades. Fixed income securities trade at different yields, reflecting differences in risk and market compensation for risk. An agency debenture, for instance, usually trades at a higher yield than a Treasury note of the same maturity. The yield spread for two-year agency debt may differ from 10-year. Corporate issues typically trade at a spread to Treasury debt, too. MBS trade at a spread. If a fund manager believes that the amount of or the market compensation for risk is likely to change, the portfolio can position to profit from changes in spreads.

MBS trades. Within MBS, securities differ along multiple risk dimensions. One MBS will differ from another in exposure to key rate durations and volatility, allowing fund managers to leverage or deleverage risk along these dimensions by taking long positions in one security and short positions in another. MBS differ, too, in exposure to risk that homeowners prepay their loans, enabling managers to leverage or deleverage this kind of risk across MBS. If investors expect changes in the availability of mortgage credit, the terms for mortgage refinancing or the pace of housing turnover, changes in government policy or programs affecting mortgage lending, or changes in regulations or accounting that affect mortgage demand, for instance, the portfolio can position to leverage or deleverage return from these events.

Credit trades. The corporate, structured, and sovereign credit markets embed exposure to interest rates and the ability of the borrowers to repay their debt. They embed legal and political risks around the ability of bondholders to recover their loans or restructure their debt. The general strength of the economy, the particular strength of an industry or government, the specifics of a given issuer all influence asset performance. Politics, regulation, and law can all move prices. Managers can position within credit portfolios to try to earn excess return from change along some or all of these dimensions.

In all of these positions, the fund manager has to believe that the position will deliver targeted return and risk more efficiently than existing positions. That also means that the manager has to believe the position will perform better in the most likely future states of the world.

Managers of equity funds use similar strategies to pick stocks or to shift portfolio exposure to various industries or to broader factors embedded in equity market performance. Similar to fixed income managers, the net result is a mix of expected return and risk that sits outside the bounds of the benchmark index.

The Quality and Cost of Capital

Mutual funds can also create comparative advantage by attracting shareholders with return and risk targets that match the manager's set of investable assets and strategies. That might seem straightforward, but because mutual fund shares trade in the open market, managers often have little control over who invests. A poor fit between investor and fund can create shareholder demand for liquidity that impairs a manager's ability to invest. One often-cited reason that the average mutual fund underperforms its benchmark after subtracting fees is that a portion of its capital sits in cash. Funds could try to attract shareholders willing to invest over horizons longer than the daily liquidity required by the Investment Company Act of 1940, for instance. Investors willing to keep their capital in a fund and take pricing volatility would enable the manager to reduce cash balances needed to provide daily liquidity. That enables the manager to invest in assets that pay an illiquidity premium or in assets that return principal over longer horizons and pay a term premium. Alternatively, a fund can cater to investors who want sizable daily liquidity and will consequently take relatively low returns.

To attract suitable shareholders, mutual funds can raise capital through channels that attract investors with implicitly or explicitly different holding periods and needs for liquidity. Corporate cash managers may need frequent and unpredictable liquidity; investors in 401(k) or other retirement plans may have longer horizons and less need for liquidity. Mutual funds can reinforce their appeal to different capital bases through ancillary services that those bases value, such as banking services, technology for monitoring fund performance, or access to portfolio managers.

Mutual fund managers can use investors' various needs for liquidity and investment horizons to hold assets appropriate to the profile of their investors. If the match between investor liquidity needs and fund assets is close, the fund should end up with a comparative advantage in holding the matched assets.

Other Findings

The traditional research literature on mutual fund performance finds that funds on average do not generate excess returns or alpha after accounting for manager fees. However, much of this work makes no effort to identify funds that have or that have attempted to create comparative advantage within the bounds of the Investment Company Act of 1940.

Carhart (1997) measures the performance of 1,892 equity mutual funds from 1962 to 1993 against both a broad equity market index and a model that also includes measures for company size, book-to-market value, and performance momentum. He finds that the best mutual funds do deliver excess return over the broad benchmark after fees and expenses. That excess return goes away, however, after bringing in the other factors that Fama and French (1993) and Carhart (1997) use to account for fund performance. Net of fees, all but the very best funds underperform. And the persistence of performance in the very best funds is short-lived.

Elton, Gruber, and Blake (1995) use both a passive benchmark of aggregate bond market returns and several other variables to try to explain performance in a sample of 123 fixed income mutual funds. The other variables include measures of inflation surprise, real GNP surprise, default risk, term premium, option premium, and stock market returns. After controlling for benchmark returns, the authors find that all of the added variables except term premium predict significant increments of fund performance. This raises the same challenges to global CAPM that Fama and French (1993, 1996) and others outline, namely, that factors other than the market basket explain portfolio performance. However, through the lens of local CAPM, the other significant factors reflect managers' attempts to invest outside of the local set of feasible investment, or, in this case, outside of the set of benchmark assets.

Elton, Gruber, and Blake (1995) also find that the mutual funds delivered an average alpha of 0 basis points, or bp, before expenses and −8 bp after expenses. If the mutual funds managers were trying to diversify outside of their benchmark set of assets in order to deliver local alpha, as local CAPM would predict, they did not succeed in this study.

Gudikunst and McCarthy (1992) also combine a passive market index with several other variables to try to explain performance in a sample of 25 fixed income mutual funds. The variables in this study do not lend themselves as easily to interpretation as measures of out-of-benchmark investing. The variables include changes in benchmark duration and in credit spreads, as well as measures of each fund's return volatility and growth rate. The significance of each variable changes across some of the methods used to test their importance, but the study consistently finds that factors beyond the passive index help explain performance.

Gudikunst and McCarthy (1992) find that gross returns on the average mutual fund exceeded those of the broad market index, but returns after fees and expenses matched the index. Efforts by fund managers to provide alpha net of fees did not succeed in this study either.

Although a large body of literature argues that mutual fund performance lags passive benchmarks after fees, the work on active share suggests that accounting for a fund's measurable comparative advantage could change those results.

Conclusion

The growth of benchmarked mutual funds suggests that active management of investments for total return offers something that traditional CAPM does not capture. Work by Diamond (1984, 1996) on financial intermediation suggests that funds provide services that both investors and issuers value primarily for their lower cost. The traditional literature on investment performance would argue that funds do not deliver excess return after fees; presumably, fund returns after fees must still be better than investors can earn on their own. Funds with clear comparative advantage might add to that.

The recent rapid growth in exchange-traded funds and other passive investment vehicles with low management fees represents a significant challenge to traditional mutual funds. If funds cannot reliably deliver excess return, then competition on cost should favor ETFs in the long run. They should continue taking share from mutual funds.

Local CAPM predicts that funds should develop comparative advantage based on size, their performance benchmarks, and investment covenants. Although the available evidence on fund behavior is limited, it looks consistent with the predictions made by local CAPM. Managers have incentives to capture economies of scale. Managers have incentives to work against narrow benchmarks, to expand allowable assets and risk positions well beyond those benchmarks, and to use a wide range of investment strategies to construct return-and-risk profiles that the benchmark does not include.

Finally, mutual funds will likely come under increasing pressure to develop comparative advantage because of competition from another set of investors working under fewer constraints and where fees are less important than pure excess return: hedge funds.

9

Investing for Total Return: Hedge Funds

Both hedge funds and mutual funds invest for total return and share similar incentives to deliver targeted performance. But hedge funds, by operating outside the US Investment Company Act of 1940, have more leeway to provide that return. They also have more leeway to shape risk and diversification. Hedge funds can focus their investments more narrowly, use leverage and derivatives more flexibly, take short positions, manage liquidity more easily, and structure a wider range of compensation. But operating outside of the Investment Company Act of 1940 comes with disadvantages, too, including a higher cost of capital and more narrow access to funding. Traditional CAPM would still predict that hedge funds would provide results similar to mutual funds and local CAPM would predict higher and more reliable alpha. Unlike the literature on mutual funds, an important share of the research so far on hedge funds does show excess return.

Hedge funds consequently compete with mutual funds to offer total return, but the combination of comparative advantages and disadvantages usually makes them best suited to take risk outside of traditional benchmarks. Hedge funds compete with mutual funds and with each other to create alpha rather than beta. This creates a local market in assets for hedge funds. Competition then centers on specializing in assets or investment strategies able to deliver specific profiles of risk and return. Funds compete on proprietary access to assets and information, on different forms of leverage and hedging, by managing liquidity and quality of capital, and through the structure of compensation. Specialization, however, although potentially powerful, is often difficult to sustain in the long run. Many funds reach limits to their size and scale.

The Structure of Hedge Fund Investing

A hedge fund is more easily defined by what it is not than by what it is. It typically is not a mutual fund as defined by the Investment Company Act of 1940. That act defines a mutual fund as a company that issues shares and primarily invests the proceeds in securities. The act carves out private funds with fewer than 100 investors and funds with 100 or more investors that meet specific net worth tests. The Investment Company Act of 1940 regulates the investment companies as mutual funds or similar vehicles, with the private funds usually considered hedge funds.

The rapid growth of hedge funds suggests the sector has made a case for its own value. Assets under management at hedge funds have grown from $50 billion in 1990 to nearly $500 billion in 2000 and to $3.11 trillion at the end of 2018 (figure 9.1). That represents a compounded annual growth rate since 1990 of 15.9% and since 2000 of 10.8%. Those exceed the corresponding growth rates of both total outstanding US debt and assets under management at US fixed income and equity mutual funds.

Assets have also tended to concentrate at larger hedge funds, especially since the 2008 financial crisis. Although assets at hedge funds have jumped 122% since the end of 2008, the number of hedge funds has gone up by only 15%, and the number of funds-of-funds—funds that take stakes in other hedge funds—has dropped (figure 9.2). The average hedge fund in 2000 managed nearly $150 million and in 2018 managed nearly $400 million.

Behind the growth in assets under management and the concentration of hedge fund assets is significant turnover in hedge funds with the rate accelerating into the 2008 financial crisis (figure 9.3). Before the 2008 crisis, the annual launch of new hedge funds regularly exceeded the liquidation of existing ones by a wide margin. In 2008 and 2009, launches fell well behind liquidations. From 2010 through 2014, launches again pulled ahead of liquidations but have since fallen behind. Getmansky, Lee, and Lo (2015) note that only 47% of hedge funds launched since 1990 reach their fifth anniversary, with only 40% surviving to their seventh year or beyond. Rates of attrition vary over time and across investment strategies for reasons including a range of operational risks, mismatches between liquidity offered investors, and liquidity of assets, fund performance, and others.

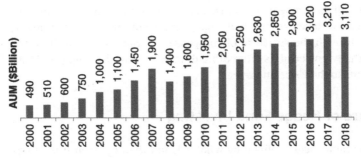

Figure 9.1 Rapid growth of assets under management at hedge funds.
Source: Hedge Fund Research (www.hedgefundresearch.com).

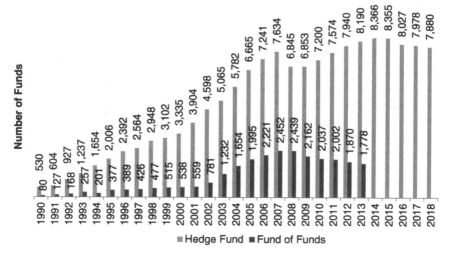

Figure 9.2 Growth in number of hedge funds and funds-of-funds has lagged growth in assets under management.
Source: Hedge Fund Research (www.hedgefundresearch.com).

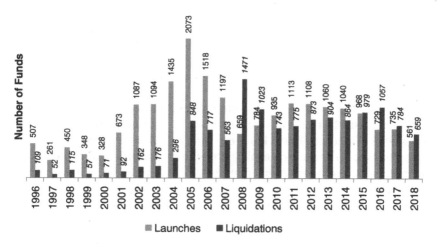

Figure 9.3 Hedge fund liquidations accelerated into the financial crisis, exceeded launches in 2008 and 2009 and since 2015.
Source: Hedge Fund Research (www.hedgefundresearch.com).

A Relative Lack of Constraint on Hedge Fund Investing

The Investment Company Act of 1940 puts limits on mutual funds that do not apply to hedge funds, setting grounds for clear competition:

- *Diversification.* A mutual fund has to have at least 75% of its assets in positions where no more than 5% of the fund value is in the securities of any one issuer and no position represents more than 10% of the voting shares of the issuer. Beyond the constraint on voting shares, that limits a mutual fund to a minimum of 15 issuers. The fund can also meet this requirement by investing in other registered investment companies, such as mutual funds or exchange-traded funds, government securities, registered private securities, or the fund can hold cash or its equivalents. A fund can declare itself nondiversified and meet the diversification against 50% of asset value, which implies a minimum of 10 issuers. A hedge fund can concentrate its capital more narrowly, giving up diversification but potentially building the scale and expertise needed to exploit narrow opportunities.
- *Concentration.* A mutual fund may not put more than 25% of its market value in the securities of issuers from any one industry unless the fund discloses that approach; in that case, the fund always has to hold more than 25% of its value in that industry. There is no limit on hedge funds in this area, allowing industry specialization.
- *Leverage.* A fund cannot issue debt but can borrow up to 33% of its asset value from a bank, limiting leverage to approximately 1.5:1. This does not apply, however, to the underlying assets or funds or ETFs, which can have embedded leverage. Hedge funds have no intrinsic limit on leverage other than the risk tolerance of their investors.
- *Derivatives.* A fund can use swaps, futures, and other derivatives with some restrictions, namely, that it has sufficient cash or equivalents set aside against its potential liability and that it limits exposure to broker/dealer counterparties. Hedge funds again do not have explicit limits on the use of derivatives, although common practice requires counterparties to derivative trades to hold enough cash or equivalents to cover their potential losses on the position.
- *Short selling.* A mutual fund can sell short if it has a tri-party collateral agreement sufficient to cover its liability. A hedge fund can short sell without any limit other than those imposed by common practice.
- *Commodities.* A mutual fund must get 90% of its income through passive investment, and commodities do not qualify. But investing in ETFs that hold commodities is allowed. Hedge funds can invest in commodities directly or indirectly.
- *Daily redemption.* Mutual funds have to provide daily net asset value and allow daily redemptions payable within seven days, which often forces funds to keep

some cash on hand. Hedge funds do not have to provide daily net asset value or redemptions and often can keep investors' capital locked up for long periods with significant advance notice required to cash out an investor. This allows hedge funds to hold illiquid assets.

- *Illiquid assets.* Because of the need for daily liquidity, mutual funds have to limit illiquid assets to 15% of holdings. The act defines as illiquid any asset that cannot be sold at fair market value in the normal course of business within seven days. Closed-end funds, however, have no limit. Hedge funds have no limit on illiquid assets, including assets that could take weeks, months, or even years to sell.
- *Compensation.* Mutual funds can charge a fixed fee on assets under management without having to qualify the investors, but charging any kind of performance fee requires investors to have minimum income or net worth. Hedge funds can make any compensation arrangement that its investors will accept.

Hedge funds consequently can use all of the assets, instruments, and investment strategies available to a mutual fund as well as tools deemed by regulation as off limits for mutual funds. This creates clear boundaries that hedge funds can exploit in competing against mutual funds, including use of leverage, asset specialization, derivatives, investment in illiquid assets, and so on. Local CAPM would predict that hedge funds would use every advantage available.

The success of any hedge fund, however, like the success of any other type of fund, can lay the ground for its own demise. Good performance over time tends to attract more capital. The capital could flow into the successful fund or into funds that mimic the strategy. Capital flows can add liquidity to a local market, but they also lower likely return. If the asset or strategy is scalable enough and fits within appropriate boundaries, even mutual funds can enter the market. At that point, falling marginal costs and lower fees can hand the advantage to mutual funds, squeezing hedge funds out.

Role of Performance Benchmarks and Investment Covenants

The performance benchmark and the investment covenant for a hedge fund should play the same role as they do for a mutual fund and govern the return, risk, and investment strategies jointly targeted by the investor and manager. But setting these terms for a hedge fund is complicated by the tendency of funds to take risks outside of broad market indices. Hedge fund returns often reflect partial exposure to broad equity, fixed income, currency, commodity, and other markets (Liang, 1999). Factors identified by Fama and French (1996), Carhart (1997), and others reflecting security selection and specialized investment strategies also seem to explain some hedge fund performance. Hedge fund returns can reflect exposure to leveraged versions of broad portfolios and to a range of option strategies, too (Agarwal and Naik, 2005).

If the goal of a hedge fund is to provide performance uncorrelated with major asset classes or other systematic risks, then a benchmark may be useful only for guiding the manager on what *not* to do. Traditional benchmarks, or betas, and other systematic factors, or exotic betas, may be useful for figuring out the part of fund returns attributable to market exposure rather than manager skill. Funds that purport to strip out all beta and deliver uncorrelated excess return should arguably get benchmarked to a simple riskless absolute return. Fees for beta should be low, and fees for uncorrelated excess return should be justifiably higher.

The choice of benchmark is also complicated by the ability, or lack thereof, of investors to independently create the return-and-risk profiles that hedge funds offer. This is an important practical issue. Good benchmarks for any fund should capture the return-and-risk profile that the investor could deliver internally, without investing in the fund. The reach of the benchmark should reflect the capacity of the investor. That creates a clear measure of the additive contribution of the manager. The benchmark return is only worth the expense that the investor might incur to create it on his or her own. Return in excess of the benchmark, however, is truly valuable.

Finally, setting a benchmark is further complicated by the typical link between hedge fund compensation and excess return. Funds usually charge a management fee and a performance fee, the former a fixed percent of assets and the latter a percent of returns in excess of a hurdle rate or benchmark. The management fee might be 1% to 2%, but the performance fee can be 15% to 50%. Usually the fund can collect the performance fee only when fund performance exceeds a benchmark net of any prior cumulative losses. That means that losses can keep a manager from collecting a performance fee until returns catch up and move ahead. A large share of manager compensation consequently depends on the benchmark, making the benchmark a critical financial variable for the fund.

Peculiarities of Reported Hedge Fund Returns

Evaluating hedge fund performance and potential value to investors is clouded by the lack of any requirement to publicly report returns. Fund investors and the US Securities and Exchange Commission see results, but disclosure to anyone else is purely voluntary. Hedge funds nevertheless end up volunteering a lot. Because the Securities Act of 1933 bars hedge funds from a wide range of marketing activities, many funds voluntarily report returns and other data to commercial databases to help attract clients. Anyone can subscribe to these databases. The most widely used databases include Lipper TASS, Morningstar Hedge/CDISM, Hedge Fund

Research, Russell Mellon, Wilshire (Odyssey), and others. These databases provide most of what the market knows about hedge funds.

Voluntary reporting of returns creates some well-known and powerful biases in hedge fund databases, starting with backfill bias. Funds can backfill or report previous returns when they start reporting to the data provider. Because the funds use the databases to market themselves, there is a temptation to start reporting only when a fund has a compelling track record. Bad track records may never get disclosed.

Hedge fund databases also include potential extinction and survivor bias. Funds can voluntarily stop reporting either because they want to close the fund to new investors or, more likely, because poor performance has put them on the path to shutting down. Funds that stop reporting can effectively extinguish or cut off a tail of poor results, even if the database provider keeps their prior performance in the database. Some databases exclude extinct funds. In that case, a record of poor performance disappears. Only the strong survive.

A number of analysts have estimated the backfill and survivor biases (Ibbotson, Chen, and Zhu, 2011; Getmansky, Lee, and Lo, 2015). Getmansky, Lee, and Lo estimated the impact of reporting bias for the historic returns on hedge funds in the Lipper TASS database from January 1996 through December 2014 and show that the combination of backfill and survivorship biases cut average returns from 12.6% to 6.3% (table 9.1).

Ibbotson, Chen, and Zhu found in the TASS database from January 1995 through December 2009 that the combination of these biases cuts historic returns from a naive 14.88% to 7.70%.

Table 9.1 Corrections for survivor and backfill bias lower average hedge fund returns

From 1996 to 2014	#fund-months	Annualized Mean	Annualized Volatility	Skewness	Kurtosis	Maximum DD	ac(1)	Box-Q(3) p-value
Naive Estimate	351364	12.6%	5.9%	−0.25	4.41	−14.9%	0.28	0.00003
Remove Survivorship Bias	927690	9.7%	5.6%	−0.22	4.96	−15.0%	0.26	0.00009
Remove Backfill Bias	195816	11.5%	8.1%	−0.54	9.02	−19.9%	0.32	0.00000
Remove Both Biases	505844	6.3%	6.3%	−0.50	5.72	−20.5%	0.25	0.00056

Note: Summary statistics for cross-sectionally averaged returns for the Lipper TASS database with no bias adjustments, adjustments for survivorship bias, backfill bias, and for both from January 1996 through December 2014. Data show number of fund months, annualized mean return and volatility, skewness, kurtosis, maximum drawdown, first-order autocorrelation, and *p*-value of the Ljung-Box Q-statistic with three lags.
Source: Getmansky, Lee, and Lo (2015).

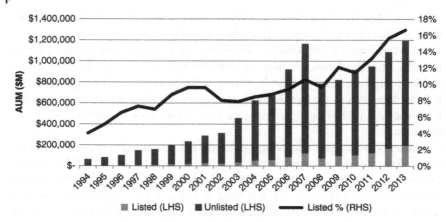

Figure 9.4 A rising percentage of hedge funds have chosen public listings. *Source:* Sun and Teo (2019), Table 1.

Publicly Traded Hedge Funds

The companies or partnerships that manage hedge funds occasionally raise public equity (figure 9.4). Public equity arguably allows the owners of fund management companies to better attract and retain staff with equity incentive plans and to build better operating processes. It also creates potential conflict among the interests of owners, manager, and investors. Owners typically want earnings growth, which might come more reliably through rising assets under management than through performance. Managers might have the same incentive, but managers of private funds also usually have their own capital invested alongside outside partners', creating better incentives for performance. Sun and Teo (2019) find that funds managed by publicly listed firms significantly underperform funds managed by private managers, even after adjusting for risk. They also offer evidence that the weaker performance is due to weaker performance incentives for the public managers. However, listed firms tend to raise more capital and launch more funds, generating more management fee income for shareholders.

Sources of Comparative Advantage

Hedge funds can develop comparative advantage from the same set of factors available to mutual funds or any other fixed income portfolio:

- Scale, cost, and compensation
- Leverage
- Funding terms

- Hedging
- Quality and cost of capital
- Information
- Access to assets
- Tax and accounting rules
- Political and regulatory environment

Scale, Cost, and Compensation

Cost is a less obvious source of advantage for hedge funds except to the extent they get access to specialized investments, strategies, or information at a lower cost than the investor might bear directly. In this case, untangling cost from access is difficult. All funds, of course, have clear incentives to spread fixed costs over larger operations, and the fixed costs for legal, compliance, audit, administration, facilities, data, and technology can be substantial. But traditional operating scales and falling marginal costs alone are, at best, a small source of advantage for a hedge fund. A hedge fund is unlikely to succeed simply by keeping marginal costs low. Some work argues that hedge funds consequently underinvest in operations. Feffer and Kundro (2003) claim that half of hedge fund failures are due to events that good process and operations might prevent—misrepresentation of investments, misappropriation of funds, unauthorized trading, and inadequate resources.

The structure of hedge fund compensation can create comparative advantage by more closely aligning the incentives of managers with hedge fund performance. Most hedge funds get a management fee of 1% to 2% of asset value and an incentive fee of 15% to 50% of performance above some threshold. Usually the threshold is the historical peak value of the assets managed for each investor in the fund. A fund getting a 2% management fee and a 20% incentive fee, for instance, might take in $1 at the start of an investment period and produce returns of an additional $1. The fund would get $0.02 in management fees and $0.20 in incentive fees. If the fund started the next period managing $2 and lost $1, it would get $0.04 in management fees but no incentive fees. The fund would continue forgoing incentive fees until the value of the fund again exceeded $2, known as the high-water mark for that particular investor. An investor entering the fund later would have a different high-water mark. The incentive fee operates like a call option on fund assets with strikes tied to the different net asset values, or NAVs, where investors enter the fund. The manager becomes a co-investor with incentives different from those offered by a management fee alone.

Some analysts caution that the call option created by incentive compensation can lead managers to increase the volatility of fund returns just to improve the chance of exceeding the high-water mark (Anson, 2001). This is a fair concern. A riskier portfolio can help exceed a high-water mark, but it also increases the chances that the manager starts the next period even further behind the mark. The incentive to take risk may be mitigated by investors' withdrawal policies. When fund volatility is high and withdrawal likely, the value of incentive compensation is highest. When volatility is low and withdrawal unlikely, the management fee can be more valuable than incentive compensation (Goetzmann, Ingersoll, and Ross, 2003).

Low marginal cost and the structure of hedge fund compensation eventually can conflict with the best interests of investors. Funds generally show declining returns beyond a certain size, and fund managers have incentives to maximize compensation. If fund assets rise faster than performance declines, the difference grows between best size for performance and best size for marginal cost and compensation. Ideal size for performance could be much smaller than the size that maximizes management fees and lowers costs. Funds broadly tend to stop growing when performance settles around the average for the funds' peer group (Yin, 2016).

Leverage, Funding Terms, and Hedging

Hedge funds have no legal or regulatory limits on leverage, funding, and hedging, making all of these potential sources of advantage in competition with mutual funds and other investors. But all hedge funds face practical limits on all of these fronts.

Leverage is often limited either by the conventional terms of lending against a particular kind of asset or by overall limits on lending to the fund itself. The bilateral and tri-party markets for repurchase agreements determine leverage, cost of funds, and maturity for lending against particular assets. Terms in the securities lending markets are similar. These markets allow investors at times to put down as little as 1% to 2% of the purchase price for US Treasury debt and 3% to 5% of the price of agency MBS and borrow the rest to get levels of leverage far in excess of those that most other investors could take in other assets. Leverage on other forms of debt or equity are lower. Nevertheless, limits on lending to the fund itself usually reduce effective leverage. Many lenders in the repurchase or securities lending markets hesitate to allow more leverage at a hedge fund than they would take themselves, effectively limiting leverage to levels prevailing at banks and broker/dealers, which can be much lower than the levels offered in the funding markets.

Most hedge funds have limited sources of funding. Because the fund managers themselves usually have very little equity and no public rating, the fund typically cannot get unsecured loans or issue debt to finance assets. Funding is usually limited to the repurchase or securities lending markets, which tend to offer floating-rate financing with short maturities. That exposes hedge funds to any tightening of terms in those markets.

Hedge funds often do have lots of flexibility to hedge or use derivatives, but it is limited by the conventional terms in those markets. Parties to derivatives contracts increasingly have to put down margin at the outset of a transaction and as the market value of the position varies over time. The initial and variation margin protects their contract counterparties. Margins tie up capital that could otherwise be used to invest. Limits to counterparty exposure could also reduce hedge fund access to hedging instruments.

Work focusing on hedge fund leverage finds it more influenced by broad factors outside of a fund, such as leverage at investment banks, rather than by the particulars of a fund itself (Ang, Gorovyy, and van Inwegen, 2011). Others find that hedge funds adjust leverage as broad market liquidity ebbs and flows and that the funds best at timing liquidity outperform the worst by 4.0% to 5.5% a year after adjusting for risk (Cao, Chen, Liang, and Lo, 2013).

Quality and Cost of Capital

The quality of hedge fund capital depends on terms for withdrawing investor funds, and the cost of capital depends on investor expectations for return, risk, and correlation with other assets. Hedge funds usually have more stable capital than mutual funds but less stable capital than other institutional investors. And the cost of hedge fund capital is usually high relative to other investors'.

Most hedge funds require investors to keep their capital invested for some minimum time, usually at least one year but potentially several, and almost all require some kind of advance notice, such as 30, 60, or 90 days, for quarterly or less-frequent withdrawal. The minimum time or lockup and the notice period allows the fund manager to invest in less liquid assets and to keep cash balances low and invested balances high. All of this should accrue to fund performance.

Most hedge fund covenants also allow gates and side pockets. Gates enable the fund manager to suspend withdrawal indefinitely to avoid asset sales in a distressed market where prices arguably would not reflect fundamental fair value. This can protect investors, especially ones with no interest in liquidating their position. Side pockets enable the manager to put certain assets in a separate account until market conditions allow a sale at fair value; existing investors hold an interest in the side pocket, new investors do not. Gates and side pockets also enable the fund manager to manage liquidity. Of course, they also preserve the management fee, which could put the manager in conflict with the investor.

Aragon (2007) found that funds that lock up capital for some minimum time produce excess returns of 4% to 7% higher than funds without these restrictions. But Ang and Bollen (2010) viewed these restrictions as limits on investors' option to withdraw funds and estimate the cost of a two-year minimum and a three-month notice period as equivalent to 1% of invested capital. They also argue that the ability to impose gates in a volatile market can be worth a lot more. These limits may all create expectations of higher return.

The cost of hedge fund capital depends on investor expectations and on uncertainty, transparency, and confidence about fund performance. Because hedge funds usually take less transparent, larger, and less liquid risks and often use proprietary strategies, investors usually expect higher return. Because hedge funds also have less regulatory oversight than other institutional investors, investors have to provide more oversight themselves and need some compensation for it. Expected return sets the cost of hedge fund capital, and those returns often are multiples of the returns expected from mutual funds and other institutional portfolios. Lack of transparency and volatility of return contribute to a higher cost of capital for hedge funds (see, for example, Jurek and Stafford, 2011).

Larger and older hedge funds generally have a lower cost of capital than smaller and newer funds, which have to compensate investors for operational risk. Larger and older funds are more likely to have better staffed and tested operations less prone to the mistakes that put funds out of business.

Information and Access to Assets

Better information and better access to assets or to investment strategies that the investor otherwise cannot get may be the most distinct potential advantage of hedge funds. Hedge funds' ability to hold concentrated portfolios creates incentive for the fund to build specialized intellectual capital and investment process that more generalized portfolios, such as mutual funds, cannot justify. This enables the hedge fund to take more active positions within a benchmark set of assets or take positions in assets outside of a benchmark. And specialization reduces the time and marginal cost to evaluate new positions. The potential for hedge funds to provide quick evaluations of unique assets or transactions also encourages current holders or issuers of those investments to approach hedge funds before other investors, especially if the seller needs a quick response. Better information and better access to assets creates a diversifying investment that generates excess return against most broad market indices.

Hedge funds may have the greatest competitive advantage in assets or markets where information is costly to develop. That likely describes relatively new, complex, or idiosyncratic assets about which most investors are partially informed at best. With fewer portfolios informed about the prospects for periodic returns, informed hedge funds should have the greatest return on information. That is a central feature of any market where information is expensive and investor beliefs differ (Grossman and Stiglitz, 1980).

Advantages in information and access may be the hardest advantages to sustain because the performance of the fund often signals an investment opportunity to other investors. Even if the fund keeps its performance private, the price action in the asset may signal the fund's changing views of performance prospects. Information that flows through a fund's marketing materials, trading partners, or former employees can chip away at informational advantages as well. Part of the difficulty in surviving as a hedge fund may be related to the erosion of these advantages and the reduction in returns as other investors come in. Either returns fall below levels expected by investors or the fund moves into areas where it has no comparative advantage.

Tax and Accounting, Politics, and Regulation

Tax and accounting rules rarely offer comparative advantage to hedge funds because most operate as partnerships with taxes imposed on the partners and use straightforward market value accounting for interest, dividends, and capital gains. Most other institutional investors can choose to use the same approach to tax and accounting, although many have other approaches available, too.

Regulation of hedge funds generally has been light compared to other institutional investors, and that has been an occasional source of advantage. Under the 2010 Dodd-Frank legislation, US funds with more than $100 million in capital have had to register with the Securities and Exchange Commission and file regular reports on assets managed, leverage, counterparties, positions, valuation practices, and so on. Funds do not have to report returns. Hedge funds can choose levels of leverage, liquidity, reporting, and compensation that suit the return and risk targets of their investors rather than regulators. That can give hedge funds more flexibility in holding or trading certain assets.

The impact of politics on hedge funds also has been relatively light. Compared to most other institutional investors, hedge funds do not attract the same range of investors or control the same share of debt or equity markets. With perhaps the notable exception of the fund Long-Term Capital Management in 1998, hedge funds have limited ability to distort markets or pose systemic risk to the financial system. They consequently attract limited political interest.

Predictions of Local CAPM

Hedge funds broadly have comparative advantage in investing in assets outside of broad market indices or in using investment strategies within those indices that mutual funds or other institutional investors cannot execute easily, such as strategies using asset concentration, leverage, derivatives, short positions, and illiquid assets. These assets and strategies effectively define the local market in hedge fund investments. Within that market, funds can differentiate by information, expertise, and access to assets or by quality and cost of capital.

Local CAPM predicts that hedge funds would compete in investing outside of benchmark assets, particularly because performance incentives create material reward for generating excess return. This leads to incentives similar to those faced by mutual funds:

- *To use incentive compensation and other mechanisms to align managers with investors.* This has no direct impact on local markets beyond making them more efficient, but it helps hedge funds compete on performance.
- *To invest in assets outside of broad market indices as much as possible.* Hedge funds have to offer excess return relative to exposures available in broad market indices. This would include investing in assets outside of broad indices, broadening exposure limits within indices, or allowing concentrated positions. This enables the manager to create return and risk configurations well beyond those in the benchmark. It also enables the managers to move from one asset class or market or investment strategy to others as opportunities for excess return change.
- *To use illiquid assets, leverage, hedging, and short positions.* This also enables the manager to create return and risk configurations well beyond those in the benchmark or in most mutual funds. Illiquid assets compensate for a high cost of converting to cash. Leverage magnifies the risk configurations of a portfolio, and hedging and short positions change the mix of net risk within a portfolio.
- *To improve the quality and lower the cost of capital.* Longer lockups, gates, side pockets, advance notice requirements, and limited windows for liquidity reduce demands for liquidity. Other services, such as regular reporting and access to portfolio managers, help improve transparency and trust and lower the risk of sudden withdrawals. All of these help keep capital in the fund longer, improving its quality and possibly lowering its cost.
- *To focus on markets where information is costly.* This enables a hedge fund to build up concentrated positions beyond the scope of mutual funds or other portfolios and fully extract return on information.

The Formal Literature

Research on hedge funds has grown with the rising balance of assets under management, and elements of that research bear on the predictions of local CAPM.

The Impact of Incentive Compensation

Although no research has examined whether incentive fees lead managers to develop specific comparative advantages, Ackermann, McEnally, and Ravenscraft (1999) have studied the relation between incentive fee and risk-adjusted performance. They find that an increase in incentive fees from zero to 20% leads to an average increase in a fund's Sharpe ratio of 66%.

Liang (1999) looked across funds at the link between average monthly returns and incentive and management fees. He found that returns rise significantly with incentive fees, a 1% increase in incentive fee predicting a 1.3% increase in average monthly return. Performance does not change significantly with management fee, Liang found, suggesting that incentive fees link compensation clearly to performance, whereas management fees do not.

Agarwal, Daniel, and Naik (2005) take a more nuanced approach to incentive fees, distinguishing them based on their distance from the high-water mark. This is equivalent to approximating the delta of a call option, or the sensitivity of the option's value to a change in the value of the underlying asset. Agarwal and his colleagues define delta as the expected change in manager compensation for a 1% increase in the value of the fund. They find that the closer the funds' performance is to the high-water mark, or the higher the delta, the better the performance.

Out-of-Index Sources of Excess Return

Fung and Hsieh (2004) study the factors that might adequately benchmark hedge fund performance. They focus on creating hedge fund indices, but the work speaks to sources of return beyond the standard factors of stocks, bonds, and cash. This suggests that hedge funds do create return by taking exposures well beyond the standard asset benchmarks. They find other sources of diversifying return for portfolios of conventional assets:

- *Momentum.* This generates return when asset prices trend, which Fung and Hsieh model as a portfolio of lookback puts and calls, or, more specifically, straddles. Momentum strategies do well when conventional markets are distressed, and they provide a valuable diversifying return. Fung and Hsieh allow for momentum strategies in stocks, bonds, and commodities.
- *Fixed income.* These strategies vary, but Fung and Hsieh proxy these by changes in the yield on the 10-year Treasury note and by the spread between the 10-year and Moody's Baa index to capture both interest rate sensitivity and the tendency of these funds to take credit and liquidity risk.
- *Equity.* These strategies get proxied by the S&P and by the difference between returns on large- and small-cap equity.

Fung and Hsieh (2004) found that a combination of conventional benchmarks and these extra factors explain between 55% and 80% of hedge fund returns. They also found that the explanatory power of these factors varies over time, which signals that hedge funds change the risks they take. And they further found that after accounting for return from these risk factors, hedge funds provide no significant alpha. However, exposure to these alternative risk factors may be the primary contribution of hedge funds. In that case, exposure becomes alpha.

Liang (1999) finds that hedge funds provide returns largely uncorrelated with conventional asset classes. He regresses hedge fund performance on returns in eight asset classes: for equity, US equity (the S&P 500), international equity (MSCI World Equity Index), and emerging market equity (MSCI Emerging Market Index); for debt, US debt (Salomon Brothers Government and Corporate Bond Index) and international sovereign debt (the Salomon Brothers World Government Bond Index); for currency, the US Federal Reserve Bank trade-weighted dollar index; for commodities, the gold price; and for cash, the one-month Eurodollar deposit rate. The share of variance explained ranged from 20% to 77%.

Other authors focus on targeted hedge fund strategies. Mitchell and Pulvino (2001) focus on merger arbitrage. This involves buying the stock of a target company and shorting the stock of the acquirer on the assumption that the merger will close. Fung and Hsieh note that this strategy has a low correlation with the S&P except where the index drops sharply. In normal markets, the success or failure of a particular merger is idiosyncratic and diversifiable, but in a down market the risk that mergers get called off becomes systemic. The authors note that merger arbitrage resembles a short position in an out-of-the-money put on the S&P. Merger arbitrage consequently provides exposure to a unique form of optionality.

Many hedge funds' performance correlates with short positions in put options on major market indices. Agarwal and Naik (2004) compared hedge fund returns with strategies of rolling monthly sales of puts and calls on the S&P 500 Index. They found that fund returns resemble a rolling short position in puts, further evidence that hedge funds provide exposure to risk factors outside of major indices.

Ibbotson, Chen, and Zhu (2011) found strong indications of alpha in their study of performance in 6,169 hedge funds that reported to the TASS database from January 1995 to December 2009 (table 9.2). After correcting for survivorship and backfill bias, the authors tested for returns in excess of those provided by traditional stocks, bonds, and cash. They found statistically significant alpha overall and in four of nine strategies—equity market neutral, event driven, fixed income arbitrage, and long-short equity. Of course, they also found that hedge fund returns include a sizable amount of beta to conventional indexes, meaning that managers get paid in part for providing passive exposure.

Ibbotson and his colleagues (2011) appealed to the potential for hedge funds to provide exposure to risk that an investor might not otherwise get:

> A substantial portion of alpha can always be thought of as betas waiting to be discovered or implemented. Nevertheless, because hedge funds are the primary way to gain exposure to these nontraditional betas, the latter should be viewed as part of the added value that hedge funds provide as compared with traditional long-only managers. (pp. 18–19)

Table 9.2 Hedge fund alpha and systematic beta estimates January 1995–2008

Subcategory	Compound Annual Return	Annual Alpha	Betas (sum of betas = 1)			
			Stocks	Bonds	Cash	R^2
Convertible arbitrage	7.41%	2.79%	0.34	−0.21	0.87	0.35
Emerging market	8.81	4.66	0.65	−0.67	1.02	0.39
Equity market neutral	7.08	2.86*	0.08	0.04	0.87	0.17
Event driven	8.33	3.94*	0.31	−0.29	0.99	0.52
Fixed-income arbitrage	6.57	2.91*	0.11	−0.16	1.05	0.12
Global macro	7.67	2.54	0.16	0.26	0.58	0.09
Long–short equity	9.99	4.79*	0.49	−0.29	0.80	0.55
Managed futures	5.03	0.57	−0.05	0.59	0.46	0.10
Dedicated short	−0.34	1.91	−0.90	0.35	1.55	0.56
Overall equal weighted	7.70%	3.00%*	0.34	−0.21	0.87	0.48

*Significant at the 5 percent level.
Notes: This table reports regression results for equal-weighted indices' (live plus dead, no backfill) post-free returns. The betas for stocks and bonds are the sums of their betas and their lagged betas.
Source: Ibbotson, Chen. and Zhu (2011).

Ibbotson and his colleagues also test for alpha after controlling for the seven factors that Fung and Hsieh (2004) found contributing to hedge fund returns. These data also show alpha at a level similar to that also found by Fung and Hsieh (table 9.3).

Hedge fund alpha also seems to persist across a variety of market conditions, according to Ibbotson's work. Except for 1998, Ibbotson and his colleagues find aggregate alpha in hedge funds from 1998 through 2008 (figure 9.5). That includes the dot.com bubble and its crash and the housing bubble and its crash.

The models that find alpha in hedge fund performance after controlling for stocks, bonds, and cash or for Fung and Hsieh factors may simply be missing an important factor. Bondarenko (2004) argues that hedge funds commonly take volatility risk, which commands a high premium. He uses traded options to build a measure of the market price of volatility risk and finds evidence that hedge funds regularly sell this risk. After controlling for this, alpha in his study goes away.

Use of Illiquid Assets, Leverage, Hedging, and Short Positions

Aragon (2007) attributes a significant part of alpha to hedge fund investment in illiquid assets. He studies funds that have different lockups and finds that funds with lockups annually return 4% more than funds without. Funds holding the

Table 9.3 Fung-Hsieh seven-factor model January 1995–December 2009

Factor	Proxy	Beta	t-Value
Bond trend-following factor	Return of PTFS bond look-back straddle	−0.008	−1.21
Currency trend-following factor	Return of PTFS currency look-back straddle	0.013	2.46
Commodity trend-following factor	Return of PTFS commodity look-back straddle	0.014	2.04
Equity market factor	S&P 500 monthly total return	0.265	12.65
Size spread factor	Wilshire Small Cap 1750 Index return—Wilshire Large Cap 750 Index monthly return	0.199	5.99
Bond market factor	Monthly change in the 10-year Treasury constant maturity yield	−2.523	−0.46
Credit spread factor	Monthly change in the Moody's Baa yield less 10-year Treasury constant maturity yield	−29.858	−4.65
Annual alpha		4.94%*	4.3
R^2		0.63	

*Significant at the 5 percent level.
Notes: This table reports results from the seven-factor model for equal-weighted indices' (live plus dead, no backfill) post-fee returns. PTFS stands for primitive trend-following strategy. The three trend-following factors were downloaded from David A. Hsieh's website: http://faculty .fuqua.duke.edu/~dah7/HFRFData.htm.
Source: Ibbotson, Chen, and Zhu (2011).

most liquid shares show either negative or insignificant alpha. Aragon also finds that liquidity restrictions predict underlying asset liquidity, suggesting that funds investing in illiquid markets use restrictions to screen for investors with low liquidity needs. Getmansky, Lee, and Lo (2015) argue that

> Illiquidity is one of the most important characteristics of certain hedge fund investments. . . . it is also central to how many financial investments generate their returns. Taking on illiquidity risk is one of the most effective ways for long-horizon investors to build wealth. (p. 32)

Lo (2001) and Getmansky, Lo, and Makarov (2004) outline a novel measure of hedge fund liquidity that uses the serial correlation of returns. They argue that past returns in an efficient market should contain little information about future returns because traders would drive expected excess returns to zero. Returns should be uncorrelated unless trading frictions, such as illiquidity, exist that

Return (%)

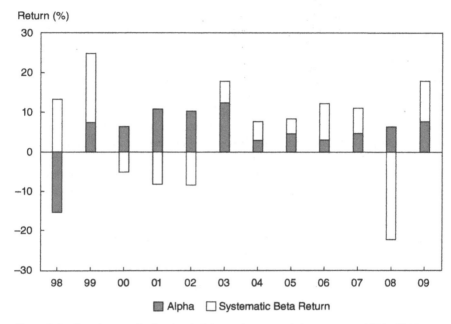

■ Alpha □ Systematic Beta Return

Figure 9.5 Year-by-year hedge fund alpha and systematic beta returns 1998–2008
Source: Ibbotson, Chen, and Zhu (2011).

prevent traders from exploiting information. Illiquidity might prevent traders from acting quickly or in sufficient size. Kruttli, Patton, and Ramadorai (2014) used this measure to help predict hedge fund returns in commodities, currencies, bonds, and equities.

Finally, Fung, Hsieh, Naik, and Ramadori (2005) look at the ability of hedge funds to generate alpha by using returns from funds of hedge funds. These data avoid survivorship bias because even failed funds remain in the portfolios of funds of funds. These authors find that performance in funds of hedge funds from 1995 to 2004 is largely explained by exposure to the Fung and Hsieh factors with no alpha leftover except for the brief period between October 1998 and March 2000. However, roughly a fifth of funds in the study do deliver statistically significant positive alpha. These funds tend to deliver more persistent excess return, are less likely to liquidate, and are more likely to attract added capital. However, as more capital flows into these alpha funds, their likelihood of delivering further alpha tends to fall. The authors interpret this finding as consistent with the model of Berk and Green (2004), which theorizes that managers able to deliver excess risk-adjusted return face declining returns to scale. As capital flows into these managers, average excess return falls and eventually disappears.

Hedge funds also take advantage of illiquidity by requiring investors to lock up their capital for long periods before withdrawal or to provide significant advance notice of withdrawal. Liang (1999) finds that the longer the lockup period, the better the fund's returns. Lockup prevents early redemptions, reduces the need to hold idle cash, and enables managers to focus on longer horizons.

Ang, Gorovyy, and van Inwegen (2011) found use of leverage across most relative value, equity, event-driven, and credit hedge funds. The amount varies over time. Most of the variability historically coincides with changing market conditions. As investment bank credit or equity underperforms, or as S&P returns drop, as equity volatility picks up, or assets become riskier, leverage drops. And when those variables go in the opposite direction, leverage rises. Hedge fund leverage historically has also moved opposite to the trend in banks, investment banks, and the finance sector at large. When leverage in these sectors ran low in the years before 2008, leverage at hedge funds ran relatively high. In early 2007, hedge fund leverage started to drop while bank, investment bank, and finance sector leverage rose toward a peak in early 2009. The changing leverage at hedge funds could signal conscious decisions by managers to adjust risk to changing conditions or decisions forced by lenders tightening or loosening their willingness to lend. Nevertheless, the broad use of leverage by hedge funds is consistent with predictions of local CAPM.

Ang and his colleagues also provided evidence of extensive hedging at hedge funds. They measured leverage several ways, including one way that accounts only for assets owned and another for assets owned against short positions or hedges. The measures show substantial although not universal short positions and hedging.

Improving the Quality and Lowering the Cost of Capital

Use of illiquid assets and, to a lesser extent, leverage only makes sense if investors plan to stay invested. Hedge fund lockup and notice periods along with gates and side pockets improve the stability of capital, and all funds include some mix of these features. These reduce the risk that capital flees but do not necessarily lower required returns. In fact, compensation for limits on liquidity can raise required returns. Hedge funds can lower the cost of capital by building relationships with clients that lower the risk of withdrawals at least over short periods of poor performance.

Focusing on Markets Where Information Is Expensive

Hedge funds' heavy focus on illiquid assets is a proxy for markets where information is expensive. Illiquidity usually comes with sizable imbalances in information between sellers and buyers, requiring time and effort before both feel comfortable trading. Extensive use of illiquid assets signals that hedge funds recognize that an important part of their value is to collect and use information for the benefit of their investors.

In general, the literature strongly suggests that hedge funds use a range of tools to create comparative advantage: leverage and funding, options and other hedging instruments, unique access to assets, and lockup and notice periods to improve the stickiness and quality of capital. Accounting and regulatory treatment also confer some advantages.

Conclusion

The flexibility of hedge funds opens the door to returns in excess of those provided by traditional assets. Hedge funds seem to take advantage of that flexibility, deploying a range of strategies that create comparative advantage over mutual fund rivals. Relative to stocks, bonds, and cash, most studies show hedge funds historically have delivered material excess return. Controlling for the strategies that many hedge funds seem to use, the excess return is less reliable. Nevertheless, if hedge funds deliver returns through strategies that investors cannot access on their own, it is clearly valuable and integral to the approach predicted by local CAPM. Portfolios that include hedge funds consequently realize a higher efficient investment frontier.

10

Investing for Banks, Thrifts, and Credit Unions

With banks and other depository institutions, the investment problem changes substantially. If mutual funds and hedge funds generally distinguish themselves by the assets they manage, banks distinguish themselves by the liabilities. Banks have to manage their investments, loans, and other assets against liabilities that vary idiosyncratically from one institution to another and that usually have no observable market price. Managing for total return consequently becomes difficult if not impossible. Instead, a depository portfolio tends to manage the spread between asset income and liability expense. Accounting, regulation, and equity valuation all tend to encourage banks to focus on this spread.

Because of the incentives to manage asset income against liability expense, the attributes of the liabilities limit the investments that a bank can make within the bounds of acceptable risk. Bank liabilities shape portfolio behavior the same way that performance benchmarks shape mutual funds and that return thresholds and high-water marks shape hedge funds. The liabilities both limit bank portfolio behavior and confer comparative advantage. Bank liabilities, in other words, largely define the local asset market where banks can credibly compete.

The Structure of Bank Investing

Banks or their equivalent take different forms in the US ranging from holding companies to trust companies, savings and loan associations to credit unions, and so on. All are largely in the business of taking in funds and providing credit. That puts all banks in the business of leveraged investing. Banks raise or accumulate equity, borrow money, and use the combined funds to acquire assets (table 10.1). In early 2019, for example, the average US bank had $1 in equity for every $8.62 in assets.

Table 10.1 The aggregate US bank balance sheet

Assets	Liabilities
$18.1 trillion	$16.0 trillion in debt
	$2.1 trillion in equity

Assets	Liabilities
55.4% loans and leases	77.0% in deposits
20.6% securities	6.3% in wholesale funds
9.4% cash	5.3% in other liabilities
14.6% other	11.4% in equity

Source: FDIC, Statistics on Depository Institutions, data for all FDIC-insured institutions reported as of March 31, 2019, available at www.fdic.gov.

Most of the funding comes from individuals and businesses depositing money in the bank with the rest coming from other sources. Most of the assets come from loans and leases made to businesses, consumers, and other banks. But a material share of assets also comes from securities and other investments.

Although banks provided 30% of outstanding US lending as of the end of 2018, signaling their importance as financial intermediaries, their debt portfolios have grown more slowly than the debt market overall. Bank debt securities and loan portfolios since 1980 have grown at a compounded annual rate of 5.5% and total US debt securities and loans outstanding have grown at 6.9%. In fact, banks have steadily lost their footing in US credit since the late 1970s when their share of outstanding balances stood at more than 50% (figure 10.1). Banking as a model for lending and investing has come under pressure.

It is telling, too, that banks have consolidated steadily since the early 1980s. The consolidation started shortly after US federal regulators stopped controlling the interest rates that banks could pay on savings, checking, and money market accounts, and the Federal Reserve allowed interest rates to rise dramatically. The volatility of US interest rates since the early 1980s has added to the challenge of managing the spread between bank assets and liabilities. The number of FDIC-insured commercial banks has dropped from more than 14,000 to less than 6,000, and the number of branches has generally continued to climb (figure 10.2). Access to banking services did not change as much as the number of institutions providing it. Consolidation suggests steadily increasing competition between banks for deposits and continuing efforts to reduce operating costs through scale. It also suggests sharper competition from other providers of credit.

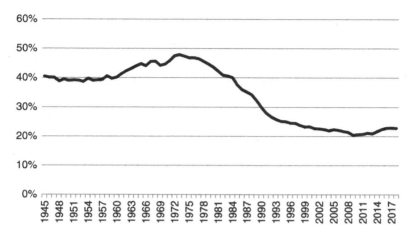

Figure 10.1 Private depositories' share of US debt has fallen since the 1970s.

Note: Data shows private depositories' debt and loan assets as a share of domestic nonfinancial and financial debt and loan liabilities.
Source: Federal Reserve Financial Conditions of the United States, Z.1, data series accessed as of March 7, 2019, available at www.federalreserve.gov.

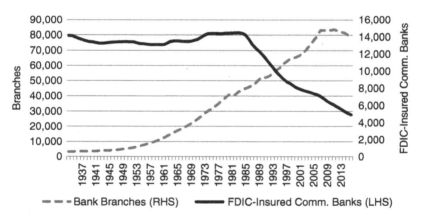

Figure 10.2 Steady consolidation in US commercial banking since the early 1980s
Source: FDIC, Historical Bank Data, accessed June 3, 2019, available at www.fdic.gov.

Basics of Disintermediation

Bank loan and securities portfolios arise out of the business of standing between the users and the suppliers of funds, arguably one of the oldest forms of investing. The users or borrowers of funds range from businesses to consumers, other banks, governments, and so on. The form of funds used can range from loans to letters of credit, from guarantees to the proceeds from selling the bank securities. The suppliers or lenders of funds can be other businesses, consumers, banks, or governments that have idle cash. The suppliers deposit cash in checking, savings, or other deposit accounts, take out certificates of deposit, make loans to the bank, buy debt securities issued by the bank, or use other means. The bank wants to take in funds at one rate and lend them out at a higher rate, the difference after operating expenses being the bank's profit. The funds taken in become the bank's liabilities; the funds loaned out or invested become assets (figure 10.3).

Although mutual funds and even hedge funds also intermediate between users and suppliers of funds, banks distinguish themselves by promising suppliers the right to withdraw \$1 for each \$1 deposited. Depositors expect the bank to protect principal. The bank consequently bears the interest rate, credit, liquidity, and other risks of making loans and investing in securities. Investors putting money in mutual and hedge funds, however, do expect to put their principal at risk.

Some theories of financial markets question the need for intermediaries such as banks or other depositories and argue that users and suppliers of funds could transact directly. Others argue that banks and other intermediaries make financial markets more efficient by solving asymmetries or imbalances in information between different market participants. The theoretical case for banks follows a few different lines (Stein, 2014).

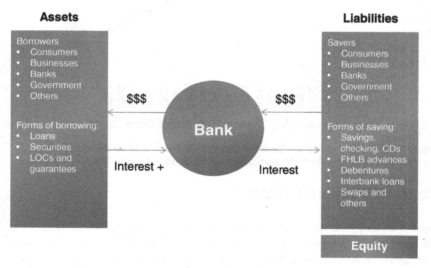

Figure 10.3 Banks stand between users and suppliers of funds.

Diamond (1984, 1996), for instance, has made an elegant case for intermediaries' ability to lower financing risks and costs through investment sourcing, monitoring, and portfolio diversification, among other services. As long as the net returns from investing with the intermediary exceed the net returns that an individual investor could get—net of the individual's cost to source, monitor, and manage directly—the investor will still keep putting money in. A bank's borrowers and the issuers of securities bought by banks benefit from banks' services as well, mainly because the banks reduce the cost of raising sufficient funds. Banks in turn will compete to lower relevant costs and develop other comparative advantages.

Gorton and Pennacchi (1990) make the case that banks protect uninformed investors by taking on a portfolio of risky assets and then splitting portfolio cash flows between informed investors who take equity risk in the bank and uninformed investors who hold debt or deposits. The uninformed investors can use the debt as a safe, tradable claim on the bank. The debt becomes a medium of exchange.

Diamond and Dybvig (1983) presented yet another view that banks enable households unsure of their future consumption needs to invest more efficiently in projects with long payoff horizons. The bank manages that uncertainty.

Regardless of the theoretical underpinnings, all banks manage assets against liabilities and take on the complexity that comes from differences in cash flow. If a bank could take in and lend out $1 and get it back with certainty just as the depositor needed to withdraw, then banking would be straightforward. That rarely if ever is the case. Depositors have both systematic and idiosyncratic needs to withdraw funds. And the users of funds, too, have unique needs: borrowers' horizons can differ; some may need funds at a fixed rate and others need floating and, among other differences, some borrowers may default. If the asset and liability cash flows mismatch significantly or if the provider of the asset defaults, then the bank has to hold equity to repay the depositor. If the mismatch or default is large enough, the bank goes out of business.

Although banks once managed their balance sheets by roughly trying to match the cash flows of assets to the cash flows of liabilities—traditional gap analysis—common practice has recast the problem as one of managing the balance sheet's net risk exposures. This involves estimating sensitivities to risk factors for both assets and liabilities. The balance sheet then becomes characterized by its net exposure to risks including interest rates, credit, liquidity, and so on. Banks summarize their largest exposures in a few metrics that measure the duration or interest rate sensitivity of a few critical parts of their business:

- Equity
- Leverage
- Net interest income

These become benchmarks of bank portfolio performance in the same way that market indexes serve as benchmarks for performance in mutual funds and hedge funds. Remarkably, these benchmarks force banks to make important trade-offs because management, outside of narrow circumstances, cannot set interest rate risk to zero on all benchmarks at once. Management must take interest rate risk somewhere. Each benchmark deserves a brief explanation.

Duration of Equity

A bank's net risk exposure ultimately is borne by its providers of equity, and the sensitivity of equity to shifts in interest rate risk gets measured by the duration of equity. Duration in this context usually means sensitivity to interest rates, not length of time. As an example, take a bank with the balance sheet shown in table 10.2.

Each side of the balance sheet has some sensitivity to any change in interest rates. If the prevailing market rate of interest goes up and banks can make a $100 five-year loan at 6% annually, for example, then a $100 five-year loan paying 5% would have a market value of less than $100. The change in value for the $100 five-year loan paying 5% is estimated by its duration.[1] Similarly, if the prevailing

Table 10.2 A stylized example of a bank balance sheet

Assets	Liabilities
$100 in a 5-year loan paying 5% annually with a 4.17-year duration	• $90 in a 4-year term deposit costing 4% annually with a 3.49-year duration • $10 in equity

Note: Example taken from Toevs and Haney (1986).

---

1 Duration means the percentage change in the present value of a cash flow if all interest rates shift by 100 basis points. For example, take a $100 two-year bond paying a 2% annual coupon with a 2% yield to maturity. The duration, D, is equal to the present value-weighted cash flows divided by 1 + yield-to-maturity:

$$D = [(\textstyle\sum_1^t t \times PV_t)/(\sum_1^t PV_t)]/(1 + \text{YTM}) = \left[\frac{1 \times \frac{\$2}{(1 + 2\%)^1} + 2 \times \frac{\$102}{(1 + 2\%)^2}}{100} \right]/(1 + 2\%) = 1.94156.$$

A 100 bp shift in all interest rates would change the price of the bond by approximately $1.94 or 1.94%. Cash flows without embedded options also show positive convexity, meaning duration gets shorter as rates rise and longer as rates fall, so the actual change in price for this cash flow would be less than $1.94 or 1.94%.

four-year deposit rate also went up and the bank has to pay 5% annually for a four-year term deposit, then the value of a deposit costing 4% would rise, partially offsetting the lower value of the loan. The deposit has duration, too. If all interest rates rose by 100 basis points, the asset position would drop in value by approximately $4.17 and the liability position would rise by $3.14. The net loss of approximately $1.03 would come out of equity, leaving the bank with $8.97. If rates rose further, equity would continue to decline, eventually threatening the bank's solvency. If rates dropped instead, equity would rise.

To ensure the bank's solvency, it has to measure and manage its duration of equity, D_{equity}. That duration depends on the amount of net risk on the balance sheet and the amount of supporting equity, as highlighted by a simple formula:

$$D_{Equity} = \frac{[(Asset\,Amount \times D_{Asset}) - (Liability\,Amount \times D_{Liability})]}{Equity\,Amount}$$

In the case of the example,

$$D_{Equity} = \frac{[(\$100 \times 4.17\%) - (\$90 \times 3.49\%)]}{10} = 10.29\%$$

For a parallel shift in interest rates of 100 basis points, the value of the bank's equity will shift by 10.29%.

Although this version of the formula focuses on sensitivity to parallel shifts in interest rates, it could just as easily focus on non-parallel shifts in key rates or on shifts in convexity, volatility, spreads, prepayments, liquidity, and so on. Bank equity entails leveraged exposure to shifts in all of these key risks.

By choosing the amount and duration of assets and the amount and duration of liabilities, a bank determines the risk borne by shareholders. A bank can set duration of equity so that the value of equity rises as interest rates rise or so it rises as interest rates fall. It all depends on arranging asset and liability durations to produce the appropriate amount of net risk. If assets have a shorter duration than liabilities, then rising interest rates raise the value of bank equity. Banks with this kind of exposure are often described as asset sensitive because assets reprice faster than liabilities. If liabilities have a shorter duration, then rising rates lower the value of bank equity. Banks of this sort are often described as liability sensitive because liabilities reprice faster than assets. Based on duration of equity and the probability of future shifts in embedded risks, bank shareholders can determine whether they are getting a fair market rate of return.

Duration of Leverage

Besides shareholders, bank management also has to meet equity requirements set by regulators. Regulators increasingly require banks to maintain a minimum equity-to-assets ratio as a simple way to ensure that banks have enough capital to survive catastrophic market conditions (see Federal Reserve Board, 2013). Because shifts in asset or liability value affect leverage, bank management has to consider not just duration of equity and the fair return to net risk but also the effect of net risk on leverage. As Toevs and Haney (1986) point out:

> Asset-to-equity ratios remain unchanged only when both elements in them either remain unchanged or change proportionally. That is, when interest rates cause the market value of assets to increase by 1%, the market value of portfolio equity must also increase by 1% for the asset-to-equity ratio to remain unchanged. (p. 320)

The duration of leverage amounts to the difference between the duration of equity and the duration of assets:

$$D_{Leverage} = D_{Equity} - D_{Asset}$$

Referring again to the previous example:

$$D_{Leverage} = 10.29 - 4.17 = 6.12$$

For a parallel shift of 100 basis points in interest rates, equity shifts by about 10.29%, whereas assets shift by around 4.17%. Leverage changes by about 6.12%. In the case of falling interest rates, leverage goes up. If the bank reduces the duration of its assets to 3.49%, then the duration of equity also becomes 3.49%. The duration of equity and assets now equals each other. The duration of leverage drops to zero, eliminating the exposure of bank leverage to changes in interest rates.

It should be clear from this example that a bank cannot set both duration of equity and duration of leverage to zero unless it also sets the duration of assets and liabilities to zero. Outside of that narrow circumstance, the bank will have to take risk with either equity or leverage.

The duration of leverage enables bank management to track the return and risk profile of the institution, but it involves as much art as science. Most loans and most retail deposit liabilities have no observable market price, and coming up with exact prices can involve significant cost and complexity. Coming up with simplified estimates of loan and liability price and risk is more realistic, however, and some commercial bank analytic systems produce price and risk estimates routinely.

Duration of Net Interest Income

Bank management also typically targets net interest income as an important and visible source of return to the risk borne by equity. Even though bank

Differences in leverage also create differences in ability to change the risk profile of the balance sheet as market conditions vary.

Regulators also limit leverage by assigning risk weights to different assets based usually on asset credit risk (table 10.3). Most bank loans today require 8% capital, but risk weights modify that. An asset with a 100% risk weight requires the bank to hold 100% of the baseline 8% amount, or 8% capital. One with a 50% risk weight requires holding only 50% of the baseline 8% amount, or 4% capital.

Table 10.3 Bank risk weights for selected assets

Asset	Basel III Standardized Approach Risk Weight	
Cash, US Treasury debt, obligations of the US Federal Reserve, Ginnie Mae MBS	0%	
Assets guaranteed by the FDIC or NCUA	20%	
Assets guaranteed by foreign governments or their central banks	OECD Country Risk Class	Risk Weight
	0-1	0%
	2	20%
	3	50%
	4-6	100%
	7	150%
	OECD Member: No CRC	0%
	Non-OECD Member: No CRC	100%
	Sovereign Default	150%
US agency debt or MBS	20%	
US state or municipal debt	20% for general obligations	
	50% for revenue obligations	
US bank debt	20%	
Broker/dealer or corporate debt	100%	
Consumer debt	100%	
Residential mortgages	50%	
Commercial real estate	100%	
High-volatility commercial real estate	150%	
Securitizations	20% or higher based on the simplified supervisory formula approach (SSFA) and subject to due diligence requirements	

Note: Percentage of the 8% baseline capital requirement; RWA charges do not include loss reserves.
Source: DavisPolk (2013).

Regulators have laid out a detailed menu of weights. All US banks have to score their assets by their regulatory risk weights and make sure they have adequate capital against their total risk-weighted assets. A bank that held a $1 position in a 100% risk-weighted asset and another $1 in a 50% weighted asset would have to hold $0.12 in capital:

$$\text{Minimum risk-weighted capital} = \$1 \times 100\% \times 8\% + \$1 \times 50\% \times 8\%$$
$$= \$0.08 + \$0.04$$
$$= \$0.12$$

Risk weighting encourages banks to hold assets with less credit risk by requiring less capital. But those assets could carry substantial amounts of other risk, including interest rate risk, optionality, spread risk, liquidity, and so on. Because risk weights depend largely on credit, they give banks comparative advantage in holding assets with low credit risk but substantial amounts of other risk. Agency MBS is one example of an asset with low credit risk but potentially material amounts of interest rate, option, and liquidity risk. Agency MBS get a 20% risk weight, allowing banks to hold 1.6% capital against those positions or leverage them more than 50 times. At the end of the first quarter of 2019, banks insured by the FDIC allocated 10.19% of their balance sheet to agency MBS—the single largest asset allocation at least measured by type of issuer.

Capital required by regulators confers both advantage and disadvantage across banks, but lenders to banks also care about capital. Although lenders to banks try to protect themselves from the risk of default in various ways—securing the loans with collateral, putting covenants in the loans to limit bank activity that might put the bank at risk, and so on—they still care about leverage. These lenders can influence leverage through the risk premium they require on loans to more leveraged banks. But because banks historically get the majority of their funds from insured deposits—an average of 77% in the first quarter of 2019, for instance, for US banks—the influence of other lenders on leverage is limited. The rules set by the agents for depositors, that is, the regulators, dominate.

Funding Terms

Apart from leverage, banks also draw sizable advantage from their menu of ways to fund themselves (figure 10.4). Deposits make up 77% of average FDIC-insured institution funding as of the first quarter of 2019, but banks also draw on interbank lending, Federal Home Loan Bank lending, repurchase agreements and securities lending, securitization, senior unsecured debt, subordinated debt, and so on. Each of these sources have unique strengths and weaknesses, and a bank's mix of funding has a powerful impact on its plausible portfolio of assets if bank management wants to keep duration of equity, leverage, and net interest income on target.

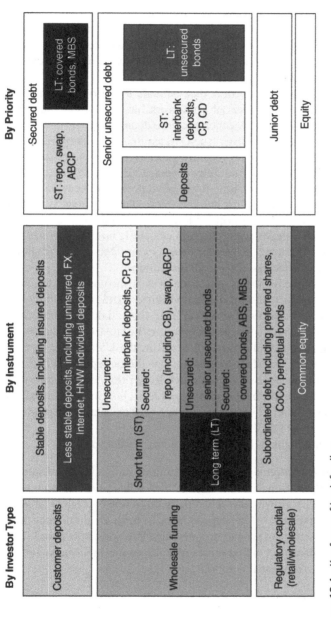

Figure 10.4 Key forms of bank funding

Note: ABCP = asset-backed commercial paper; ABS = asset-backed securities; CB = central bank; CD = certificate of deposit; CoCo = contingent convertible; CP = commercial paper; FX = foreign exchange; HNW = high net worth; LT = long term; MBS = mortgage-backed security; ST = short term; The example presented here is for an economy without deposit preference.
Source: IMF staff.

Deposit Funding

Deposits arguably constitute the most unique form of bank funding. Checking, saving, and money market funds can walk out the door on demand at any time without notice or penalty. As of early 2019, FDIC-insured banks held nearly $13 trillion in deposits. Regulators recognize the importance of deposits to the safety and soundness of a bank, and equity investors frequently value banks based largely on the value of their deposits (Sheehan, 2013).

Regulators have created frameworks that estimate the attributes and value of deposits. Perhaps the most influential framework has come from the Office of Thrift Supervision (2001), or OTS, which provides detailed guidelines for valuing deposits and calculating deposit lives. The OTS assumes that its approach works properly across all institutions. More recently, Basel III (Basel Committee on Banking Supervision, 2010) lays out a liquidity coverage ratio, or LCR, requiring the largest banks to have enough liquidity to cover all potential needs for cash over 30 days assuming short-term funding markets freeze. The LCR assigns availability factors to deposits and other sources of liquidity. Stable deposits get an availability factor of 85%, less stable deposits get 70%, and wholesale funding gets 50%. These availability factors imply average lives for these types of deposits. And similar to the OTS framework, the factors apply to all institutions.

Literature on the effective terms and value of deposit funding is limited, but some recent work has started to lift the veil. Sheehan (2013) analyzed five banks that provided monthly balances across all of their demand deposit accounts. The data cover account behavior for five years or more in the late 1990s and early 2000s. Three of the banks were among the 100 largest in the US and two were large credit unions. He found that the expected average life of deposits varied significantly across institutions but usually ran much longer than projected using OTS calculations. For instance, the projected average life of checking deposits at all five institutions ran longer than 17 years even though OTS calculations would project less than three (figure 10.5).

Sheehan (2013) highlighted the differences across institutions:

> The importance of differences across institutions cannot be understated. For example, institutions like E*Financial have relied primarily on internet funds and have grown relatively rapidly, attracting depositors largely based on paying relatively high deposit rates. In contrast, Commerce has emphasized a strategy of providing convenient locations, hours, and services. One should expect to find substantial differences in the behavior of core deposits across these institutions. (p. 212)

Sheehan also estimated the interest rate sensitivity of core deposits at these five institutions and calculated their value based on the banks' ability to retain deposits at rates below those on Treasury debt or on other funding benchmarks. Sheehan

Figure 10.5 Estimated average lives for demand deposits run longer than OTS calculations.

Note: CHK = checking, BCHK = business checking, NOW = NOW accounts, SAV = savings accounts, MMA = money market accounts. Each letter represents a different depository. OTS represents estimates based on OTS calculations. Average lives stated in years with the OTS lives taken from OTS (2001) whereas the other lives are calculated based on forecasted monthly retention of balances.
Source: Sheehan (2013), Table 4.

argued that the banks should be willing to pay substantial premiums to obtain the balances in their core deposit accounts, and that those premiums generally should go up with interest rates as the cost of deposits lags other parts of the funding markets. He estimated that the banks studied would pay premiums of between 10.4% and 33.1% in his base scenario, for instance, and much higher values in most cases as rates rise (figure 10.6). The base premiums and their projected value in different scenarios vary substantially across institutions.

Sheehan concluded:

> to the extent that deposits are raised in less competitive markets, one should expect profit margins to be higher and potentially to remain higher as long as barriers to entry or switching costs exist in those markets. The implication is that long-term profits of financial institutions beyond a normal rate of return may be more likely to stem from the liability side of the balance sheet than from the asset side as long as banks have greater monopoly power on the liability side. (p. 219)

Sheehan's work clearly has limits. Although the bank data capture the US recession that ran from March to November 2001, they do not capture the stresses of 2008 and later years where persistence of deposits both across and between banks

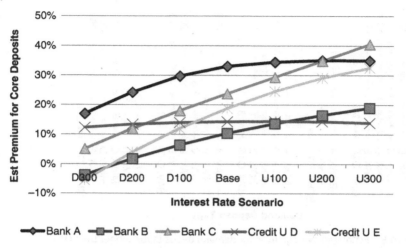

Figure 10.6 Projected price premiums for core deposits at selected depositories

Note: Weighted average value of core deposits per dollar. A base premium of 33.1%, for instance, indicates that the bank should pay $1.331 per $1 for the average deposit. The premium reflects each institution's deposit mix, interest rate sensitivity, and cost to service the mix of accounts.

Source: Sheehan (2013), Table 6.

may have changed. The study also misses the near-zero rates of 2008 through 2015, which have nearly eliminated any room for banks to price retail deposits below wholesale rates and accrue value. The relatively flat yield curves of the years studied also may have narrowed the range of compelling alternatives to bank deposits, enhancing the persistence of deposits. The work also focuses on a handful of self-selected depositories rather than a broader representative sample. Nevertheless, it is an extremely valuable case study of deposit attributes and value and hopefully will bring out more work in this area.

Despite its limits, Sheehan's work highlights material differences across even this small set and the potential comparative advantage conferred by deposit funding alone. Deposits vary in their persistence, interest rate sensitivity, interest expense, and the cost to attract and service them.

Driscoll and Judson (2013) used a much larger set of data over a longer period to show that rates on bank deposits are much less sensitive than wholesale market rates. Their data spanned 1997 to 2007 and captured weekly rates at nearly 900 institutions on 10 different types of deposits. Their key findings:

- Using fed funds and Treasury bill rates as wholesale benchmarks, the average deposit rate drops relatively quickly as market rates fall but rises slowly when market rates rise; deposit rates are downward flexible but upward sticky, increasing the value of deposits as rates rise.

- Rates on certificates of deposit change roughly every two months or less while rates on money market deposit accounts change every five months and rates on interest checking every nine months, arguably reflecting corresponding levels of competition from alternatives; wholesale funding consequently looks less valuable than retail.
- The frequency of change can vary significantly across branches; 25% of branches change MMDA rates every eight months or less frequently, and the same percentage changes interest checking rates yearly or less frequently, suggesting sizable differences across banks and branches in the rate of sensitivity and value of their deposits.

This work complements Craig and Dinger (2011), who also used a robust dataset to show that the probability of a change in deposit rates depends on market share with banks—particularly small banks—changing their retail deposit rates less frequently in markets where they have the strongest share. It also complements Yankov (2012), who found evidence of monopoly pricing power in the rates offered on certificates of deposit.

Depending on the attributes of any bank's core deposits, the bank may have comparative advantage or disadvantage in holding a given set of assets. A bank that found persistent deposits with little interest rate sensitivity would have something close to long, fixed-rate funding. That makes the bank a plausible holder of long, fixed-rate assets. A bank with inexpensive deposits regardless of persistence or sensitivity could hold relatively safer and more liquid assets with lower yields and still reach average bank income targets. Alternatively, a bank with a low cost of deposit funding could take on riskier assets and exceed average targets. Banks with deposits that come and go quickly could be restricted to buying only short or highly liquid assets. And banks with a high cost of deposit funding could be forced into buying generally riskier assets.

Banks also raise funds through certificates of deposit with defined maturities. Most banks charge a penalty of three- to six-months of interest for early withdrawal, so certificates of deposit usually approximate longer fixed-rate funding. Certificates of deposit can extend the average life of a bank's funding base. If the bank raises the certificate of deposit from its retail base, it also stands to get high rates of reinvestment into new certificates as current certificates expire. That further extends the effective life of the deposit. If the cost of interest, servicing, and sourcing on the certificate is below the cost of alternative funds, this source of funds accrues to the value of the bank and its portfolio. If the bank raises the certificate in more competitive wholesale markets or from certain retail segments such as wealthier households, it may be forced to compete on rate to retain these deposits, and the effective average life and value may be lower.

Finally, banks do take in deposits above the limits for government insurance, and these may be among the shortest and least valuable. These deposits often come from corporations or individuals with temporary surplus cash or expecting an imminent expense. The cash can flow out as easily as it flows in. More important, if the bank fails, uninsured depositors get in line with every other unsecured creditor of the bank to recover their funds. Uninsured deposits consequently can be very sensitive to the changing risks of the bank's balance sheet.

Wholesale Funding

Wholesale funding can be either short or long term and either unsecured or secured by a bank's assets. This creates another layer of funding tools with attributes and costs that can differ materially from deposits. Depending on the flexibility and cost of this funding, it can extend the range of assets that a bank can hold or change the net return and risk on an existing asset base. As of mid-2019, 13% of US commercial bank funding came from wholesale sources.

Most lending in the wholesale markets helps banks manage the balance sheet more fluidly than deposit funding. Most fed fund loans, for instance, are overnight. The borrowers tend to be banks that need cash to meet banking reserve requirements or to clear financial transactions. Most fed fund lenders tend to be banks with excess reserves. Foreign banks, government-sponsored enterprises, and other eligible institutions can also lend. The transactions can start between two institutions that already have a relationship or can go through a fed funds broker. And the transactions typically occur without a contract. The parties instead reach a verbal agreement based on their history of doing business together. The borrowed amounts usually are subject to counterparty credit limits. These conventions allow a fast flow of funds at the lowest possible cost—in contrast to the generally slower and more expensive process of building a deposit base.

Other sources of wholesale funds include repurchase agreements or repo, securities lending or swaps, and asset-backed commercial paper. All of these approaches use securities held by the bank to quickly raise funds with terms often better than the bank might get in the unsecured market. Repurchase agreements, for instance, involve selling a security to a counterparty at a spot market price while agreeing to buy it back later at another prearranged price. Between the sale and repurchase dates, the bank holds cash. The difference between the dates constitutes the term of the effective loan and can vary from overnight to weeks or months. The difference between the spot and repurchase price, with adjustments for carry in the security, constitutes the effective interest rate. Repo markets lend against only a percentage of the market value of a security. Repo lenders might lend 98% of the value of a US Treasury note or 98% of the value of an agency mortgage-backed security and lend only 95% of an investment-grade corporate bond. This protects the lender if the borrower fails to repurchase and the lender has to liquidate the collateral. Repo lending rates also vary by the quality of the security with US Treasury debt and MBS getting the lowest rates and corporate other assets getting higher rates.

Beyond the institutional details of the repo market, however, these markets enable banks to raise funds quickly and efficiently for purposes other than meeting banking reserve requirements and securities settlement. Secured funding also enables a bank to raise funds based on the quality of the secured assets rather than the quality of the overall balance sheet—an advantage for a bank with a low credit rating but at least some high-quality assets. Among other things, banks can use repo markets to fund the purchase of securities even in the immediate absence of sufficient deposits. The repo and securities lending markets also enable banks to turn their better assets into cash quickly without any selling and without the impact on earnings that a sale might trigger. But secured funding can come with a hidden cost. By encumbering certain bank assets, it prevents other lenders to the bank from liquidating the encumbered assets if the bank ever fails. Unsecured lenders may need extra compensation for their limited recourse to the entire asset base, raising the cost of unsecured funds.

Long-term unsecured funding usually comes from issuing senior bonds that rank just below insured depositors in the line of creditors if the bank ever fails. Banks able to issue senior bonds can often raise substantial amounts of funds at much longer maturities than provided in other markets and without posting assets as collateral. But usually only the most highly rated and well-known banks can issue senior bonds at attractive rates.

Banks that need long-term funding but lack either the necessary ratings or reputation can find secured funding from other sources: the Federal Home Loan Bank system in the US or covered bonds in Europe, or securitization. These can be important sources of funds. Each deserves a brief review.

The Federal Home Loan Bank system in the US and covered bonds in Europe broadly serve the same purpose, although they have different institutional histories. Both avenues allow banks to borrow funds secured or collateralized by mortgage loans. Both allow the bank to keep the loans as an asset on balance sheet. In the case of the FHLBank system, each bank in an FHLBank district becomes a member and an equity investor in their local FHLBank, which is organized as a co-op, and the system can raise funds for members by issuing debt. In the case of a covered bond, the individual bank issues debt as a general obligation of the bank but secured by the mortgage loans. In both cases, the bank ends up with funds secured by a portfolio of loans with terms that depend both on the bank and the loans. And the bank has to manage any differences in credit risk, interest rate risk, or other attributes between the loans and the liability.

Securitization also allows a bank to raise funds secured by a portfolio of loans. But securitization usually depends on the portfolio alone rather than partially on the bank. And securitization can remove assets and risks from the bank balance sheet altogether. Securitization involves selling assets to a trust that stands beyond the reach of bank creditors if the bank ever fails. This takes the assets off the bank balance sheet. The trust in turn issues debt to fund the purchase of the loans. Different classes of debt bear different amounts of credit and interest rate risk. If a bank sells the loans to the trust and buys back the classes that bear the predominant share of credit risk, for instance, it is equivalent to financing the portfolio through the sale of the other classes of debt. If the assets are of sufficient quality or if the credit classes absorb enough risk, the rate on the classes sold to other investors may be lower than the bank could get based on its own credit. And if the classes sold to other investors offset enough interest rate risk, then the bank has removed most assets and most risk from the balance sheet and bought back only the elements it wants.

Bank Funding Differences

From one economy to another, one bank to another, and across time, banks' access to and choice of funding can vary significantly. The International Monetary Fund (2013) looked at 751 banks worldwide from 1990 through 2012 and found material differences in liability mix (figure 10.7). To understand the influence on that mix, it examined factors unique to each bank as well as country-level macroeconomic, financial market, and regulatory and institutional factors. And it drew a few major conclusions:

- Unique bank attributes matter most but depend on the regulatory environment. The past mix of funding, the availability of high-quality assets on the balance sheet, and bank size and profitability have the most influence. But countries with better regulation tend to have banks with more deposit and less debt funding. Banks in advanced economies with stronger disclosure requirements tend to have higher deposit-to-asset ratios and lower loan-to-deposit ratios.
- Capital structures tend to persist, but persistence varies across time and countries. Equity funding adjusts faster than the mix of debt and deposits. And the pace of balance sheet adjustment has accelerated since 2007.
- Size matters. Large banks rely more on debt and depend less on deposits and equity, possibly because the market knows them better or assumes implicit government backing.
- More traditional banks depend less on wholesale funding. Banks with more securities and tangible assets and banks that pay dividends use less wholesale funding.

Because of their long history and important economic role, banks may enjoy the most funding flexibility of any institutional investor. The liability side of a bank portfolio consequently contributes a large share of the ultimate value of the bank's

(Percent)

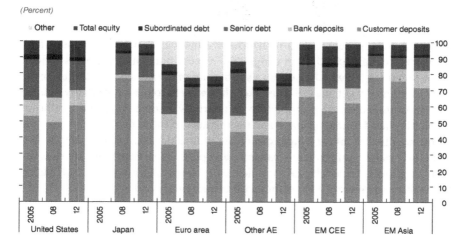

Figure 10.7   Bank liability structures across major economies and regions

Note: "Other" includes financial and accounting liabilities, such as derivatives liabilities, insurance liabilities, noncurrent liabilities, accounts payable and accrued expenses, deferred taxes and tax liabilities, and other provisions. Japan data for 2005 omitted due to data limitations. AE = advanced economics; CEE = central and eastern Europe; EM = emerging market economics. For region coverage, refer to Table 3.2.
Sources: Bank of Japan; SNL Financial; and IMF staff estimates.

total portfolio. Funding in many cases is a powerful source of comparative advantage for a bank portfolio.

Hedging

Banks have as much flexibility to hedge their risks as almost any institutional investor. Banks can use short positions, where plausible, or use forwards, futures, swaps, and options. Banks may have a slight advantage in their value as counterparty to a swap or derivative transaction. But banks arguably are at comparative disadvantage in using these tools because of the accounting treatment for derivatives and because of banks' emphasis on stable spread income.

Any advantage that banks have in derivative transactions comes largely from their quality as regulated counterparties. Regulatory oversight and accompanying disclosure helps derivative counterparties get a better view of a bank's credit. As regulations have pushed large shares of derivative transactions onto exchanges or required counterparties to post initial and variance margin for transactions done away from exchanges, the value of a regulated counterparty has dropped. Nevertheless, regulated counterparties still have some advantage.

The major limit on bank hedges comes from their accounting treatment. Under US accounting rules (KPMG, 2018), most hedges get marked-to-market each quarter with the change reported through income. Banks can avoid this treatment if the hedges pass certain tests to show hedge effectiveness, but that often proves difficult for most mortgages, which make up a sizable part of the asset base.[3] Because most bank assets do not get marked-to-market, the hedge becomes a potentially isolated and uncontrollable source of volatility in quarterly income. With the significant emphasis placed by management and the markets on stable quarterly income, the accounting treatment for hedges can create untenable risk. Even though hedges can create significant economic value for any portfolio by reshaping net risk, the joint accounting for assets and their hedges at banks does not reflect it. Hedging for banks consequently often comes with extraordinary cost.

Quality and Cost of Capital

Banks work off of permanent equity capital that requires a rate of return generally toward the lower range of the equity markets. That reflects both the liquidity of bank equity and the risk and relative transparency of the institution. Most bank equity trades in public markets, giving it relatively high liquidity. And risk at most banks falls within a modest range because of regulatory oversight. Regulatory disclosure also makes it easier for equity providers to gauge risk across banks. The net result is generally patient capital at a relatively low cost, which enables bank managers to focus on investments that can produce the required return on equity over longer horizons.

Information

Banks also can benefit from proprietary information that flows from banking activity itself. Some of that information can come from seeing cash flow both to and from individual and business deposit customers. Some comes from seeing customers' other banking activity, including various forms of borrowing. Other information may come from lending that requires individuals and businesses to disclose private information.

---

3 Derivatives on any balance sheet get marked as an asset or liability at fair value unless the reporting entity can prove that the derivatives are highly effective at offsetting the fair value or the cash flows of a hedged item. The different influences on pricing MBS and interest swaps, for instance—the price basis—makes it difficult to consistently prove hedge effectiveness. And the cash flows of MBS and most plausible hedges also differ dramatically. Getting accounting treatment for a swap as an MBS hedge, which would allow changes in the swap's fair value to flow through AOCI instead of income, consequently, is very difficult. In practice, few entities try. Interest in hedging with derivatives has increased with the introduction of last-of-layer accounting in 2018, but the practice still is limited.

to securities for liquidity and or alternatively pay more interest; banks' ability to source loans through broad deposit and cash management relationships with potential borrowers, accounting rules that usually let banks hold loans at amortized initial purchase price, and access to leverage at low cost give banks significant advantage over mutual or hedge funds and most other competing portfolios.

- *To build portfolios dominated by low- and high-capital assets.* Limits on leverage encourage banks to offset assets that require low economic capital with assets that require high economic capital.
- *To prefer short maturity rather than long maturity assets.* Concentration of bank funding in demand deposits limits asset maturity because of risk from a deposit run and forced asset liquidation.
- *To prefer floating- to fixed-rate debt.* Emphasis on net interest income and the risk of a deposit run make floating-rate debt attractive, or alternatively, fixed-rate debt that can be easily swapped to floating.

Evidence for Local CAPM

Gathering formal evidence for the predictions of local CAPM is work to be done, but informal evidence is plentiful on the balance sheets of banks representing different approaches to the US market.

Differentiation

The structure of US banking offers support for many of the predictions made by local CAPM. US banks broadly differentiate themselves by geography and lending specialization, and these translate into significant differences in funding and assets (table 10.5). Universal, regional, and community banks differ in their deposit and lending footprints and universal, custodial, credit card, and investment banks differ in degree of specialization.

The differences between these types of banks show up in representative balance sheets from early 2019 (table 10.6). Among other distinctions:

- SunTrust, SB One, and, to a lesser extent, Capital One hold relatively large amounts of loans and leases (Line 8). SunTrust and SB One come closest to a traditional model of taking deposits and making loans. Capital One makes credit card loans. These banks also hold more loans with a maturity of more than five years (line 37), which also arguably reflects lending businesses with relatively less need for liquidity.

Table 10.5 A range of US bank business models as of early 2019

Model	Territory	Major Business Lines	Examples
Universal bank	National or global	Consumer and business lending, foreign exchange, custodial services, investment banking	JP Morgan, Citibank, Bank of America, Wells Fargo
Regional bank	Regional	Consumer and business lending	PNC, BB&T, Sovereign, SunTrust, Regions, Huntington, M&T
Community bank	Local	Consumer and business lending	The Middleburg Bank (VA), Sussex Bank (NJ)
Custodial bank	Global	Custodian for investor securities and cash	Bank of New York/Mellon, Northern Trust, State Street
Credit card bank	Global	Consumer lending	Capital One, American Express
Investment bank	Global	Issuance and trading of debt, equity, foreign exchange	Goldman Sachs, Morgan Stanley

- JPMorgan and Goldman Sachs have sizable trading business, which get reflected both in trading account assets (line 10) and in repo loans or loans collateralized by securities that a client might buy from the bank's trading desk (line 7).
- Holdings in securities vary significantly across this sample of banks (line 6). State Street notably holds nearly 40% of total assets in securities and Goldman Sachs holds nearly 2%. State Street's high securities holdings likely reflect the short average duration of its deposits, which largely come from custodial accounts. Custodial accounts get cash when securities pay interest or dividends, mature, return principal, or when the owner sells holdings. Holders of custodial accounts could quickly decide to reinvest the cash, so SunTrust likely needs to hold liquid securities rather than loans.
- On the liability side, most of these banks fund with roughly 70% to 80% deposits, but the volatility of their liabilities (line 46) and the use of Federal Home Loan Bank advances (line 48) differs. Volatile liabilities largely reflect deposits with balances above the FDIC-insured limit of $250,000 and are arguably likely to flee at the first signs of bank trouble. Both JPMorgan and State Street's volatile deposits likely reflect parts of their business where the bank serves as a custodian for the investment portfolios of large institutional clients.

Table 10.6   A sample of bank balance sheets

Bank	JPMorgan Chase Bank	SunTrust Bank	SB One Bank	State Street Bank and Trust Co.	Capital One	Goldman Sachs Bank USA
Type	Universal	Regional	Community	Custodial	Credit Card	Investment Bank
FDIC Number:	NA	867	22221	14	NA	33124
	628				4297	
Reporting date:	3/31/19	3/31/19	3/31/19	3/31/19	3/31/19	3/31/19
Assets and Liabilities						
3 **Total assets**	**100.00%**	**100.00%**	**100.00%**	**100.00%**	**100.00%**	**100.00%**
4 Cash and due from depository institutions	14.80%	2.11%	1.25%	25.58%	21.31%	18.00%
5 *Interest-bearing balances*	*14.01%*	*1.30%*	*0.68%*	*23.71%*	*20.37%*	*17.88%*
6 Securities	11.60%	14.86%	10.66%	39.94%	21.80%	2.02%
7 Federal funds sold and reverse repurchase agreements	13.66%	0.03%	0.00%	0.68%	0.00%	17.29%
8 Net loans and leases	37.12%	72.55%	81.81%	10.41%	46.85%	38.84%
9 *Loan loss allowance*	*0.43%*	*0.77%*	*0.50%*	*0.03%*	*0.72%*	*0.35%*
10 Trading account assets	14.32%	1.81%	0.00%	2.05%	0.26%	18.25%
11 Bank premises and fixed assets	0.89%	1.16%	1.19%	0.77%	1.35%	0.02%
12 Other real estate owned	0.01%	0.04%	0.18%	0.00%	0.00%	0.01%
13 Goodwill and other intangibles	1.46%	3.67%	1.60%	4.20%	4.79%	0.03%
14 All other assets	6.14%	3.76%	3.32%	16.39%	3.64%	5.53%

(Continued)

Table 10.6 (Continued)

#							
15	**Total liabilities and capital**	**100.00%**	**100.00%**	**100.00%**	**100.00%**	**100.00%**	**100.00%**
16	**Total liabilities**	**85.62%**	**86.73%**	**88.36%**	**88.41%**	**88.26%**	**90.53%**
17	Total deposits	74.06%	80.83%	74.34%	79.44%	76.76%	68.91%
18	*Interest-bearing deposits*	74.06%	72.59%	58.53%	64.79%	59.13%	52.09%
19	*Deposits held in domestic offices*	74.06%	80.83%	45.47%	79.44%	76.76%	56.50%
21	Federal funds purchased and repurchase agreements	0.87%	0.11%	0.63%	0.00%	0.41%	5.55%
22	Trading liabilities	3.76%	0.12%	1.65%	0.00%	0.15%	5.24%
23	Other borrowed funds	1.73%	3.72%	1.20%	8.38%	9.45%	6.17%
24	Subordinated debt	2.17%	0.00%	0.44%	0.00%	0.41%	0.01%
25	All other liabilities	3.02%	1.95%	10.11%	0.60%	1.08%	4.65%
26	**Total equity capital**	**14.38%**	**13.27%**	**11.64%**	**11.59%**	**11.74%**	**9.47%**
27	Total bank equity capital	14.36%	13.27%	11.64%	11.59%	11.69%	9.46%
28	*Perpetual preferred stock*	0.00%	0.00%	0.00%	0.00%	0.00%	0.00%
29	*Common stock*	4.08%	0.01%	0.01%	0.16%	0.01%	0.08%
30	*Surplus*	2.96%	11.75%	5.71%	8.54%	6.26%	4.33%
31	*Undivided profits*	7.31%	1.51%	5.91%	2.89%	5.42%	5.06%
32	Noncontrolling interests in consolidated subsidiaries	0.02%	0.00%	0.00%	0.00%	0.05%	0.01%
Memoranda:							
37	Long-term assets (5+ years)	3.50%	28.66%	20.48%	30.81%	32.71%	18.27%
46	Volatile liabilities	10.19%	3.08%	47.54%	11.08%	7.07%	26.19%
48	FHLB advances	0.27%	0.00%	0.00%	8.24%	3.86%	1.93%
51	Tier 1 (core) risk-based capital	14.26%	8.67%	7.64%	9.97%	9.44%	8.30%
52	Tier 2 risk-based capital	2.63%	0.76%	0.39%	0.50%	1.14%	0.49%

Source: FDIC, Statistics on Depository Institutions, reported as of March 31, 2019, available at www.fdic.gov.

Sometimes purposefully and sometimes opportunistically, these and other banks push both the asset and liability side of their businesses into areas where they see competitive advantage.

Retail Rather Than Wholesale Funds

The average FDIC-insured bank at the end of the first quarter in 2019 funded 77% of its balance sheet with retail deposits, 10% with wholesale funds, 2% with other liabilities, and 11% with equity. The sample banks here range around that average with only Goldman Sachs slightly low at nearly 69%.

Loans Rather Than Securities

Despite steadily losing share of US nonfinancial and financial debt to securities since the early 1970s, banks still dominate the business of making loans. Banks, thrifts, and credit unions held more than 45% of the $25 trillion of loans outstanding in the US at the end of 2018, nearly 20 percentage points higher than the next largest holder (figure 10.8). Of remaining holders with more than 1%

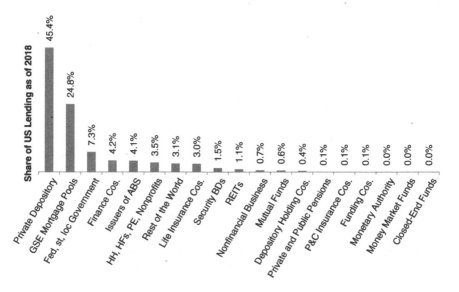

Figure 10.8 Banks hold an outsized share of US lending.
Source: Federal Reserve, Financial Accounts of the United States as of December 31, 2018, available at www.federalreserve.gov.

of outstanding loans, a number are government lenders in markets with public policy support or securitization vehicles that feed the capital markets: GSE mortgage pools (24.8%); federal, state, or local governments (7.3%); or issuers of asset-backed securities (4.1%). One largely represents foreign bank lending into the US: rest of the world (3.1%). That leaves finance companies (4.2%); households, hedge funds, private equity and nonprofits (3.5%), life insurers (3.0%); broker/dealers (1.5%); and REITs (1.1%) representing diversified private portfolios with a collective share of 13.3%. Of diversified private lenders only, banks have a 77% market share. The combination of leverage, low-cost funding, book value accounting, and access to lending opportunities gives depositories a powerful upper hand.

For the banks, with the exception of State Street, which does not have a traditional lending operation, loans constitute the single biggest asset category on the balance sheet of the small sample of balance sheets reviewed here. Yield and book value accounting make loans compelling for banks routinely evaluated based on net interest income.

Low- and High-Quality Assets

These summary balance sheets offer no window on the distribution of risk and required economic capital across the asset base. But the strategy of barbelling low- with high-risk assets is compelling. An appendix to this chapter lays out the rationale.

Short- Rather than Long-Maturity Assets

None of the banks in this small sample have more than 33% of their portfolio in assets with maturities of five years or longer, with five of the six holding less than 33% and one, Goldman Sachs, holding 3.5%.

Floating- Rather than Fixed-Rate Debt

All banks here get roughly 70% or more of their funding from deposits, which predominately have terms that the bank can set from day to day.

Conclusion

Banks have balance sheets that Sharpe-Lintner or Black CAPM would likely struggle to explain but that local CAPM handles well. Banks compete in local markets for funding and assets with clear incentives to differentiate outside of those markets. Their list of potential comparative advantages is long, and evidence that banks use those advantages is compelling. Powerful funding, leverage, asset access, and accounting advantages shape their balance sheets, as do political and regulatory disadvantages. They are a prime example of asset-liability portfolios and the power of those portfolios to dominate segments of the investable set.

Appendix: A Few Special Topics in Bank Balance Management—The Duration of Regulatory Leverage

The duration of bank leverage has even greater implications when it comes to managing the amount of capital required by regulators. Regulators often have their own view of sufficient capital apart from the view that bank management might have. If regulatory capital falls too low, management and shareholders can lose control of the bank. Regulators use the accounting value of assets and liabilities rather than their economic or market value, however, to calculate bank capital. Accounting puts a special focus on securities because securities have observable market prices and get marked-to-market value, whereas loans and deposits do not. Change in the market value of securities can flow directly into shareholder equity as measured by accountants and consequently by regulators under some regulatory regimes. Change in the market value of securities consequently shifts the assets-to-equity ratio or leverage. Small changes in the duration of a bank's securities portfolio can have a big impact on the duration of leverage. This creates a sizable risk for bank management.

Take a bank with the balance sheet shown in table 10.7, for example. Note that compared to the first example, this balance sheet substitutes a security for a loan.

Because only the security gets marked-to-market, the liabilities, for practical purposes, have zero duration. That magnifies the duration of regulatory equity:

$$D_{Regulatory\ Equity}$$
$$= \frac{[(Securities\ Amount \times D_{Security\ Portfolio}) \times (Securities\ \%\ Total\ Assets)]}{Equity\ Amount}$$

Table 10.7 A simple bank balance sheet invested in mark-to-market securities

Assets	Liabilities
$100 in a 5-year security paying 5% annually with a 4.17-year duration	• $90 in a 4-year term deposit costing 4% annually with a 3.49-year duration • $10 in equity

For the sample balance sheet:

$$D_{Regulatory\ Equity} = \frac{[(100 \times 4.17\%) \times 100\%]}{10} = 41.7\%$$

The impact of the duration of regulatory equity becomes clearer after considering the impact of changes in interest rates, r, and other risks on assets-to-equity ratios:

$$\%\Delta\ Assets\text{-}to\text{-}Equity = \left[\frac{D_{Regulatory\ Equity} - D_{Securities}}{1+r}\right] \times \Delta r \times 100$$

As the duration gap between regulatory equity and securities grows, so does the duration of leverage. Suppose interest rates rose 1%. The value of both equity and securities would drop by $4.17. Leverage, however, would rise sharply. The publicly reported balance sheet would show as in table 10.8.

Equity would fall to slightly more than 6% of assets.

This highlights an important choice for bank management: the duration of true economic bank equity and the duration of regulatory equity only match if the durations of securities and of all other assets and all liabilities are set to zero. This is extremely unlikely. Banks have to weigh the trade-off between the duration of equity the bank might prefer considering all parts of the balance sheet and the duration of equity shown in the lens of accounting.

Balancing Risk-Weighted and Economic Bank Capital

Banks will hold the minimum required amount of risk-weighted capital except when that comes in below minimum required equity-to-assets. That can happen

Table 10.8 A simple bank balance sheet after a shift in rates

Assets	Liabilities
$95.83 in a 5-year security with a 4.17-year duration	• $90 in a 4-year term deposit with a 3.49-year duration • $5.83 in equity

because many assets have low risk weights. Assets backed by government guarantees, for instance, have risk weights of 0%. If a bank chose to hold only assets with 0% weights, risk-weighted capital alone would allow the bank to hold no equity and be infinitely leveraged. But that never happens because the minimum equity-to-assets ratio kicks in. Banks consequently have to hold the larger of risk-weighted capital or minimum equity-to-assets.

The potential for minimum equity-to-assets to set a floor on capital also creates another issue for managers of bank asset portfolios. If a bank wants to add assets with risk weights below the equity-to-assets floor, or, more generally, add assets that require low economic capital, the floor could make it difficult. If the bank accumulated capital to support each asset as it came onto the books, the bank would have to recoup the cost of that marginal capital through the interest rate and general performance of the marginal asset. For example, if the bank had a 4% minimum assets-to-equity and took a new $1 asset onto its books, it would have to add $0.04 in capital even if the asset were extremely safe. That could force the bank to charge an excessive interest rate or impose restrictive terms, leaving the bank at comparative disadvantage to other lenders.

Banks have to solve this problem by balancing risk-weighted or economic capital against the equity-to-assets floor. That is, for every $1 allocated to lending that requires less capital than the floor the bank has to put $1 in a loan that requires corresponding more capital than the floor. Or, more generally,

$$\text{Minimum Percent Equity-to-Assets} = \frac{\sum_1^i w_i A_i}{\sum_1^i A_i}$$

where w_i represents the percentage economic capital required for the ith asset, and A_i represents the value of the ith asset.

11

Investing for Property/Casualty and Life Insurers

The investment issues for insurers run along the same lines as the issues faced by banks. Insurers manage assets against liabilities, but insurance and bank liabilities look very different. Insurers take in premiums and pay out claims, and banks take in funds from different sources and pay out at withdrawal or maturity. The flow of premiums and claims create insurance liabilities every bit as idiosyncratic as those managed by banks. There is no observable market value for the liabilities, of course, just like banks. But unlike banks, the cost only becomes clear when the tally of claims and expenses becomes final well after the liabilities get put in place. Managing for total return again becomes difficult. And a host of influences—accounting, regulation, equity valuation, and others—encourage insurers to manage the spread between investment income and liability expense.

The importance of spread and the emphasis on reliably paying claims make liabilities central to any insurance portfolio and set the bounds for plausible investments. This creates a local asset market for insurers, a source of comparative advantage for insurers within the local market but also the grounds for competition between insurers.

The Structure of Insurance Investing

The US insurance industry falls broadly into property and casualty, or P&C insurance, and life insurance, and insurance portfolios reflect the differences (figure 11.1). Within these broad categories comes a wide range of more narrow lines of insurance. The biggest difference between these business lines comes in their liabilities, and the differences in liabilities lead to differences in investment strategy and portfolio structure.

P&C insurers broadly cover damage and loss from fire, weather, theft, or other causes; legal liability from injury or damage to property; loss from business

Property & Casualty Insurers – All Lines

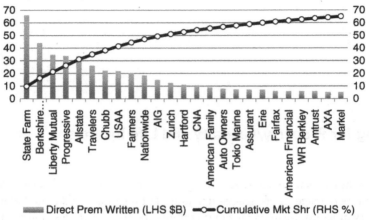

Life Insurers

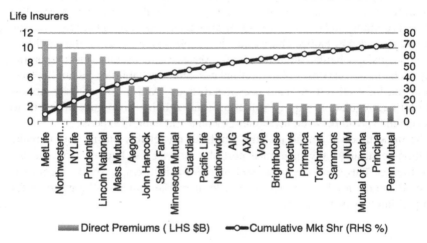

Figure 11.1 Top 25 property and casualty and life insurers
Source: National Association of Insurance Commissioners (2019).

interruption; or loss from accident or illness. That exposes the insurer to a wide range of events from the weather to traffic safety, from crime to litigation, and beyond. P&C insurers consequently have to cover a potentially volatile stream of claims, creating relatively short and relatively risky liabilities. This gets reflected in portfolios that typically hold relatively short, safe, and liquid assets.

Most P&C contracts also come up for renewal every six or 12 months. The insurer or the policyholder can choose to renew or cancel, and the policyholder can even cancel before the term is out. This gives both sides in the contract the ability to manage cost and risk, although state law limits insurer's ability to cancel without notice.

Life insurers broadly cover death benefits, provide income after disability or retirement through annuities or other investment products, and cover the cost of routine, acute, and long-term care. Life insurers consequently take on exposure to health and lifestyle risk. These risks typically unfold over much longer horizons than risks taken by P&C insurers. Because life insurers often take in premium and pay benefits years later, they also take on exposure to changes in interest rates, credit, and other risks over a long time. Some aspects of health care, such as regular doctor visits or ongoing prescriptions, look like the same steady stream of claims that a P&C insurer faces. Other aspects, such as pregnancy and childbirth or hospice care, cluster at particular points in an insured person's life. The long liabilities of life insurers get reflected in portfolios that can hold longer, more volatile, and less liquid assets.

All insurers end up in the business of leveraged investing, taking in premiums against future benefits and claims and using those premiums—along with equity and some debt—to finance an asset portfolio (table 11.1). Premiums provide most of the funding with a small amount coming from debt. The average amount of equity depends on the line of business. In the first decade of the 2000s, according to Nissim (2010), the average P&C insurer held $1 in equity for every $4 in assets, and the average life insurers held $1 in equity for every $10 in assets. The broad differences in equity across P&C and life insurers has roughly held, although P&C insurers by 2018 had reduced leverage to $1 for roughly every $3 in assets, and life insurers had raised leverage to hold $1 for roughly every $11 in assets. The

Table 11.1   Average insurer balance sheet (1999–2009)

Assets	PC	LH	Liabilities	PC	LH
Investments	63%	79%	Earned premiums held as reserves	46%	73%
• Securities	*56%*	*63%*			
• Loans	*7%*	*16%*			
Receivables	6%	2%	Unearned premiums	9%	0%
Reinsurance	10%	3%	Debt	9%	7%
Other assets	21%	16%	Other	11%	10%
			Common equity	25%	10%
TOTAL	100%	100%	TOTAL	100%	100%

Note: Other assets include intangible assets, deferred policy acquisition costs, and other assets.
Source: Nissim (2010).

significantly greater equity held by P&C companies reflects the greater volatility of the insured risk, with claims potentially swinging dramatically from year to year.

When it comes to assets, securities make up the largest category for both P&C and life insurers, although life insurers hold a healthy amount of loans. Cash and other assets follow far behind. Unlike banks, which have deposit networks and cash management services that put them in regular contact with businesses and individuals who need to borrow, insurers have more limited opportunity to lend and have to rely more on capital markets for most investments.

The size of the US industry depends on whether it's measured by number of firms, premiums, capital, or assets. The US had 2,620 licensed P&C insurers at the end of 2017 and 743 life-and-health insurers (Federal Insurance Office, 2018). The $557 billion in 2017 premiums taken in by P&C insurers slightly trails the $597 billion taken in by life insurers. But premiums capture annual flows and miss the accumulation of those flows on the balance sheet. The picture changes after considering reserves, which broadly represent premiums on balance sheet waiting to be paid out for future benefits and claims. P&C insurers at the end of 2017 held more than $636 billion in reserves, whereas life insurers held $3.3 trillion. For P&C insurers, reserves rarely build up for long because the time between premium and claim typically is short. For life companies, however, the time can be significantly longer, allowing immense blocks of premium, or reserves, to build up. The big difference in reserves gets reflected in big differences in the size of the asset bases, with P&C insurers holding $2.41 trillion in financial assets at the end of 2018 and life-and-health companies holding general account assets of $5.12 trillion (figures 11.2 and 11.3).

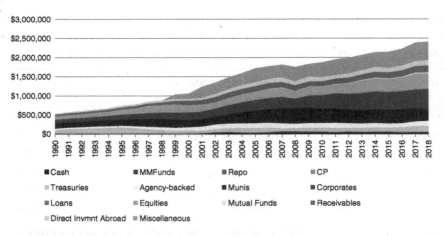

Figure 11.2   US P&C insurers' asset balance and asset mix
Source: Federal Reserve Board (2019), Table 115.

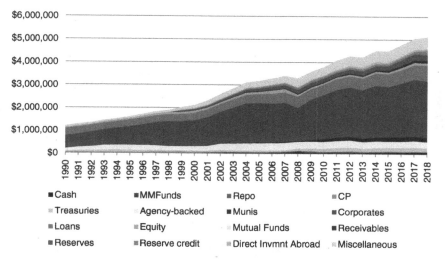

Figure 11.3 US life insurers' general account asset mix
Source: Federal Reserve Board (2019), Tables 116g.

Life insurers at the end of 2018 also held $2.45 trillion in assets in separate accounts, which are often managed for third parties in return for fees. This business takes advantage of insurers' relationships with businesses and individuals and is much more like an asset management business than an insurance business.

The current size of the insurance industry follows years of consolidation. The number of life insurers has fallen from a 1988 peak of 2,343 to a 2017 level of 781 (figure 11.4). Employment in life insurance over the same period, however, has

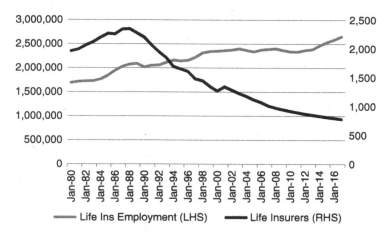

Figure 11.4 Fewer life insurers and rising employment point to consolidation.
Source: American Council of Life Insurers (2018), Tables 1.7 and 1.8.

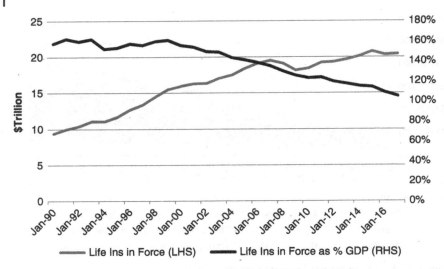

Figure 11.5 Life insurance in force has failed to keep up with US GPD.
Source: American Council of Life Insurers (2018), Table 7.9; US Bureau of Economic Analysis, Real Gross Domestic Product [GDPC1], retrieved from FRED, Federal Reserve Bank of St. Louis; https://fred.stlouisfed.org/series/GDPC1 (May 11, 2019).

gone up 28%. The size of the average insurer's workforce consequently has gone up nearly four times.

The consolidation reflects a smaller role for insurance in the broader US economy. Life insurance in force in the US generally continues to rise, but it has not kept up with growth in US GDP (figure 11.5). Life insurance in force from 1990 through 2017 roughly doubled from $10 trillion to $20 trillion (American Council of Life Insurers [ACLI], 2018), but as a share of GDP it fell from nearly 160% to nearly 100%. The sizes of both life and P&C insurance segments tend to track one another closely, so the trend for P&C insurance is likely the same.

The Basics of Insurance

Individuals or businesses could choose to set aside money and self-insure or take on insurable risks themselves, and some undoubtedly do. But the annual premium streams and the size of insurance reserves and invested assets suggest that many do not. This suggests that insurers have value as financial intermediaries and have comparative advantage in bearing both insurance and investment risks.

The demand for insurance traditionally comes from its ability to reduce variation in wealth and income (Friedman and Savage, 1948; Arrow, 1963). Rothschild and Stiglitz (1976) outline a simple case in which individuals face two future states of the world: one with a certain level of realized wealth without an accident, W, and one with an accident, W − d. The individual can buy an insurance policy by paying a premium, a_1, and will get paid a_2' if an accident occurs. That transforms the future into one without an accident, $W − a_1$, and one with, $W − d + a_2$, where $a_2 = a_2' − a_1$. This reduces the variance between states of the world, which may be worth the reduced income.

A simple example takes an individual who makes $1 every year without an accident and $0 every year with one. Accidents happen to this individual 50% of the time. If the individual pays a $0.50 annual premium and gets paid $1 after every accident, then risky income has turned into riskless income (table 11.2). Instead of making either $1 or $0 each year and $0.50 on average, the individual makes $0.50 every year.

The same rationale applies to life insurance, which protects against a complete loss of future earnings. It applies, too, to disability insurance, which protects against a reduction but not a complete earnings loss. Premiums that reflect the actuarial year-by-year odds of death or disability reduce the variability of future wealth on average to very low levels if not to zero.

When life insurers offer annuities that generate cash flow from retirement or some other point in time to the policyholder's death, the uncertainty about market conditions over that period and the buyer's lifespan transfer from buyer to insurer. The insurer then reduces the uncertainty by buying assets to generate annuity cash

Table 11.2 A simple insurance example

Year	Accident (0=No, 1=Yes)	Income without Ins	Income with Ins
1	0.0000	$1.0000	$0.50
2	1.0000	$0.0000	$0.50
3	1.0000	$0.0000	$0.50
4	0.0000	$1.0000	$0.50
5	0.0000	$1.0000	$0.50
6	0.0000	$1.0000	$0.50
7	1.0000	$0.0000	$0.50
8	1.0000	$0.0000	$0.50
9	1.0000	$0.0000	$0.50
10	0.0000	$1.0000	$0.50
Average	0.5000	$0.5000	$0.50
Variance	0.53	$0.53	$-

flows and pooling risk to get the expected rate of annual mortality. The buyer no longer has to manage against changing market rates of return or the risk of outliving his or her asset base.

The individual has incentives to take any policy in which expected wealth with insurance is equal to or better than wealth without insurance. In perfectly competitive markets, all contracts price to the actuarial odds of the insured event. Uncertainty has turned into certainty. Because expected wealth in a perfectly competitive insurance market hasn't changed, the certain outcome should dominate the uncertain one.

One key advantage that insurers have in managing actuarial risk is size. The insurer is drawing a particular sample of risk from some underlying population, and the larger the sample then the more likely the realized set of insured events will match the value in the underlying population. The variability of risk drops, which is good for the individual and good for the insurer.

In practice, insurance differs from other products in a very distinct way. Insurance helps the buyer only if some relatively rare event occurs. Other products— a meal, a car, a new pair of shoes—provide benefits immediately. A number of studies show insurance demand rises with wealth, education, and family size and declines with life expectancy and retirement benefits (Nissim, 2010). Demand also appears stronger in competitive insurance markets and weaker in markets with high inflation and high interest rates.

Insurance from the perspective of the supplier looks more complex. The insurer does not know the probability of the insured event for every individual. The insurer may know average driving habits, lifestyle, or the stability of different businesses, for instance, but around that average are insurance buyers of higher and lower risk. Once a premium is set, the insurer runs the risk of adverse selection and moral hazard. Adverse selection involves attracting individuals with event probabilities higher than the average used to set the premium—the reckless rather than the safe drivers. If the insurer is adversely selected, premiums will not cover the cost of claims. Moral hazard changes behavior by encouraging insured individuals to take more risk because they now have the backstop of the insurer's claim. Insured drivers might drive a little faster, for instance, or take rougher roads. Adequate size, careful underwriting, risk diversification, pricing, policy deductibles and exclusions, and the art of insurance contracting all try to address these risks.

The insurer consequently raises equity capital and issues insurance contracts. The contracts generate initial premium, continuing premium, or both. After covering expenses, the insurer holds net premium. The ratio of incoming premium against outgoing losses and expenses—often reported as the combined ratio, or losses and expenses as a percentage of earned premiums—measures underwriting profit or loss. The combined ratio becomes the effective cost of funds. A combined ratio above 100% means that losses and expenses have exceeded premium and that the insurer has paid a price for holding the premium. A combined ratio below 100% means the insurer has taken in premium and made money on it by paying out less! Assume, for example, a driver pays $1,000 a year for car insurance requiring $5 to administer and gets into a minor accident requiring $975 in repairs. The insurer can invest the $1,000 for roughly a year, pay $5 in expenses, pay $975 in claims, and keep $20. The insurer's cost of funds is *negative* 2%! The second year, the driver has another accident requiring $1,015 in repairs. After another $5 in expenses and $1,015 in claims, now the cost of funds is *positive* 2%. The combined ratio determines the insurer's cost of funds.

P&C insurers' combined ratio can vary significantly from year to year. From 2008 to 2017, for instance, the ratio varied from a high of 110.6 in 2011 to a low of 97.0 only two years later, a swing in implied cost of funds from 10.6% to −3.0% (figure 11.6). And because claims on some types of policies take years to resolve, the combined ratio can keep fluctuating long after the insurance contract expires.

Investing is the other critical part of insurance. The insurer invests equity capital and net premium until the time comes to pay out claims. That leaves the insurer with investment income. Timing is everything. The difference in timing between premiums received and losses paid out creates the insurer's investment window. The insurer invests the premium against two types of liabilities: unearned premium and loss reserve. Unearned premium represents premium paid in for coverage not yet provided, and, because most policy periods are short, looks like short-term debt. The loss reserve, which arises because claims lag premiums and loss events, represents expected losses net of claims already paid. The latter is a highly contingent cash flow. The insurer looks like an investment portfolio funded by premiums.

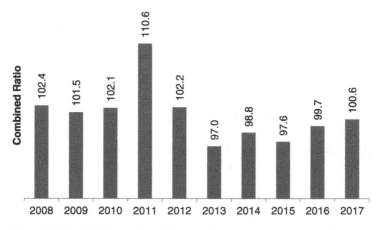

Figure 11.6   P&C insurers' combined ratio can vary significantly from year to year. *Source:* NAIC (2017).

Insurers consequently get revenue from returns on assets, r_a, and returns from underwriting, r_u. Where A is the size of the asset base and P is the size of the premium stream:

$$Insurer\ revenue = r_a A + r_u P$$

Return on equity, E, flows from revenue:

$$ROE = (r_a A + r_u P)/E$$

Note the similarity to the general formulation of $ROE = (r_A A - r_L L)/E$. With a little restating of terms, that becomes $ROE = (r_A - r_L) \times Leverage + r_L$. By analogy, insurer $ROE = (r_a - r_u) \times Leverage + r_u$. That formulation shows that returns to an insurance portfolio depend on financial and underwriting leverage. The interplay between the two led Wiltbank (1989) to write:

> Equity-holders in the firm receive compensation as either investment income or underwriting profits, but the source of their earnings does not concern them. When investment opportunities are particularly attractive, the prospect of underwriting losses produced by "inadequate" rates is counterbalanced by the higher investment income. Managers acting rationally (in the economic sense) will pursue underwriting strategies that seem suicidal but are in fact profitable. (p. 366)

Insurance consequently creates a levered corporation that issues debt and equity. It issues debt through insurance contracts. Unlike conventional debt, payment timing and amount depend on contingent events. And the insurers' customers rather than lenders or depositors hold the debt. The price of the debt should reflect the risks borne by the insurer compared to the same insured risk borne by an individual customer. If the insurer can bear the risk more efficiently than the individual—reflected by reduced volatility in the customer's wealth or income—then the individual may lend the insurer money at a rate well below market levels.

Sources of Comparative Advantage

Insurance portfolios can draw on the same set of potential comparative advantages as other investors:

- Scale, cost, and compensation
- Leverage
- Funding terms
- Hedging
- Quality and cost of capital

- Information
- Access to assets
- Tax and accounting rules
- Political and regulatory environment

Insurers' actual comparative advantages, however, are distinct.

Scale, Cost, and Compensation

Low cost adds directly to net return for any investment portfolio. And any portfolio has incentives to grow and reduce the marginal cost of portfolio staff and infrastructure. Insurers are no different. Scale also enables a portfolio to use more specialized expertise, which should broadly translate into better return, less risk, or both. Lower cost and better marginal return compound over time in an investment portfolio, so the impact over long horizons is substantial.

For the underwriting side of an insurer, scale can be a powerful competitive advantage. The larger, more representative, and more diversified the portfolio of insured risk, the smoother and more predictable the insurer's cost of funds. The cost of funds can still rise unexpectedly if catastrophe strikes—earthquake, storms, epidemic, and so on—but size reduces the idiosyncrasies.

Insurers can use compensation to align portfolio management with portfolio performance, but the metrics for an insurer are unique. The insurer has to match asset to liability performance, but liabilities can be idiosyncratic. Insurers might have one set of goals for assets held against specific liabilities and another set for assets considered part of the surplus. Some insurers try to describe liabilities in terms of one or more public benchmarks and then tie compensation to annual or even cumulative performance relative to the benchmark. This is analogous to the performance fees charged by hedge funds. But insurers have to be careful to structure incentive compensation to keep portfolio management aligned with targeted return and risk. A portfolio actively managed against a benchmark might buy and sell to maximize price performance, but that might not square well with insurers' strong incentives to maximize portfolio income net of liability costs. Unlike cost, compensation looks unlikely to be a major comparative advantage.

Leverage

Leverage reflects the required size of statutory reserves and the riskiness of the assets where the reserve is invested. If a life insurer receives a $100 premium, for instance, only $10 might go to cover the first year's insurance costs. That leaves $90 in reserve. The capital required depends on how the $90 is invested. The National Association of Insurance Commissioners, or NAIC, recommends insurers hold minimum investment capital based on asset risk. This is a good news–bad news situation. Fixed rules mean that the equity required to run an insurance business is relatively stable, unlike a capital regime that adjusts dynamically as asset risk evolves. But depending on competing investors' view of the capital needed to support evolving risk, insurers' advantage can wax or wane. When competing investors' view of required capital is high relative to insurers', insurers win by being able to use higher leverage to buy assets. When a competing portfolio's view of required capital is low, insurers lose.

The NAIC's risk-based capital, or RBC, approach started in the early 1990s after a string of insurer insolvencies. Before RBC, regulators used fixed capital standards to gauge solvency. Those standards required the same minimum capital regardless of a company's financial condition. The amounts ranged from $500,000 to $6 million depending on the state and the line of business. If the insurers' capital and surplus met the standards, it became licensed and could start writing contracts.

RBC tries to align capital with risk. It focuses not just on assets but also on underwriting and insurance, interest rate, and business risks (table 11.3).

Table 11.3 Components of insurer risk-based capital, or RBC

Life RBC	
C0	Insurance affiliate investment and (non-derivative) off-balance sheet risk
C1cs	Invested common stock asset risk
C1o	Invested asset risk, plus reinsurance credit risk net of C1cs
C2	Insurance risk
C3a	Interest rate risk
C3b	Health provider credit risk
C3c	Market risk
C4a	Business risk – guaranty fund assessment and separate account risks
C4b	Business risk – health administrative expense risk
Life RBC = C0 + [(C1o + C3a)^2 + (C1cs + C3c)^2 + (C2)^2 + (C3b)^2 + (C4b)^2]$^{1/2}$ + C4a	
P&C RBC	
R0	Insurance affiliate investment and (non-derivative) off-balance sheet risk
R1	Invested asset risk – fixed income investments
R2	Invested asset risk – equity investments
R3	Credit risk (non-reinsurance plus one half reinsurance credit risk)
R4	Loss reserve risk, one half reinsurance credit risk, growth risk
R5	Premium risk, growth risk
P&C RBC = R0 + [(R1)^2 + (R2)^2 + (R3)^2 + (R4)^2 + (R5)^2]$^{1/2}$	
Health RBC	
H0	Insurance affiliate investment and (non-derivative) off-balance sheet risk
H1	Invested asset risk
H2	Insurance risk
H3	Credit risk (health provider, reinsurance, misc. receivables)
H4	Business risk
Health RBC = H0 + [(H1)^2 + (H2)^2 + (H3)^2 + (H4)^2]$^{1/2}$	

Source: Felice (2002).

And the rules vary across P&C, life, and other lines. RBC for life insurers, with their long liabilities, for instance, covers interest rate risk, and RBC for other insurers does not.

The weighting of asset risk together with the risks of underwriting/insurance and operational risk means that insurers with safer lines of business can take more risk in their investment portfolios, and insurers with riskier business have to take less investment risk. Work by Yu (2013) suggests that asset, interest rate, and market risk nevertheless create the majority of the capital needs of a life insurer. These risks constituted 62% of the demand for capital in Yu's review with risk from affiliated insurers at 22% and risk from insurance and underwriting a distant third at 9% (table 11.4). This makes insurers very sensitive to asset capital requirements.

The NAIC categorizes asset risk in tiers based on ratings, with each tier requiring a fixed minimum capital (table 11.5). Requirements for life and P&C insurers differ, with P&C insurers holding slightly less because of the shorter expected holding period for the assets. Shorter holding periods lower the risk of losing investment principal and require less capital.

Fixed minimum capital leads insurers to a minimum spread required to hit targeted pre- or post-tax return on equity. This sets a minimum hurdle rate for the spread of assets over liabilities. Assuming a post-tax ROE target of 10%, a tax rate of 35%, a 0% cost of funds for simplicity, and the heroic assumption that the insurer uses every bit of available leverage, an NAIC Category 1 asset would need to yield only 6.2 bp to hit the ROE target (table 11.6). But as the NAIC category and capital rise, the minimum yield needed to hit the ROE target rises quickly, and by NAIC Category 6 it reaches 461.5 bp. Note that these are minimum yields. In practice, an insurer would need even higher yields to help pay for additional capital that supports operations and other functions that do not generate revenue, especially in years with underwriting losses.

NAIC ratings almost entirely reflect the probability of default and loss of invested principal, that is, credit risk. But all investments include risks other

Table 11.4 Contributions to life insurer RBC

C0: Asset Risk—Affiliates	22%
C1o: Asset Risk—All Other + C3a: Interest Rate Risk	51%
C1cs: Asset Risk—Common Stock + C3c: Market Risk	11%
C2: Insurance Risk	9%
C4a: Business Risk	7%
C3b: Health Credit Risk, C4b: Business Risk Admin Expenses	<1%

Source: Yu (2013).

Table 11.5 Asset risk requirement

Risk Category	Life: Pre-Tax RBC Factor	P&C: After-Tax RBC Factor
U.S. Treasuries	0.0%	0.0%
NAIC 1 (Aaa-A)	0.4%	0.3%
NAIC 2 (Baa)	1.3%	1.0%
NAIC 3 (Ba)	4.6%	2.0%
NAIC 4 (B)	10.0%	4.5%
NAIC 5 (Caa)	23.0%	10.0%
NAIC 6 (Ca and lower)	30.0%	30.0%
Bond size factor	Based on # of bonds	
Other selected assets		
Mortgages in Good Standing	2.6%	5.0%
Real Estate	15.0%	10.0%
Real Estate JV	23.0%	10.0%
Preferred Stock: Class 1	1.1%	2.3%
Preferred Stock: Class 6	30.0%	30.0%
Common Stock	30.0%	
Common Stock Factor	Add'l 50% charge for Top 5	

Source: CRE Finance Council, Annual Conference, June 11–13, 2012; Felice (2002).

Table 11.6 RBC and target ROE lead to minimum acceptable asset yields

NAIC Category	RBC	Leverage	Post-Tax ROE	Pre-Tax ROE	Asset-Liab Spread
1	0.40%	250	10%	15.4%	0.062%
2	1.30%	77	10%	15.4%	0.200%
3	4.60%	22	10%	15.4%	0.708%
4	10.00%	10	10%	15.4%	1.538%
5	23.00%	4	10%	15.4%	3.538%
6	30.00%	3	10%	15.4%	4.615%

than credit, such as spread volatility, liquidity, structural complexity, and so on. Insurers have incentives to take risks not reflected in NAIC ratings because the added risk leads to higher yields without requiring more capital. ROE for assets with other embedded risk, of course, goes up.

Rating agencies also have views on the capital needed to run an insurer, and agencies' views are qualitatively similar to the NAIC. But instead of setting minimum levels, rating agencies set capital to distinguish tiers of insurer risk. Stronger insurers presumably have a better ability to pay claims and should be able to attract either higher premiums or average premiums at a lower cost. This is an instance when holding more capital might lower insurer leverage but reduces the costs of funding by an amount still sufficient to raise return on equity.

Insurer capital sets the playing field against other investors but not against other insurers. Insurers will have advantage in markets where other investors have to hold more capital either because their regulators require it or because market circumstances do. Where insurers hold more capital than others, of course, it's a disadvantage.

From one insurer to another, however, regulatory and rating agency capital creates a generally even playing field. In fact, that's the broad policy goal behind regulatory capital: to discourage capital competition and avoid a race between insurers to ever-lower levels. This should give the public a well-capitalized insurance industry with limited systematic or idiosyncratic insolvency.

Funding Terms

Along with scale and diversification of insured risk and leverage, the quality of underwriting and its direct impact on effective cost of funds is a powerful driver of advantage both within and outside the insurance industry. Insurers may not know the ultimate cost of insuring a line of risk, but the relative cost of insuring different segments of a risk market is arguably more predictable. It costs less to insure better drivers than worse, stronger buildings than weaker, markets with better health care than poorer, and so on. Insurers have powerful incentives through contract design, pricing, marketing, and distribution to attract the better risks in a broad population. This kind of favorable selection not only lowers an insurer's cost of funds but also leaves the adverse risks to the competition and raises competitors' cost of funds.

The cost of funds for P&C insurers depends on the combined ratio, but policyholders may be willing to take a low or even a negative rate as a concession for lower income or wealth volatility. The combined ratio across the P&C industry in the past has dropped below 100%, indicating underwriting profits or, alternatively, a negative rate of interest.

For life insurers, the combined ratio is harder to interpret. Life insurers take in premiums years before paying out claims, so it takes a long time for a life insurance book to reach a balance between premiums in and claims out. Even with a balanced flow, the long stretch between first payment and claim means that the underlying mix of premium schedules and actuarial risks is always changing. It becomes hard to assign the combined ratio to any one vintage of contracts.

Funding costs and terms for a life insurer depend more on the type of contract written. For example:

- *Classic term life.* A classic term life insurance policy pays a fixed lump sum or death benefit over a series of one-year renewable terms, and each year the cost of the policy rises to reflect the increasing risk of death as the policyholder ages. This is similar to P&C insurance because it depends mainly on relatively stable actuarial risks. In a competitive market, the insurer should expect on average to pay out all premiums taken in, so the term of the funds and the investment horizon are short. Cost depends almost exclusively on realized actuarial risks.

- *Level term life.* A level term life policy usually charges a level premium over 10 or 15 years or longer and pays a fixed sum if the policyholder dies during that term. Compared to the premium on a series of one-year contracts, the level premium is usually higher in the beginning of the contract and lower at the end. It might seem that the term of this funding would match the term of the contract and that the cost would match present value of a series of renewable one-year contracts. But the term and cost of this funding also depends on the tendency of the policyholder to lapse or stop making payments. Lapses can occur because the original need for the insurance—to protect an earnings stream, for instance—changes or because the policyholder can no longer afford the premium. Lapses make this funding shorter than mortality alone might suggest and reduce its costs because the policyholder has paid in premium without getting a benefit.

- *Whole life.* Whole life policies vary tremendously but generally combine a term policy with a linked set of investments that compound tax-free. The insurance company manages the linked investments, and those investments create a policy's cash value. If the policyholder stops paying the whole life premiums, the policy uses the cash value to continue paying for the term policy. If the policyholder continues paying the whole life premiums, however, the cash value eventually goes to the policyholder's estate. Or the policyholder can borrow against the cash value at any time. The cost of this funding starts at the same level as term life and is reduced further by the gains to the insurer from managing the linked investments. Those gains can come from investment management fees. But they also can come from the share of asset returns, or the crediting rate, that the insurer decides to pass through to the policyholder's cash account. The insurer does not have to pass through all asset returns, and competition between insurers tends to set the crediting rate. Policyholders nevertheless may be willing to accept this loss of return because their cash value still compounds tax-free. For the insurer, however, whole life policies can create a long stream of funds at a very low cost.

- *Annuities.* Annuities also vary dramatically in the schedule of premium and later cash benefits, but almost all involve paying premium in return for later cash flow. The cash flow usually ends within some window of time around a policyholder's death. This guarantees the policyholder a stream of cash no matter how long he or she lives. For an insurer writing a large, diversified set of contracts, the future benefits should match actuarial expectations. The insurer invests the premiums in instruments expected to cover the future obligations to policyholders, and the returns on these instruments compound tax-free. For an insurer, this looks very similar to a life insurance policy except that, instead of a lump sum, the obligation is a stream of cash flows that start at a certain date and end at a date related to the policyholder's death. And because the returns on annuity assets compound tax-free, policyholders may be willing to take a lower rate of return and cede part of that return back to the insurer. This can help make annuities, too, a low-cost source of funding.

Annuities do have one aspect to them that can make them both difficult and potentially expensive to manage and can drive the funding cost down: the policyholder can withdraw the premium or principal value of the contract. Annuities usually involve significant penalties or surrender charges in early years if the policyholder withdraws more than 10% or some other small amount of the principal. But once surrender charges fall far enough, the insurer is at risk of withdrawal. And policyholders are more likely to withdraw as interest rates or other asset returns rise. That leaves the insurer with a source of funds that could actually get shorter as interest rates go up, forcing the insurer to replace those funds with more expensive funds. If the insurer also has invested in fixed income assets to cover the annuity obligations, the insurer may have to liquidate the portfolio and pay out funds as interest rates rise—potentially an expensive process because the value of fixed income will be dropping as demands to withdraw rise. Similarly, if the insurer has assumed a base rate of withdrawal, that rate might drop as interest rates fall, lengthening the effective term of the funds even though the term of the fixed income asset base may not change. This could raise the projected cost of annuity obligations just as the insurer has to reinvest portfolio coupons and maturing or prepaid principal at a lower rate of return.

The cost of paying benefits on an aggregate book of traditional life insurance, predicted by mortality trends and insurer experience, is understandably more stable than the cost of paying for benefits and withdrawals on annuities subject to withdrawal (figure 11.7). Managers of annuity funding have to manage more risk.

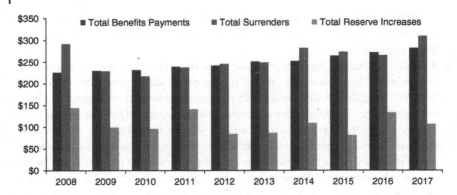

Figure 11.7 More volatility in paying for annuity surrenders than for life benefits
Source: Federal Insurance Office (2018), p. 72.

In recent years, annuities have become a much larger source of funds for life-and-health insurers than either life insurance or accident-and-health premiums (figure 11.8). This puts a premium on the ability of the insurer to anticipate the variability of annuity withdrawals and invest appropriately.

For both P&C and life insurers, the cost of funds depends, too, on the company's ratings. Ratings assess an insurer's ability to meet its ongoing insurance and policy contracts. This can be the ability to pay claims, redeem annuities, or other obligations. The higher the rating, the lower the effective cost of funds.

The length of funding ultimately depends on the lag between taking premiums in and paying claims out. In the case of P&C insurance, it is relatively short, almost all less than five years, and the large majority are less than three. In the case of life insurance, it is potentially decades long. That enables investing in very long assets, including illiquid assets where the price can swing substantially as

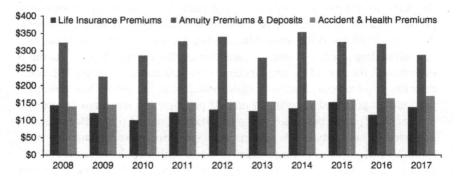

Figure 11.8 Sources of funding for life-and-health insurers
Source: Federal Insurance Office (2018), p. 71.

insurer identify better actuarial risks, educating policyholders to avoid or mitigate risk, identifying or managing fraud, or managing claims more efficiently.

Insurers arguably have little intrinsic information advantage in investing. Unlike banks that take deposits from the same individuals or businesses that might need loans, an insurer doesn't have a ready flow of assets or proprietary information on the balance sheet of those asset providers. It's possible that an insurer could capitalize on its underwriting knowledge to invest in securities that carry similar risk, but that would mean performance in the insurer's asset and liability would likely be highly correlated. If an auto insurer, for instance, invested in securities backed by auto loans or leases, an unexpected jump in auto accidents could raise the insurer's cost of funds and reduce the value of the auto asset–backed securities. The insurer would have leveraged its exposure to the insured risk.

Insurers, similar to any investor, however, can develop proprietary information or expertise. In any asset class where an insurer has some other competitive advantage, proprietary information or expertise should only help to reinforce that advantage.

Access to Assets

Insurers also likely have no intrinsic advantage in access to assets other than the advantages that come from other aspects of the investment platform—size, proprietary expertise, or something else that makes the insurer a better buyer in a particular corner of the market. Regular buyers in any asset class tend to see the widest range of offerings in that class because sellers realize that regular buyers can help turn inventory.

Nevertheless, insurers have invested heavily in corporate bonds, small-and-medium-enterprise loans, commercial real estate, and infrastructure. NAIC's securities valuation office, or SVO, helps by providing ratings on private assets to help the insurer and regulator set minimum capital. Insurers consequently get a proprietary flow of these kinds of assets for a very important reason—their advantage in holding illiquid assets.

Tax and Accounting

Tax and accounting create some of insurers' most powerful advantages.

Tax Treatment

Tax makes P&C insurers motivate buyers of tax-exempt debt and helps lower the cost of funds for life insurers. And accounting, in concert with the long liabilities of life insurers, makes those balance sheets extremely well suited to own illiquid or volatile assets.

P&C insurers pay tax on both underwriting and investment income. Underwriting income is premium revenue net of losses and expenses. And investment income is coupon, principal, and any realized capital gains or losses. Because underwriting income is not debt for tax purposes, P&C insurers do not get to deduct an underwriting loss as an interest expense (Johnson and Baxley, 2004). That exposes the full return on P&C assets to tax and creates incentives to buy tax-exempt bonds. Even then, P&C insurers pay taxes on 15% of municipal bond income while life insurers and other investors pay no tax.

By contrast, life insurers get taxed on investment income but not on the portion that they credit to reserves held against future losses or to the portion credited to the cash value of a policyholder's account. That enables the insurer to effectively deduct an interest expense (Johnson and MacIvor, 2012).

To highlight the difference between these tax treatments, take a P&C insurer with a 101% combined ratio that invests in a 2% par municipal bond. The P&C company pays taxes on the full 2% coupon. At a 35% tax rate, the company nets 1.30% after taxes. All else being equal, the company would buy any tax-exempt bond with a coupon above 1.372% because $1.372\% * (1 - 15\% * 35\%) = 1.30\%$. A life company that credits 1% to the policyholder pays taxes only on 1%. At a 35% tax rate, the life company nets 0.65% after taxes. All else being equal, the life company would buy a tax-exempt bond only with a coupon above 1.65% to get the same net 0.65% after taxes. Tax-exempt bonds consequently are much more valuable for a P&C than for a life insurer.

Tax treatment of life insurance policies with cash value also helps attract premiums. A policy with cash value involves the policyholder paying more premium than needed to cover the immediate cost of insurance. Investment returns on the extra premium compound tax-free, a big advantage over trying to cover the insurance cost outside of the insurance policy with taxable investments. Moreover, the policyholder has the option of withdrawing the cash value of the policy later, possibly when the policyholder is paying a lower tax rate.[1] Assume, for example, that the actuarial cost of a 30-year life insurance policy runs at $100 for each decade. If 10- and 20-year interest rates stood around 5%, the policyholder might pay upfront $100 for the first decade, $100/(1 + 5\%/2)^{20}$ or $61.03 for the second, $100/(1 + 5\%/2)^{40}$ or $37.24 for the third. If the policyholder had to pay a 35% tax rate each year, then he might pay upfront $100 for the first decade, set aside $100/(1 + (5\%/2)(1 - 35\%))^{20}$ or $72.44 for the second, and $100/(1 + (5\%/2)(1 - 35\%))^{40}$ or $52.47 for the third. The policyholder has incentive to pay the insurer upfront.

---

1 Withdrawals up to the amount of premium paid in are tax-free because the policyholder paid taxes on those monies before using them to pay the insurer.

Accounting Treatment

Accounting encourages insurers to hold some assets but not others (table 11.7). Assets held at amortized cost enable the insurer to take the assets' yield-to-maturity into quarterly income without having to report changes in price in either shareholder equity or income. That enables the asset to make a smooth and steady contribution to income even if it varies significantly in price, an ideal way to account for a volatile or illiquid asset. Assets accounted for at the lower of cost or market also make a smooth contribution to income, although changes in price flow through to shareholder equity. Assets held at market value show up in income quarterly.

Because life insurers hold all assets except NAIC 6 at amortized cost, the balance sheet is well suited to holding volatile or illiquid positions. P&C insurers have some leeway, but assets at NAIC 3 or below can show up in shareholder equity and potentially threaten regulatory capital requirements.

No matter the accounting treatment, selling an asset creates gains and losses that flow through income and add volatility. That imposes an indirect penalty on trading activity, and subtly discourages it.

Table 11.7 Asset accounting treatment

Risk Category	Life	P&C
U.S. Treasuries	Amortized cost	Amortized cost
NAIC 1 (Aaa-A)	Amortized cost	Amortized cost
NAIC 2 (Baa)	Amortized cost	Amortized cost
NAIC 3 (Ba)	Amortized cost	Lower of cost or market
NAIC 4 (B)	Amortized cost	Lower of cost or market
NAIC 5 (Caa)	Amortized cost	Lower of cost or market
NAIC 6 (Ca and lower)	Lower of cost or market	Lower of cost or market
Other selected assets		
Mortgages in Good Standing	O/S Principal	O/S Principal
Real Estate	O/S Principal	O/S Principal
Real Estate JV	O/S Principal	O/S Principal
Preferred Stock: Class 1	Amortized Cost	Amortized cost
Preferred Stock: Class 6	Lower of cost or market	Lower of cost or market
Common Stock	Market value	

Source: Felice (2002).

Political and Regulatory

The states regulate insurers heavily with some influence from federal authorities and rating agencies. State regulators set standards for market conduct, insurer and agent licensing, premiums, policy language, solvency, and consumer protection. Most states also require all licensed insurers to participate in a residual market of individuals or businesses that could not get insurance through usual private providers.

The complexity of insurance regulation is a clear advantage to incumbents and a disadvantage to new entrants. Insurers that need to build geographically diverse books of business have to deal with state regulators in each jurisdiction. They also have to deal with rating agencies, which serve as proxy national regulators, and, for large insurers under Dodd-Frank, with the Financial Stability Oversight Committee and its power to designate an insurer as a systemically important financial institution. The insurer has to meet the capital and risk standards of all of these regulators, who may not coordinate their rules, so the insurer ultimately has to meet the highest standard. Although regulatory complexity protects incumbents and deters new entrants, it adds cost and risk to an insurance portfolio that other portfolios do not bear.

Insurers have regularly used the ongoing regulatory interest of states to discourage efforts at federal regulation. But federal policymakers regularly enact changes that affect the demand for life insurance, such as introducing 401(k) plans where tax-deferred compounding of returns competes with life insurance or changing marginal tax rates, which also affects the appeal of tax-deferred investments.

Predictions of Local CAPM

Based on the comparative advantages and disadvantages of an insurance investment platform, local CAPM makes a few predictions easy to explore with readily available data:

- Life insurers will prefer assets with long maturities; P&C insurers will prefer assets with short maturities.
- Life insurers will prefer illiquid assets; P&C insurers will prefer liquid.
- P&C insurers will invest in muni bonds because of tax advantages.
- All insurers will prefer fixed income to equity, particularly life insurers.

Evidence of Local CAPM

The clear differences between the investment portfolios of life-and-health and P&C insurers speaks to the influences that create local markets in assets.

Life Insurer Preference for Long Maturities; P&C Preference for Short Maturities

The evidence for long maturities in life portfolios is straightforward. Life insurers routinely buy debt with long maturities to match the long liabilities of life and disability policies and annuities. Life insurers in 2017 showed a familiar pattern, making 40% of new debt investments in maturities of 20 years or longer and another 33% in maturities between 10 and 20 years (figure 11.10). Outstanding life insurer investments showed a shorter average maturity, understandable as purchases from earlier years approach maturity over time.

Evidence on the shorter maturities of P&C portfolios is indirect. As US interest rates generally declined from 2008 to 2017, the net yield on invested life insurance assets declined from approximately 5.47% to 4.58% while the net yield on P&C insurance assets declined from 4.20% 3.03%. Because US debt yields typically rise with maturity in most markets, the higher yield in life portfolios suggests investment in relatively longer maturities and the lower yield in P&C portfolios suggests investment in relatively shorter maturities. Further, the larger drop in portfolio net yield suggests P&C insurers held shorter maturities and had to reinvest principal at steadily lower interest rates.

Life Insurer Preference for Illiquid Assets; P&C Preference for Liquid

Measuring the liquidity of an asset is a subtle exercise with the best work weighing the influence of trading volume, the spread between bid and ask prices, and the

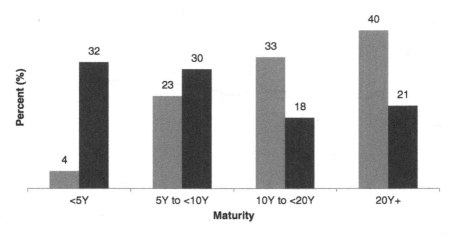

Figure 11.10   Life insurers tend to invest in debt with long maturities.
Source: American Council of Life Insurers (2018).

sensitivity of that spread to large flows of buying or selling (Amihud, Mendelson, and Pedersen, 2005). It is still possible to broadly categorize assets into relatively more or less liquid.

The Federal Reserve's quarterly Financial Accounts of the United States reports investment portfolio assets for both P&C and life insurers, and those assets fall broadly into the relatively liquid and illiquid. The liquid includes cash, money market mutual funds, repurchase agreements, commercial paper, and Treasury and federal agency securities. The illiquid include municipal and corporate debt and all loans.

Life insurers hold a consistently higher share of their investment portfolios in illiquid assets than do P&C insurers (figure 11.11). Since the mid-1990s, life insurers have held more than 70% of their portfolio in illiquid assets and P&C insurers have held between 40% and 50%. The higher share for life insurers reflects the broader set of assets that the NAIC allows the company to hold at amortized cost rather than market value as well as the shorter and less predictable liabilities that P&C insurers have. Investors holding assets at amortized cost can ignore changes in market value in their public reporting, making it easier to hold illiquid assets subject to sudden jumps in market value. For P&C insurers, shorter and less predictable liabilities argue for holding securities that the portfolio can easily sell.

P&C Holdings of Municipal Bonds

The special tax treatment of municipal bonds in P&C insurance portfolios creates incentives to invest, and P&C insurers typically respond. P&C insurers have held

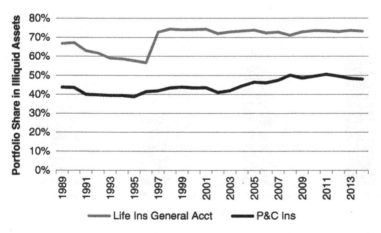

Figure 11.11   Life insurance portfolios hold a larger share of illiquid securities.
Note: Liquid assets for this analysis includes cash, money market mutual funds, repurchase agreements, commercial paper, and Treasury and federal agency securities. Illiquid includes municipal and corporate debt and all loans.
Source: Federal Reserve Board (2019).

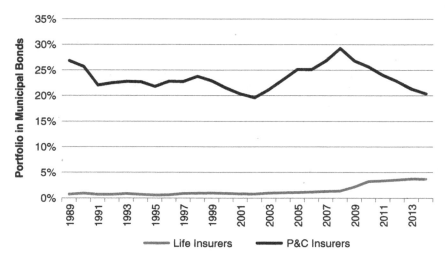

Figure 11.12 P&C insurers hold more than a quarter of their portfolio in municipal bonds, and life insurers hold less than 5%.
Source: Federal Reserve Board (2019).

between 20% and 30% of their portfolio in municipal bonds for the last quarter century, and life insurers have held less than 5% (figure 11.12).

Preference for Fixed Income

The need to cover regular insured claims makes fixed income a better asset than equity. And for life insurers, tax-deferred compounding makes fixed income and its regular cash flow even more attractive. Both life and P&C insurers invest a majority of their portfolios in fixed income, with life insurers investing a consistently higher share (figure 11.13).

Local CAPM also makes other predictions that will need further research:

- Life insurers will dominate broad parts of the market in times of stress.
  Life insurers' ability to hold most assets at amortized cost insulates them from sharp swings in market value that often come with market stress. Life insurers do have to consider security or loan rating because that sets minimum required capital, and life insurers have to consider the ultimate ability of the debt to pay principal and interest. However, debt or other investments temporarily trading at distressed prices but still likely to pay principal and interest are well suited to life insurance portfolios.
- Life insurers' annuity portfolios will have low exposure to MBS.
  One of the biggest risks for an insurer's set of annuity contracts is the risk of early redemption, and that risk rises as interest rates go up and gives the policyholders

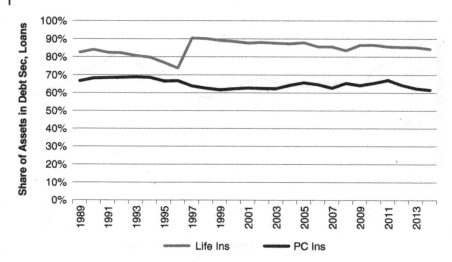

Figure 11.13 Both life and P&C insurers hold a majority of assets in fixed income. *Source:* Federal Reserve Board (2019).

the opportunity to trade into new annuities at higher rates. Annuity redemptions can force the insurer to sell debt as rates rise, generating a loss on the investment. This problem is especially acute with MBS, which, as rates rise, tend to fall in price faster than Treasury or corporate debt. Higher rates generally reduce prepayments in MBS and extend the security's expected cash flow. Insurers managing annuities should hesitate to hold MBS against their annuity book.

- All insurers will prefer A to AA or AAA assets.

  Insurer preference for A assets is a simple reflection of NAIC capital rules, which require the same capital for A, AA, and AAA assets. Because A generally offers more yield, insurers should prefer A for its resulting higher return on equity.

Conclusion

Insurers take in premiums, pay out claims, and invest in the interim. The timing and magnitude of the premium and claim streams defines a market of assets that make suitable investments. This market is the local market for insurance portfolio investment. The local market may differ for P&C and life insurers, but it is still unique and reinforced by other aspects of insurer balance sheets. Leverage, a potentially low or even negative cost of funds, along with accounting and regulation create sustainable advantages for insurers. Along with banks, insurers show the potential for asset-liability managers to dominate segments of the investable set.

12

Investing for Broker/Dealers

Beyond investing for total return as a mutual or hedge fund or against bank or insurance liabilities, a long list of portfolios work off of other investment platforms. These platforms usually exist because of comparative advantages they bring to investing in specific types of assets. These platforms further fragment the set of investable assets into distinct local markets. Broker/dealers, or brokers, for short, stand out as an interesting example of these platforms and broaden the application of local CAPM to analyzing portfolio behavior and asset pricing. In the course of standing between buyers and sellers of assets, brokers often become important investment portfolios in and of themselves.

The value of a broker usually varies with the expense, in time and money, of finding parties willing to buy or sell assets or participate in other transactions. When the broker brings its own capital to the business of buying and selling, the broker bridges the gap between the time a seller wants to sell and the time a buyer wants to buy. The gap varies from market to market, lasting seconds in some or minutes, hours, days, weeks, months, or longer in others. And during that time, the broker holds a portfolio with all the risks and rewards of any other. The capital and funding needed to hold the portfolio are necessary but not enough on their own for sustainable advantage. Scale and diversification, leverage, and information are core competitive advantages for brokers. Brokers consequently most closely resemble hedge funds in their market role. Rather than specializing in a particular type of asset, however, brokers specialize in any asset transitioning from one holder to another. Returns to the role reflect the risk and reward of managing that transition. The most successful brokers capitalize on the information embedded in markets.

Broker Market Structure

The US today has more than 3,800 brokers registered with the Financial Industry Regulatory Authority, or FINRA, although the number has declined steadily for more than 15 years (figure 12.1). The total number of registered representatives

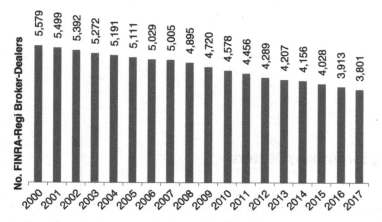

Figure 12.1 The number of FINRA-registered firms has steadily declined.
Source: FINRA; SIFMA Fact Book (2018).

working at brokers has been more stable, however, suggesting that industry operations keep getting more concentrated. The consolidation likely reflects the rising
costs of running a broker and the incentives to spread costs over a bigger operation.

Broker net revenue, assets, and capital remain highly concentrated (figure 12.2).
Less than 5% of brokers generate nearly 60% of net revenue and hold more than
70% of equity and more than 80% of net capital and assets. Concentration of equity
and net capital has increased noticeably since the 2008 financial crisis. Separating

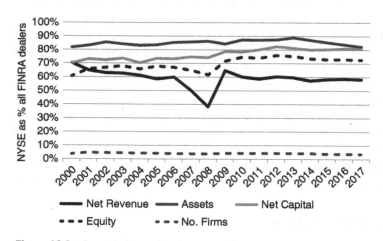

Figure 12.2 A small share of brokers control most revenue, assets, and capital.
Note: 2000 data based on all broker/dealers registered with the SEC; 2001 onwards data
based on all broker/dealers registered with FINRA filing a FOCUS report.
Source: SIFMA Fact Book (2018).

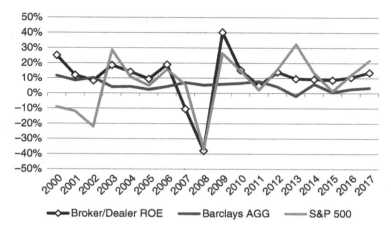

Figure 12.3 Broker return on equity has varied significantly with returns in debt and equity markets.

cause and effect is difficult. Although more assets can lead to more revenue, and more revenue to more equity and net capital, it is also possible and even likely that cause runs in the other direction: more capital leads to more revenue. More equity and net capital enables control of more assets and information, and more assets and information lead to more revenue.

Return on equity at the largest firms varies considerably from year to year often in rough parallel with returns in equity and debt markets (figure 12.3). Brokers have exposure to these markets, although the form is unclear. Brokers may own assets outright, or, alternatively, run businesses with returns that vary coincidentally with equity and debt, or both. Annual returns in the S&P 500 and the Bloomberg Barclays US Aggregate Bond Index explain more than half the annual variance in broker return on equity (table 12.1). From 2000 to 2017, a 1% change in returns on broad fixed income assets coincided with a 2.51% change in

Table 12.1 Broker ROE shows aleveraged return to fixed income (2.51x) and a deleveraged return to equity (0.78x)

	R-Square	Adj R-Square	F Stat	P-Value
ROE Regression	0.59	0.53	10.58	0.00
	Coefficients	*Std Err*	*T Stat*	*P-Value*
Intercept	−0.08	0.06	−1.35	0.20
Barclays AGG	2.51	0.92	2.72	0.02
S&P 500	0.78	0.17	4.59	0.00

Note: N=18.
Source: SIFMA (2018); Damodaran (2019); author regression of annual ROE on annual returns in the Bloomberg Barclays US Aggregate Bond Index and the S&P 500 Index.

broker performance, and a 1% change in equity returns paralleled a 0.78% change in broker return. Brokers over that period effectively held leveraged positions in fixed income and deleveraged positions in equity.

Revenues for Brokers

Even though the main business of a broker is making markets, or intermediating between buyers and sellers of assets, that business breaks down into several tightly linked streams of revenue:

- Portfolio investing
- Fees and other revenue from primary and secondary market-making
- Net interest income from asset finance
- Other hard or soft revenue

Portfolio investing usually starts when brokers deploy capital as an essential element of standing between buyers and sellers. If the broker acts only as an agent, trying to find the best assets at the best prices but owning nothing directly, then the role involves no investing. But few brokers operate as agents alone.

Because buyers and sellers rarely arrive in a market at the same time, brokers usually need to bridge the timing gap between the ultimate parties and a transaction. The broker buys from the seller, holds the asset, and resells later. Occasionally a broker will sell first without already holding the asset, hoping to buy the asset from someone else before the first sale settles. But usually brokers buy assets and build up an inventory in anticipation of demand.

Once brokers hold inventory and begin buying and selling out of their own account, they become portfolio investors. A broker may trade in and out of inventory continually, but the broker nevertheless still has continual market exposure through a changing mix of similar assets. The data bear this out, showing that brokers tend to hold a substantial portfolio of assets, although the level varies significantly (figure 12.4). Between 2013 and 2019, for example, the largest brokers held between $200 billion and $400 billion of fixed income assets. Holdings rose quickly starting in 2018 as the US started issuing Treasury debt to fund a growing deficit. And not surprisingly, most of the rise in dealer holdings came from larger positions in Treasury debt. Net holdings in debt and equity securities explain some if not most of the clear sensitivity of broker returns to performance in the debt and equity markets. Trading gains and losses are often the most volatile part of broker net revenue (figure 12.5).

Similar to any portfolio, brokers take the risk and return of the assets in their account. Brokers initially may measure this as a series of standalone positions on each trading desk. Management may view the capital or balance sheet allocated

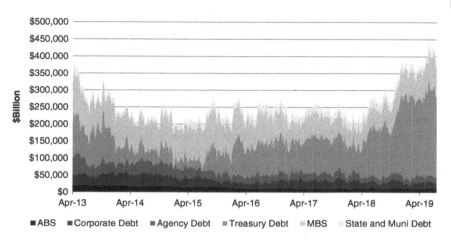

Figure 12.4 Brokers hold substantial net positions in fixed income assets.
Source: Federal Reserve Bank of New York, Primary Dealer Statistics Historical Search.

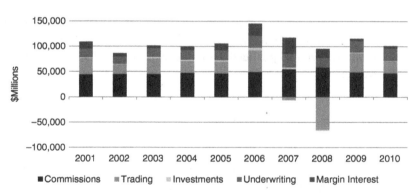

Figure 12.5 Trading gains and losses can be the most volatile part of broker revenue.
Source: SIFMA (2015).

to trading Treasury debt, for instance, as separate from capital for trading mortgage-backed securities or corporate debt or both. But brokers involved across multiple markets have the same issues as any diversified portfolio. Relative return, risk, and correlation should play a central role in driving allocation of capital across competing asset classes. Each broker's portfolio of inventory has to deliver return with tolerable risk.

Returns from inventory often get conflated with revenue from providing liquidity in primary or secondary markets, although conceptually the revenues from providing liquidity are separate. In new issue markets, where brokers issue new equity and debt, fees and price concessions show up as underwriting revenue.

In the secondary markets, where equity and debt trade after new issuance, any difference in the bid price paid to a seller and the ask price received from a buyer shows up in trading revenue. Brokers do not quote an explicit bid or ask price in many markets, however, and the bid-ask has to be inferred from consecutive pairs of buys or sells or through other methods. The return to providing liquidity can prove hard to measure and hard to separate from the return and risk of the positions themselves.

Brokers also often find themselves in the business of financing assets for buyers, or lending money so buyers can purchase assets from the broker. The buyers invest some of their own money and then borrow the rest of the purchase amount secured by the value of the asset itself. This is a portfolio investment business for the broker because the broker effectively ends up with a portfolio of loans secured by a wide range of assets. The broker can use its own cash to make a loan or can borrow funds from other investors, ending up with a leveraged portfolio of loans. Asset finance produces another distinct stream of revenue.

Brokers also can earn hard revenue or contractual fees for providing services such as research, specialized analysis, software, transaction clearing, settlement, and so on. But brokers also can offer services without charge in the hope that the client will direct a disproportionate share of trading or other business to the service provider. The value of services provided without charge gets conflated into other streams of revenue.

The Volcker Rule

Brokers affiliated with US banks since 2014 have had to manage new limits on portfolio investing. Policymakers want to stop brokers from taking proprietary trading risks that might impair a bank affiliate or any other affiliate with access to federal deposit insurance or the Federal Reserve's discount window. The Dodd-Frank Wall Street Reform and Consumer Protection Act included Section 619, commonly called the Volcker Rule, limiting proprietary trading and investing. The rule, among other things, strongly encouraged brokers to hold inventory positions for 60 days or less and in amounts proportional to expected client demand. Volcker also requires proof that instruments used to hedge risk actually do the job and are not simply speculative investments. The rule outlines strict reporting requirements so regulators can evaluate compliance. Among other things, brokers have to report inventory turnover as well as the volatility of daily trading profits, with unusually low turnover or high volatility possibly signaling proprietary trading. Although the specifics of Volcker might eventually change, it limits brokers from building large portfolios beyond the needs of making markets. It limits risk, but it also limits broker returns.

The Role of Broker as Financial Intermediary

The large number of brokers points to their value as financial intermediaries. Buyers and sellers occasionally make themselves known by advertising themselves, but often they are hard to find. The time and expense of finding a willing counterparty on agreeable terms is arguably the value added by a broker. Anything a broker can do to trim that time and expense adds to their value.

Sources of Comparative Advantage

In their inventory and asset finance portfolios, broker/dealers draw on the same set of potential comparative advantages as other investors:

- Scale, cost, and compensation
- Leverage
- Funding terms
- Hedging
- Quality and cost of capital
- Information
- Access to assets
- Tax and accounting rules
- Political and regulatory environment

In many respects, brokers have comparative advantages and disadvantages similar to hedge funds. The biggest difference arguably is in the type of information advantage. Brokers should have the best market information in an asset class, including the activity of the most informed investors. Hedge funds should have the best information on the fundamental risks of the assets themselves.

Scale, Cost, and Compensation

Brokers get the same operational cost benefits from size and scale as any portfolio and have to manage the same potential drag from increasing complexity. But the costs benefits of scale for a broker are less important that potential information benefits.

Brokers can use size and scale to improve the flow of information about the preferences or even the pending transactions of a wider set of buyers and sellers, and this is arguably the most important return to scale for a broker. Information quality improves both within and across assets. This is especially true if the broker transacts with the most informed investors or those with the best information on likely future asset performance. Trading with informed investors is most valuable in markets where information is expensive, where the number of informed investors is low, and where trading from relatively uninformed investors is high (Grossman and Stiglitz, 1980). Brokers get early access to information embedded in the price and volume of informed transactions. It helps the broker's own asset selection and allocation. And if other investors become aware that the broker is trading with informed investors, those investors will want to trade with the broker, too, for the information embedded in the broker's own transactions. Trading volume can beget more trading volume in a network effect. If the broker can scale across markets, the quality of information on potential linkages across markets improves, too. Information may be the most valuable comparative advantage of a broker, and the better brokers collect and use that information carefully within and across markets. Scale improves that information.

Brokers also have flexibility to align compensation with performance much the same way that fees at hedge funds can align fund managers with investors. Incentive compensation acts like a call option on broker performance, making management at least a partial investor alongside shareholders. But unlike hedge funds, brokers usually do not require that performance reach a high-water mark before triggering incentives. Annual performance bonuses instead create a sequence of one-year options on portfolio performance, encouraging management to take risk in the broker portfolio and raise the value of its performance options. Management can try to moderate the basic optionality through long vesting schedules or by having the ability to claw back compensation, but the basic optionality is there. To the extent that management reduces the link to portfolio performance, compensation starts to look more like fees on assets under management and should encourage behavior closer to that of mutual fund managers.

Leverage

Brokers also have significant flexibility to determine capital and leverage. The US Securities and Exchange Commission, which regulates brokers, sets minimum capital for brokers. Brokers can hold the larger of $250,000 or a certain percentage of net debt or, alternatively, the larger of $250,000 and a certain percentage of funds owed to customers.[1] The SEC mainly tries to make sure brokers have enough liquid assets to pay off customers if the broker business fails. For larger brokers that do not hold customer funds, regulatory capital requirements are minimal. For practical purposes, shareholders and lenders dictate capital requirements. Lenders, in particular, will often set minimum equity, and brokers will usually calculate equity under generally accepted accounting principles, or GAAP, and then subtract a haircut or percentage from each asset held on the broker's

---

1 SEC Rule 15c3-1 sets broker capital requirements.

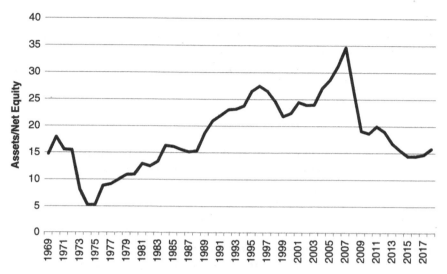

Figure 12.6   The average broker has held between $5 and $35 of assets for every $1 of equity.
Source: Federal Reserve Board, Financial Accounts of the United States, accessed June 6, 2019.

balance sheet. The SEC sets those haircuts. The haircut implicitly imposes a capital requirement for each asset.

The average broker since the early 1970s has held between $5 and $35 in assets for every $1 in equity, making brokers at times among the most leveraged portfolios in the markets (figure 12.6). But those average figures may hide as much as they reveal. Average leverage includes leverage on both the inventory portfolio and the asset financing portfolio, which is likely the much more leveraged of the pair. It also includes leverage on brokers affiliated with banks and ones unaffiliated, the latter likely the more leveraged of the pair. And it includes leverage on equity and fixed income brokers, the latter again the more leveraged of the pair. Nevertheless, broker/dealers clearly use leverage extensively, likely giving them clear advantage in some markets. However, this advantage may be no greater than the one held by hedge funds.

Funding Terms

Most brokers fund their inventory positions by borrowing against their assets, the same way that hedge funds might. Some of the largest brokers or ones affiliated with banks may fund by issuing unsecured debt. There is no broker deposit base or stream of premium income. Because most brokers fund their inventory portfolios in wholesale markets based on the same assets that any other investor might present, their funding generally offers no comparative advantage. Larger brokers may get slightly better terms by funding through interdealer broker markets, and primary dealers may get proprietary access to Federal Reserve funding programs. These advantages, however, are small and insufficient to overcome the funding advantages of banks or insurers.

Hedging

Brokers do have some comparative advantage in hedging mainly because nearly all of their assets get marked-to-market, creating none of the conflict that banks and insurers run into in aligning the marks on assets and their hedges. Brokers constantly balance the daily marks against assets and hedges, trying to offset one with the other. Hedging does leave room for brokers to take proprietary portfolio risk because hedges can offset some or all of the risk in an inventory portfolio. Broker management can intentionally create a mismatch between asset and hedge to create exposure to the unhedged or residual risk. Regulators in recent years have picked up their efforts to identify and discourage proprietary mismatches. The Volcker Rule tries to reign in proprietary trading of hedges. Brokers nevertheless have a hedging advantage over mutual funds, banks, and insurers but arguably not over hedge funds.

Quality and Cost of Capital

Although brokers can attract permanent capital by issuing private or public equity, the volatility of their earnings means that investors usually demand a high rate of return. The permanence of the capital is an advantage compared to mutual and hedge funds, but the cost is not. Mutual funds likely have a lower cost of capital, and hedge funds a similar cost. Most banks and insurers also have permanent capital at a much lower cost than brokers.

Information

Information overwhelmingly is the most important advantage of operating as a broker. Most other competing portfolios can match or exceed a broker along most other dimensions of comparative advantage, but that is harder to do when it comes to information. Brokers get information from a continual flow of market and financing transactions. These transactions partially disclose client holdings, their inclination to buy or sell, often their view of risk and reward in the market, and the tendency of clients to transact in complementary or offsetting ways across markets. By sitting at the center of a hub of information, brokers tend to attract more counterparties willing to trade one piece of information for another, improving the richness of the broker's information flow. The early and proprietary access to the flows of the most informed investors gives brokers the opportunity to extract excess return from traded asset classes. When information is expensive, when the number of informed investors is low, and when trading from relatively uninformed investors is high, the opportunity is greatest.

The information that flows through a broker is not easy to capture, however. It comes through sales, trading, research, and asset finance across different markets. Unless a broker has some formal or informal mechanism for capturing information and recognizing its various implications for asset values, a large part of the information and the opportunity to position an inventory or financing portfolio against it gets lost.

Access to Assets and Tax and Accounting

Brokers have no clear advantage in access to assets through the inventory portfolios they own, but they do have advantage in their asset financing portfolios. Inventory comes from the same publicly traded markets available to almost any investor, eliminating comparative advantage. But few other investors have the same opportunities to lend against securities.

Efficient lending against securities requires intimate knowledge of the daily price volatility of the securities, their liquidity in markets under stress, and, of course, knowing who owns the securities and might need to borrow against them. The broker lends the client money secured by the value of the securities. If the securities have a market value of $100, for example, the broker might lend $95. The $5 difference between the market value and the loan is the investor's equity in the investment, also called *the initial margin on the loan*. If the value of the securities drops to $98, the investor typically has to either add another $2 of securities to bring market value back to $100 or repay part of the loan. The value added to offset a drop in market value is called *variance margin*. Properly run, a repo or securities lending book needs little or no capital from the broker because the broker requires the investor to post initial and variance margin. Margin effectively creates the capital needed to ensure full repayment of the loan. If the investor does not repay, the broker can sell the security to recover full loan proceeds. Because a securities lending book effectively is self-capitalizing, even a small spread between the interest on the loan and the cost of funds can produce a high return on broker equity.

As for tax and accounting, brokers come out on par with any other portfolio that frequently marks asset and liabilities to market. Against banks and insurers that can hold illiquid assets without marks for long periods, brokers are at distinct disadvantage.

Political and Regulatory Environment

Brokers have attracted more political attention since Bear Stearns, Lehman Brothers, Merrill Lynch, and others failed or nearly failed in 2008. The US recession that followed highlighted the connection between brokers and the broader economy and created public interest in their stability. The Securities and Exchange Commission had long-standing authority over the securities industry, but the Dodd-Frank legislation passed in 2010 extended the authority of the Federal Reserve to any systemically important financial institution. Brokers affiliated with banks have to meet the additional requirements of all the regulators that oversee banking, including requirements of the Volcker Rule. Independent brokers consequently face less political and regulatory oversight than a competitor affiliated with a bank, but more than hedge funds.

Predictions of Local CAPM

Local CAPM and its emphasis on portfolios that build on comparative advantage would make a range of predictions:

- *Market share.* Share of trading volume will become most concentrated in markets where information is expensive, where the number of informed investors is low, where trading from relatively uninformed investors is high, or where some combination of all of these factors holds. In these markets, the information gathered by trading with informed investors is the most valuable, and all investors will have incentive to trade with the most informed brokers.
- *Inventory or portfolio size.* Brokers with more scale or share within or across markets, and consequently more proprietary information, will have disproportionately larger inventory portfolios.[2]
- *Asset finance portfolio size.* Brokers with more scale or share within or across markets will have disproportionately larger asset financing portfolios.
- *Preference for liquid assets.* Because of mark-to-market accounting, and because of the Volcker Rule for bank-affiliated firms, brokers will prefer to hold liquid assets or assets with risks that can be offset with liquid hedges. Bank-affiliated brokers will show stronger preference than independent brokers for liquid assets because the Volcker Rule and its time limits on holding inventory discourage brokers from holding illiquid assets.

---

2 This implies that inventory within a market grows as a nonlinear function of market share and that inventory across markets grows as a nonlinear function of markets covered.

Informal Findings

Research that looks at brokers as portfolio investors is limited, but some work shines light on the predictions of local CAPM.

Market Share

Brokers' share of trading volume does differ significantly across markets. The Federal Reserve tracks primary dealer trading volume and breaks it down, among other things, by the share going to the top five in each market (figure 12.7). In early 2019, share varied from less than 45% in parts of the Treasury market to more than 90% in the market for student loan asset–backed securities. The top five share generally is lowest in markets for government debt and higher in markets for corporate, state, municipal, and mortgage- and asset-backed debt. In the markets for Treasury, corporate and state, and municipal debt, where securities mature or return investors' original principal on a scheduled date, the top five share tends to rise with the maturity of the debt. It is tempting to argue that the market for government debt is the most transparent, lowering the cost of information and the ability of brokers to build share. It is also fair to argue that securities with longer maturities and more price sensitivity have fewer investors, making information about owners and trading flows more expensive and improving the opportunity for brokers to build share.

Portfolio Size and Asset Preference

Evidence that brokers' inventory or asset finance portfolios rise disproportionately as share and proprietary information rise will have to wait for further study. One angle on the issue could look at the relationship between broker share of trading and broker inventory size. If brokers get proprietary advantage from trading flow, then brokers would have incentive to deploy capital for holding inventory rather than to offset daily trades, usually by selling to another party. Adjusting for the amount of capital available, high-trading volume should lead to larger inventories.

Preference for Liquid Assets

Bank-affiliated brokers have become much more sensitive to liquidity under the Volcker Rule. Darrell Duffie at Stanford University predicted that bank-affiliated brokers under Volcker would step back from the corporate bond market and independent brokers would step in (Duffie, 2012). Corporate bonds vary significantly

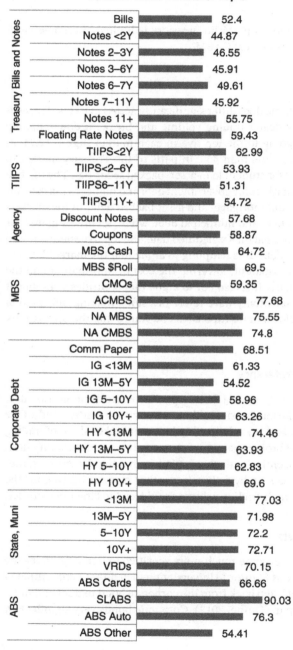

Share of Trans Vol 2Q19: Top 5

Treasury Bills and Notes	Bills	52.4
	Notes <2Y	44.87
	Notes 2–3Y	46.55
	Notes 3–6Y	45.91
	Notes 6–7Y	49.61
	Notes 7–11Y	45.92
	Notes 11+	55.75
	Floating Rate Notes	59.43
TIIPS	TIIPS<2Y	62.99
	TIIPS<2–6Y	53.93
	TIIPS6–11Y	51.31
	TIIPS11Y+	54.72
Agency	Discount Notes	57.68
	Coupons	58.87
MBS	MBS Cash	64.72
	MBS $Roll	69.5
	CMOs	59.35
	ACMBS	77.68
	NA MBS	75.55
	NA CMBS	74.8
Corporate Debt	Comm Paper	68.51
	IG <13M	61.33
	IG 13M–5Y	54.52
	IG 5–10Y	58.96
	IG 10Y+	63.26
	HY <13M	74.46
	HY 13M–5Y	63.93
	HY 5–10Y	62.83
	HY 10Y+	69.6
State, Muni	<13M	77.03
	13M–5Y	71.98
	5–10Y	72.2
	10Y+	72.71
	VRDs	70.15
ABS	ABS Cards	66.66
	SLABS	90.03
	ABS Auto	76.3
	ABS Other	54.41

Figure 12.7 Share of trading captured by the top five brokers varies significantly.
Source: Federal Reserve Bank of New York, Quarterly Market Share Data of Primary Dealer Transactions.

in liquidity, with larger and newer issues trading much more frequently than smaller and older issues. Hendrik Bessembinder at Arizona State University and his colleagues looked at broker trading in corporate bonds between 2006 and 2016 and found strong evidence that Volcker had significantly lowered bank-affiliated brokers' willingness to commit capital to corporate bond trading while increasing independent broker allocation (Bessembinder, Jacobsen, Maxwell, and Venkataraman, 2018). The difference between bank-affiliated and independent brokers was the strongest on days with the most market stress, when differences in liquidity between bonds become more pronounced. Volcker arguably has created local markets in corporate bonds across brokers depending on asset liquidity.

Conclusion

By standing between buyers and sellers of assets, brokers tend to evolve into portfolios of inventory assets and asset finance loans. Leverage, financing, hedging, and most other sources of potential comparative advantage leave brokers at least on par with hedge funds. Brokers do have proprietary access to information in trading flows and asset finance and better market information for monitoring and managing the risks in those portfolios. Brokers capitalizing on information flowing through their platform can turn it into an exceptional source of advantage in monitoring and managing an inventory portfolio, too. The better brokers become masters of transforming market information into excess return.

13

Investing for Real Estate Investment Trusts

In the same way mutual funds and hedge funds allow investors to pool capital and hold a portfolio of securities or other assets, so real estate investment trusts, or REITs, pave the way for portfolios of real estate and mortgages. REITs cater to the peculiarities of these assets and represent a fascinating case of a focused investment platform creating a very local market in the targeted investments. Real estate and mortgages often trade in illiquid markets and can require sizable borrowing to finance the investment. These assets make a poor fit with mutual funds and hedge funds, where investors usually can withdraw capital much faster than any fund could reasonably sell most real estate. Mutual funds also usually limit borrowings to levels well below the norm in real estate and mortgage finance. Although banks and insurers own real estate and mortgages, too, REITs are uniquely well positioned to compete.

REIT Market Structure

Policymakers intended REITs to broaden investing in US commercial and residential real estate. Traditionally, only the largest investors could raise the capital, arrange the financing, and bear the market and operating risks of owning office buildings, shopping centers, apartments, and other large developments. The Cigar Excise Tax Extension Act of 1960 included, among other things, changes to the US tax code to pave the way for REITs.[1] Diversified, competitively financed portfolios of professionally managed real estate and mortgages came within reach for a wide set of individuals and other investors for the first time. To attract individuals, policymakers elected not to tax REITs like corporations. Banks and insurance companies, for instance, pay corporate taxes on net profits from holding real estate and mortgages and put whatever is left over in the pool of potential dividends.

---

1 Formally P.L. 86-779.

REITs, by contrast, do not pay the corporate tax and must distribute most net profits directly to shareholders, who then pay individual taxes. Compared to owning shares in a bank or insurer with a portfolio of real estate and mortgages, REITs can be a way for individuals to own these assets without paying taxes at the corporate level. The corporate tax exemption and other features make REITs efficient holders of leveraged real estate and mortgage debt portfolios.

To qualify as a REIT in the US, a portfolio needs to meet a series of asset, income, and ownership requirements (table 13.1). The asset requirements basically ensure the REIT stays focused on real estate and mortgage debt and avoids wandering into other assets. The income requirements ensure the REIT distributes almost all of its net income instead of holding onto earnings and building up capital like a corporation. And the ownership requirements ensure that REITs serve groups of investors instead of becoming private clubs for a few large holders of real estate.

REITs generally specialize in portfolios of commercial or residential real estate or in portfolios of mortgage debt, although some have blended both exposures into hybrid positions (figure 13.1). Equity REITs take investor capital and buy commercial and residential property, often going to banks or the capital markets for debt financing. Mortgage REITs take investor capital and buy mortgage loans or mortgage-backed securities, often getting financing through repo or other arrangements.

US REITs get their equity capital either by raising it privately or by publicly issuing common stock or preferred equity. Unlike mutual funds or hedge funds subject to redemptions, REITs, like most banks or insurers, raise permanent capital. REITs often trade on public exchanges, and investors can easily scale their holdings up

Table 13.1 REITs have to meet asset, income, and ownership requirements

Assets	• At least 75% of the value of the REIT's assets must come from (i) real estate assets, (ii) cash or equivalents, and (iii) government securities. • At least 55% of the REIT's assets must consist of entire properties or, if a pool of assets, the entire pool. • At most 20% of the REIT's assets can come from taxable REIT subsidiaries, with no restriction on assets held by the subsidiary.
Income	• At least 90% of income must be distributed as a dividend. • For REITs that invest in debt, at least 75% of REIT gross income must come from interest on mortgage loans or MBS; dividends from subsidiaries can make up the rest. • At least 95% of income just comes from sources that qualify for the 75% asset test, dividends, interest, payments on certain hedges, gains from sale of stock, securities, or hedges.
Ownership	• There must be at least 100 beneficial owners. • No more than 50% of the value can be owned directly or indirectly by five or fewer individuals.

Source: Laws (2015).

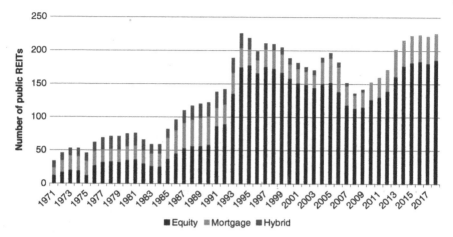

Figure 13.1 Equity REITs grew aggressively from 1985–1995 and again after 2008. *Source:* National Association of Real Estate Investment Trusts (2019).

or down. Liquidity for REIT investors comes through selling shares in public or private markets. As of mid-2019, daily public trading volume in the $1.262 trillion FTSE NAREIT All REITs index averaged around $7.5 billion daily.

The major draw of REITs for investors usually is income, although appreciation in portfolio property or mortgage debt can add to total return. Because REITs take equity and borrower money to invest in assets that spin off various forms of income—rents, lease payments, interest, and so on—the spread between income and interest and operating costs combine with available leverage to set REITs' core investment performance. Raising income, lowering debt and operating costs, and managing leverage are the key levers on REIT returns.

Over time, US REITs have become somewhat specialized, catering to investor interest in clearly defined exposure to particular commercial property or mortgage debt. Specialized exposure gives investors a free hand to build real estate and mortgage asset allocations suited to the investors' own risk-and-return target rather than taking the one built into a single REIT's diversified portfolio. The market tracks at least 18 separate categories of publicly traded US REITs, with further specialization typical within each category. The operating challenges, risk, return, and correlation all differ (figure 13.2).

A few shifts in public policy have made REITs progressively more competitive over time and have spurred growth (Feng, Price, and Sirmans, 2011):

- Laws governing REITs originally required REITs to hire outside companies to provide asset management services. The Tax Reform Act of 1986, however, allowed REITs to put together in one organization all the expertise needed to

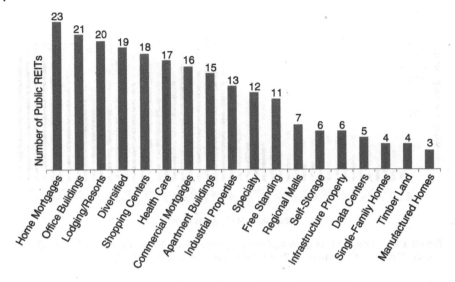

Figure 13.2 The market tracks at least 18 different types of US REITs.
Source: National Association of Real Estate Investment Trusts (2019).

manage assets. That expertise included, among other things, purchasing and financing real estate, originating mortgage debt, operating properties, and actively managing portfolio risk and return. Internal management made REITs much more efficient and profitable and led to an immediate surge of new players.

- REITs also sometimes had trouble building diversified property portfolios because current owners would have to pay taxes on gains from selling to a REIT. In 1992, Taubman Centers Inc. created the first umbrella partnership REIT, or UPREIT, allowing owners to transfer property to a REIT without an immediate taxable gain. The UPREIT created an operating partnership that owned almost all of the transferred property, with property owners getting units in the partnership. The owners of operating units could exchange them for REIT stock, which would be a taxable transaction. The UPREIT gave property owners control over the timing of taxable gains, leading to another surge in REIT formation.

Both the number and market capitalization of public REITs in the US have grown steadily, and so have assets controlled by REITs. The number of public REITs from 1985 to 2018, according to the National Association of Real Estate Investment Trusts, has run from 59 to 226. Public REIT market capitalization over that run has grown at a compounded annual rate of 16.1%. And total assets at all REITs, according to the Federal Reserve, have grown at a compounded annual rate of 14.2%. Meanwhile, total outstanding residential mortgage debt has grown at a compounded annual rate of 6.1%, commercial mortgage debt at 5.2%, and multifamily or apartment mortgage debt at 5.9%. REIT assets have grown far faster than outstanding mortgage debt, although REITs also hold real estate equity. Nevertheless, the rapid growth of REITs argues for clear advantages in holding real estate and mortgage debt.

Since launching in the US, REIT structures have developed throughout Asia, the Middle East and Africa, Europe, and North and South America. REITs have become a distinct, global platform for owning real estate and mortgage debt.

Sources of Comparative Advantage

REITs compete along the same dimensions as any other investment portfolio but take their most important advantages in the US from liquid and permanent equity, flexible leverage, flexible hedging, and favorable tax status. These advantages enable REITs to hold leveraged positions in illiquid target assets more easily than most alternative platforms. The particulars:

- Scale, cost, and compensation
- Leverage
- Funding terms
- Hedging
- Quality and cost of capital
- Information
- Access to assets
- Tax and accounting rules
- Political and regulatory environment

Scale, Cost, and Compensation

The benefits of scale accrue to REITs like they would to any investment portfolio, along with eventually diminishing returns. REITs only need enough scale to efficiently spread fixed costs and build expertise in the targeted real estate or mortgage debt market. Given frequent specialization, REITs should have well-defined administrative, operating, underwriting, investment, and risk management requirements with limited coordinating costs. Compared to portfolios managing multiple independent asset classes, most REITs should be less complex. And to the extent specialization truly separates distinct markets, the first mover should be able to get optimal scale and hold a marginal cost advantage. That should limit the number of viable REITs in a well-defined property or mortgage debt market to just a few. REITs should be able to compete on cost with other much larger investment portfolios unless larger portfolios choose to subsidize relevant marginal costs.

REITs can use compensation to align the management team with investors. Internally managed REITs have clear accountability to investors, and equity grants to management and other performance incentives can tighten the alignment. Externally managed REITs have more room for conflict with investors, especially if REIT management has other responsibilities and sources of income. Some REITs fall within larger asset managers where the interest of other clients could compete for the time and attention of the REIT team, and where other portfolios could compete for real estate or mortgage assets. In general, all else being equal, the market tends to value internally managed REITs more.

Proper scale and specialization should enable REITs to take more return out of target assets compared to smaller mutual funds or more broadly focused banks and insurers, although REITs would hold no advantage over similarly focused hedge funds. Compensation also could give REITs an advantage over mutual funds, banks, and insurers, although hedge funds could match REITs on incentive alignment.

Leverage

Unlike banks and insurers, REITs have no regulatory limits on leverage. But equity investors and lenders to REITs informally limit leverage. Equity investors limit leverage by pricing in risk and lenders by setting loan terms.

REITs that own commercial or residential property usually take out mortgages on terms competitive with or slightly better than most other owners. The scale, expertise, track record, and need for ongoing funding usually makes REITs favored borrowers. And REITs have clear incentive to lower debt costs because each penny saved gets multiplied in REITs' leveraged returns.

REITs that own mortgages or mortgage-backed securities usually borrow through repo markets, where allowable leverage can go much higher than banks or most insurers. REITs that can manage the effective interest rate risk that comes with leverage—risk identical to banks' duration of equity—can hit targets for dividends and return on equity beyond the reach of less leveraged investors.

Informal limits give REITs more leverage than mutual funds and more flexibility than banks and insurers, a powerful competitive advantage for REITs in owning targeted assets. Only hedge funds can match REITs on leverage, although other factors ultimately give REITs the edge.

Funding Terms

REIT funding depends almost entirely on the type and quality of assets. REITs that own real estate directly can borrow against property, with the amount of leverage reflecting prevailing conventions and market conditions. REITs that own mortgage debt or mortgage securities can borrow against their assets, too, with terms determined by repurchase agreements or other markets for collateralized lending.

Funding arguably represents a comparative disadvantage for REITs because banks and insurers have less expensive and more stable sources of funds, especially compared to REITs that use repurchase agreements to borrow against securities. REITs again end up roughly on par with hedge funds in the funding markets.

Hedging

REITs that invest in mortgage securities hedge a substantial part of their interest rate risk with futures, swaps, swaptions, and other derivatives. Although all REITs have to pay close attention to net interest income, which drives dividends but might discourage expensive hedging, many also emphasize the net asset value of their businesses. Measuring performance with net asset value encourages the REITs to mark to market both assets and liabilities, enabling the markets to offset one another. High dividends may not amount to much if largely offset by falling net asset value. Mortgage REITs in particular often report the duration gap, or difference in interest rate sensitivity of assets and liabilities. The nominal gap can seem small, but, after taking leverage into account, the duration of equity can be substantial. A nominal duration gap of one year means the net change in value of asset and liabilities if interest rates move 100 basis points would only be 1%. But if the REIT is 10 times leveraged, or only has 10 points of equity, a 1% net change in assets and liabilities becomes a 10% change in equity. It is the duration of equity that matters.

The emphasis on net asset value and the active use of hedges gives REITs advantage over banks and insurers constrained by their focus on stable accounting income. REITs can more actively trade and hedge assets. Hedge funds, again, can do the same.

Quality and Cost of Capital

Similar to banks and insurers, public REITs can raise liquid permanent capital, which also helps reduce its cost. Because REITs have to distribute 90% of their net income, however, they cannot build capital through retained earnings but instead have to raise more equity in order to grow.

Access to public equity puts REITs on par with banks and insurers, although the inability to retain earnings limits their ability to grow equity. When the market trades equity below book value, which it can do for long periods, REITs may not be able to grow equity at all. A REIT trading below book value in theory could liquidate all assets and liabilities, buy back all equity, and still have money left over. No equity investor should invest \$1 when the market immediately values it at less than that. REITs trading far enough above book value to cover the cost of issuing new shares, however, should issue equity. The intrinsic value of REIT equity trading below book value and the risk of equity issuance from REITs trading above book value keeps equity broadly trading in a wide band around book value.

Access to public equity does create clear advantage relative to hedge funds. In fact, access to permanent equity is arguably the most important and only advantage a REIT has over a hedge fund. In distressed markets, the value of REIT equity might drop but it cannot be withdrawn. For a hedge fund without adequate notice provisions or otherwise unwilling to put up gates on withdrawals, equity can disappear altogether.

Information and Access to Assets

REITs have no intrinsic advantage over other investors in information on real estate and mortgage debt other than any that comes from scale and specialization. Scale and specialization can put any portfolio at the front of the line for any asset in which the seller thinks a large, informed investor can act quickly and take the entire transaction. But the real estate and mortgage debt markets have a wide range of large, specialized investors. REITs arguably stand at a disadvantage to banks and insurers that may know more about local property markets, builders, and borrowers through regular lending and other banking activity.

Tax and Accounting Rules

Exemption from corporate tax arguably is the most important REIT advantage. Earnings from REITs get passed through to investors and taxed at the individual level. Corporations pay taxes on earnings from real estate and mortgage debt, and investors then pay another round of taxes on any dividends.

The tax exemption gives REITs an advantage over corporations in owning a portfolio of qualifying assets but still leaves REITs on par with mutual funds, hedge funds, and other private partnerships that pass through gross earnings directly to partners. REITs did pick up a potential tax advantage over mutual funds, hedge funds, and private partnerships in the Tax Cut and Jobs Act of 2017. The legislation created a 20% deduction for income passed through to REIT investors. An investor paying a 37% top tax rate would end up paying only 29.6% after the deduction, making REITs marginally more attractive to shareholders with high marginal tax rates.

Publicly traded REITs report according to the same accounting standards set for banks and insurers, so REITs have no clear advantage or disadvantage from accounting.

Political and Regulatory Environment

US REITs get much less scrutiny from regulators than banks and insurers do, trimming the cost and complexity of the business. REITs do have to meet SEC regulations and potential scrutiny from the Financial Services Oversight Committee, but REITs do not report to banking regulators. A relatively light regulatory burden helps REITs.

REITs are not completely immune from regulatory battles, however. In mid-2012, several public mortgage REITs started getting access to funding from the Federal Home Loan Bank system, which also makes loans to banks secured by mortgages and mortgage-backed securities. The REITs created captive insurers, which the Federal Home Loan Bank system had admitted as members since its founding in 1932. Membership allowed access to the system's low-cost, flexible financing. From mid-2012 to January 2016, the system admitted 27 captive insurers, 25 of which were owned by REITs, finance companies, or other entities not directly eligible for membership. System loans to captives between 2011 and late 2015 went from $11 billion to $35 billion. In January 2016, after many banks argued REITs' thin capital and limited regulation put the system at risk, the system stopped admitting captives, requiring some REIT captives to withdraw within a year and others within five years.

Predictions of Local CAPM

Local CAPM would predict REITs should have outsized influence on pricing in their target assets. Scale and specialization give REITs clear ability to compete on cost with most mutual funds, banks, and insurers. Leverage gives advantage over mutual funds and puts REITs at least on par, often at an advantage, with banks and insurers, although cost of funds is a disadvantage. Hedging accrues to REITs' advantage in managing risk, and tax becomes a powerful plus. Permanent capital puts REITs ahead of hedge funds except in the most liquid mortgage securities. REITs should be able to extract returns from target assets more reliably than competing platforms.

Informal Evidence

REITs' strong growth relative to the set of investible assets is probably the best informal evidence of REITs' ability to create competitive advantage and a local market in their target assets. REITs give individuals direct access to complex, often illiquid assets that need financing, something most individuals would not be able to create on their own. They are a case study in local CAPM.

Some work does look at the ability of REITs to compete with banks, insurers, broker/dealers, and other potential investors in different assets. Samuel Hanson and his colleagues argue that REITs and other portfolios that use repo and other short-term funding are best suited to hold liquid assets that the portfolio can sell quickly, if needed, to repay funding (Hanson, Schleifer, Stein, and Vishny, 2014). In fact, agency mortgage-backed securities, which are second only to Treasury debt in liquidity, make up an important part of many mortgage REITs. There is an element of chicken-and-egg in the argument because the ready availability of repo for liquid assets may encourage the REIT to buy them in the first place. Nevertheless, Hanson and his colleagues acknowledge the funding structure of REITs and other portfolios has a powerful influence on the composition and behavior of their investment portfolio.

Conclusion

REITs take advantage of their special tax status to carve out a local market in real estate, mortgage loans, and mortgage-backed securities. They clearly compete with banks, insurers, and mutual and hedge funds in some of those assets. The marginal demand for those assets from REITs almost certainly has shaped asset value.

14

Investing for Sovereign Wealth Funds

When Kuwait launched a fund in 1953 to invest surpluses from the sale of oil, it marked the first fund to invest broadly on behalf of a government and its citizens. Suddenly an investment portfolio played a public rather than private role. Its managers worked not in the interests of individual investors or shareholders but for the current and future generations of citizens and the government representing them. Funds working for public cause in the US and worldwide numbered 85 by 2019 and invested $12.1 trillion, a group subject to their own limits and shaping local markets like any other investor (Prequin, 2018).

Sovereign wealth funds face the same challenges as private portfolios but with different emphasis. Many funds try to stabilize government income and expenses subject to boom and bust as prices of major national resources vary. Others amount to national savings accounts or currency reserve portfolios. Some serve as pension funds or invest in national infrastructure. Sovereign wealth funds bring the broad advantages of size and scale. To the extent they operate with disadvantages, those flow from the occasionally competing incentives of pure investment performance and public policy. Observers that want investment portfolios to serve the public good, however, might not see disadvantage at all.

The Structure of Sovereign Wealth Funds

Kuwait and Kiribati, a Pacific island nation with phosphate deposits, stood alone as the only sponsors of sovereign wealth funds until high oil prices in the 1970s brought another round of new funds. The 1997 Asian financial crisis and Russia's default on its debt the next year then started a decade in which funds formed primarily to help countries manage excess currency reserves (figure 14.1). The 2008 financial crisis triggered another round of new funds. The world's 25 largest sovereign wealth funds in 2019 managed $10.3 trillion in assets (table 14.1).

1953 Kuwait*	1981 Singapore***	2000 Iran*	2002 Equatorial Guinea*	2006 Bahrain*
1956 Kiribati**	1981 Singapore****	2000 Mexico*	2004 Sao Tome and Principe*	2006 Libya*
1974 Singapore***	1983 Brunei*	2000 Qatar*	2004 Australia***	2006 Chile**
1976 United States*	1993 Malaysia***	2000 Trinidad, Tobago*	2005 Timor-Leste*	2007 Chile**
1976 Canada*	1996 Norway*	2000 Ireland***	2005 Korea***	2007 China****
1976 UAE*	1996 Botswana**	2001 Kazakhstan*	2005 Korea****	2008 Russia*
1980 Oman*	1999 Azerbaijan*	2001 New Zealand***		

Figure 14.1 Launch date, sponsor, and objectives of world SWFs to 2008
Note: Investment objectives (stars): 1 = Oil and gas, 2 = Other commodity, 3 = Fiscal surplus, 4 = FX reserves.
Source: Kunzel, Lu, Petrova, and Pihlman (2011).

Sovereign wealth funds often pursue more than one objective, with emphasis sometimes changing over time. Funds typically fall in one of several categories: stability funds, savings funds, currency reserve funds, pension funds, and development funds. But the objective most specific to a sovereign wealth fund and arguably best addressed by this approach is to buffer government finances vulnerable to commodity boom and bust in countries or other political enterprises without reliable access to bank or capital market debt. We begin with sovereign funds committed to acting as counterweight to boom-and-bust: stability funds.

Stability Funds

Countries, states, or other territories with significant natural resources often find themselves riding a rollercoaster. As the price of the resource and the associated income go up and down, tax revenues parallel and amplify the boom and bust of the economy. Governments end up spending in markets with rising demand and rising prices and then cutting back as demand and prices fall, making the cycle more severe. Even if government spending itself does not follow boom and bust, depositing government funds in banks during a boom encourages lending during a boom and withdrawing funds tightens credit during a bust. Unless the government has the ability to save or borrow, its revenue and spending cycle becomes part of the problem rather than part of the solution.

Table 14.1 The world's largest sovereign wealth funds in 2019

Rank	Name	Country	AUM ($B)
1	Government Pension Investment Fund	Japan	1407.00
2	Government Pension Fund Global	Norway	993.10
3	China Investment Corp.	China	940.00
4	Abu Dhabi Investment Authority	UAE	739.63
5	State Administration of Foreign Exchange	China	690.00
6	National Pension Service	South Korea	568.90
7	APG Groep	Netherlands	547.00
8	Kuwait Investment Authority	Kuwait	527.10
9	GIC Private Ltd.	Singapore	510.00
10	Qatar Investment Authority	Qatar	303.70
11	Canada Pension Plan Investment Board	Canada	292.00
12	Public Investment Fund	Saudi Arabia	260.00
13	National Council for Social Security Fund	China	247.41
14	Saudi Arabian Monetary Agency-Investment Portfolio	Saudi Arabia	236.50
15	PGGM	Netherlands	236.00
16	Investment Corp. of Dubai	UAE	233.90
17	Caisse de Depot et Placement du Quebec	Canada	232.00
18	Temasek Holdings	Singapore	230.00
19	Mubadala Investment Co.	UAE	227.00
20	Employees Provident Fund	Malaysia	195.00
21	Caisse des Depots et Consignations	France	174.00
22	AP Funds	Sweden	145.30
23	Korea Investment Corp.	South Korea	142.00
24	Ontario Teachers' Pension Plan	Canada	142.00
25	Public Investment Corp.	South Africa	134.70

Source: Sovereign Investor Institute (2019).

Boom and bust from natural resources or any other cause can also take a balanced economy and make it more narrow and fragile. This is often called the Dutch disease after the discovery by the Netherlands in the early 1960s of large natural gas fields in the North Sea. The surge in oil and gas exports drove up the value of the Dutch guilder and made the country's traditional exports more expensive. Those exports began to shrink, and the Netherlands domestic economy started revolving increasingly around the goods and services in demand by the booming oil and gas sector. The income base of the economy began to narrow.

But the Netherlands has not been alone. Oil-rich countries caught strains of the Dutch disease in the 1970s when the price of oil surged and local manufacturing and agriculture shrank. And Colombia caught a version in the late 1970s when a failure of Brazil's coffee crop drove up Colombia's coffee exports at the expense of manufacturing exports (Ebrahimzadeh, 2018). Government can try to counter Dutch disease by buying up foreign currency to slow or stop appreciation of the domestic currency, or, if a resource surge looks permanent, it can try to smooth transition away from the weakening traditional exports. The government, however, usually does not want to magnify the problems.

In an economy subject to boom and bust, the public can manage government revenue by splitting it into a permanent part, equivalent to a stable percentage of gross domestic product, and a cyclical or boom-and-bust part that averages to zero. The public also chooses a fiscal revenue target—a surplus, a balanced budget, or a deficit. Any revenue that comes in above the target gets invested in the sovereign wealth fund, and any deficit gets funded by withdrawals or borrowing against the fund.

The estimates of permanent revenue, the fiscal spending target, and the volatility of commodity swings all have a big impact on a stability fund. If the government routinely targets excess revenue, for instance, it will have to tap the sovereign wealth fund only in extreme cases of falling resource prices. The fund becomes more of a savings vehicle with longer investment horizons and lower needs for asset liquidity. If the government instead targets deficit, the fund may need to ride to the rescue more often and consequently may need to invest to shorter horizons with more liquidity.

With a fund in place, the government has a chance to add ballast to the economy, and it almost certainly has to do this by investing outside the country. Investing domestically magnifies boom and bust by bidding up local resources during booms and depressing prices during busts. By investing internationally, the fund draws off local demand during booms and brings government demand back during busts. It also smooths currency fluctuation by selling more local currency in booms to buy foreign investments and buying more local currency in busts using proceeds from sale of foreign investments. And by smoothing demand and exchange rates, a stability fund can also relieve pressure on monetary policy, making the central bank more effective, too (Brown, Papaioannou, and Petrova, 2010).

A stability fund also has to invest in assets negatively correlated with the price of the country's key natural resources or other factors that drive economic growth. These assets ideally should appreciate when the domestic economy is weak and depreciate when the domestic economy is strong and the fund is investing heavily. A stability fund effectively owns the stream of tax revenue from one or more key natural resources and has to blend this with diversifying assets to hit a targeted risk and return.

The most unique feature of any stability fund is the pattern of deficit spending in the sponsoring government. The fund may or may not be able to extract excess return from a particular asset class, but it should be able to create a more efficient portfolio than either of the alternatives: holding the country's natural resources alone or building an investment portfolio divorced from the resource.

Savings Funds

Savings funds come into play when a public and its government hold natural resources that could be depleted one day, and the country decides to save and invest current revenues for future generations. The savings often come from cutting current government spending with the expectation that the future value of invested savings will help support government services long after the original resource has played out.

The clearest potential advantage in a savings fund is the likely long investment horizon. Unlike a stability fund, a savings fund may not have to come to the rescue of a government struggling with deficits. It may be able to own illiquid assets and tolerate the fluctuation in value that comes along with that. It may be able to buy or provide funding to assets selling at depressed values or otherwise out of favor. These seem to be attributes of Norway's sovereign wealth fund, which in part has a mandate to save and invest the value of Norway's oil and gas resources (Chambers, Dimson, and Ilmanen, 2012).

Similar to any fund largely investing for total return, the targeted risk and return, the performance benchmarks, and the fees all figure into portfolio construction.

Currency Reserve Funds

Sovereign wealth funds also have played a central role in managing foreign exchange rates. In a world where all currencies float freely against one another, of course, this role does not exist. The supply and demand for currency fluctuates with economic growth, investment opportunity, interest rates, international trade, monetary and fiscal policy, and so on. But in countries sensitive to trade balances, the value of the currency can make a big difference. If the local currency rises in value, local exports become more expensive worldwide. If the value of the currency falls, local exports become cheaper. In emerging markets where the economy developed based on the low cost of exports or in mature markets with large export sectors, keeping the local currency inexpensive has often been critical to continued growth.

Central banks or sovereign wealth funds commonly develop currency reserves to manage exchange rates. If the country exports more than it imports and sees net strong demand for its local currency, it can print and sell local currency and buy up foreign currency to build foreign exchange reserves. To limit local inflation in that case, the central bank or sovereign wealth fund can sell bonds denominated in the local currency and absorb the local excess, a process known as sterilization. This incidentally establishes a cost of funds for the currency reserve fund because it needs to cover the cost of interest on the securities used for sterilization. Sterilization often is expensive because the central bank is selling local currency and buying foreign currency in a market with local inflation pressure and, presumably, rising interest rates. Sterilization also may reduce the impact of a currency intervention (Goldberg, Hull, and Stein, 2013). Using a stability fund to absorb local currency and convert it into foreign investments may be less expensive than sterilization. If trade flows eventually reverse and the country eventually imports more than it exports and sees its currency depreciate, it can sell foreign currency and buy up its local exchange.

Central banks and sovereign wealth funds also build up foreign exchange reserves to protect the economy from foreign capital flight. During the Asia currency crisis of 1997, for instance, debt issued by Asian countries in US dollars became an Achilles heel when foreign investors refused to take proceeds from maturing issues and roll into new debt. Because the local currency had depreciated against the dollar, the Asian governments had to repay the dollar debt at extremely high cost in local currency, threatening to send the issuers into default. After that crisis, many Asian countries built up substantial dollar reserves to protect against a repeat of crisis (figure 14.2). They could use the foreign exchange to repay maturity debt or buy up local currency to counter the depreciation.

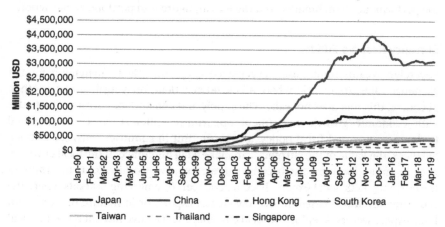

Figure 14.2 Foreign exchange reserves in Asia have built up since the mid-1990s. *Source:* Data from Bloomberg, LP.

Pension Funds

Pension funds that invest to ensure benefits for all citizens in retirement are less common under the umbrella of sovereign wealth funds. Public pension funds have a longer history, however, of investing on behalf of public employees and generally do not serve a policy goal other than attracting talent to public service and ensuring benefits for a specific group. Because the benefits promised to public employees often do not have an immediate cost to taxpayers, public pensions sometimes serve as valuable currency for attracting and keeping public employees with costs largely borne by future taxpayers. If future taxpayers resist the bill when it arrives, portfolio management often has to take substantial risk to get the correspondingly higher returns needed to cover imminent benefits. It can be a difficult portfolio problem to solve.

Properly funding a public pension can pull resources away from other priorities. But a well-designed and -executed national or public pension fund can improve public welfare by helping attract and retain better public servants. Poorly designed or executed funds can require taxpayers to fund shortfalls between pension asset value and benefits due. If the tax bill comes at a time the government already is running a deficit, it can put extra strain on taxpayers or fiscal balances.

Other than the usual competition for funding, pensions have less interaction with other parts of government than stability, savings, or foreign exchange reserve portfolios. Pensions target very specific liabilities.

Development Funds

Some countries sponsor development funds to allocate resources to important social and economic projects. Most of these funds invest in domestic government ventures that otherwise would have no other sponsors. These funds largely set priorities in specified public policy areas and monitor progress. Other than through the costs and benefits of funded investments, these funds have limited impact on other parts of government.

The Challenges of Governance and Public Support

Giving control of substantial capital to a sovereign wealth fund requires that the public ensure the fund is acting in the broadest public interest. The public needs to understand the fund's goals and activities and monitor results. Investment performance inevitably varies, and public confidence needs to hold through performance ups and downs. Building and holding public trust depends on the political norms in the sponsoring country, but a few principles are likely to hold:

- *Clarity on ownership, oversight, and management.* The government typically owns and oversees the fund with day-to-day management assigned to the Treasury or Ministry of Finance.
- *Clear rules on funding.* The flow of funds from government budgets into a sovereign wealth fund should be transparent and the rules and process clear.
- *Clear investment goals.* Clear specification of allowable assets, asset allocation, rules for rebalancing, and performance benchmarks all help the public understand the process and the results. Among other things, benchmarks set clear risk-and-return expectations. The authority and process for amending any of these elements should be clear, too.
- *Clear rules for withdrawing proceeds.* The rules governing transfer of interest, dividends, capital gains, and portfolio principal back to the government should be clear, too, to avoid the impression the government might raid the fund. The authority and process for amending these rules also should be clear.
- *Regular communication.* The public and its representatives should have access to regular reports on portfolio inflows, outflows, holdings, trading, and investment performance. Regular discussion of investment outlook helps the public understand the fund's view of risk and opportunity. When any material aspect of portfolio funding, investment, or distribution changes, the funds should disclose and explain the change. Even simple things such as reporting holdings and performance in local currency help public understanding.

The challenges of governance are significant because the public may not be familiar with portfolio investing and its implications for government budgets, import and export flows, foreign exchange, and monetary policy. The activities of a sovereign wealth fund arguably cannot run ahead of public understanding.

The Issue of Government or Individual Control

All sovereign wealth funds centralize management of public capital and, no matter how well governed, raise the issue of whether the public would be better served by distributing the capital to the public. There's a case for either side of the issue.

The strongest claims for central management all center on scale and its various benefits: lower marginal cost, more specialized staff, access to more funds on better terms, hedging, access to better information, and so on. A central place for all of this is much more efficient than distributing the functions.

The other strong claims for central management center on coordinating with other parts of government. If a stability fund invests government surplus, it can also fund deficits by selling or borrowing against assets. Once a surplus is distributed to the public, however, it's not clear the government can easily get it back. If a foreign exchange reserve fund needs to buy or sell currency to stabilize exchange rates or counter a flight of foreign capital, it's not clear a decentralized system could do that efficiently.

The weakest claims for central management focus on serving as trustee for future generations. This case argues that the government can best take the interest of future generations into account in saving and investing proceeds of current resources and distributing them to later generations either through government services or directly. But it's not clear the collective judgment of individuals looking out for their children or grandchildren is any worse than government judgment and arguably may be better on average.

The strongest claim for giving control to individual citizens is that individuals arguably are the best judges of their current and likely future needs and of the combination of risk and return best suited to meet them. The sovereign fund could distribute principal directly to citizens and rely on them to allocate between immediate spending or saving, inviting, of course, the objection that many citizens would not feel equipped to invest. Individuals who spent or invested poorly might still look for public support. Alternatively, the savings and pension mandates of sovereign wealth funds could be met by setting up accounts for individual citizens and giving each a choice of investments offered by a screened menu of managers. Each citizen could build his or her own portfolio out of the available choices or make choices within asset allocations or investment horizons or other limits that would ensure each citizen invested efficiently for his or her preferred level of risk. This would also use the scale of the sovereign wealth fund to negotiate competitive fees and provide investment education, research, and other services.

It is harder to see giving individual control for stability or reserve funds. Those funds need to be able to coordinate closely with other parts of government. It is possible that governments could rely on individuals to invest independently or from a screened menu of investments and then tax or draw from accounts to fund fiscal deficits or currency intervention. But the practical reaction to having individual funds withdrawn probably would tie government hands.

Sovereign wealth funds have come up with different answers for this question. Some distribute funds only to the government, which may spend on government programs or distribute to the public. Some distribute to individuals over long horizons. And some, such as the Alaska Permanent Fund, distribute directly to citizens. The history of sovereign wealth funds is too short for conclusive evidence on where to strike the balance.

Sources of Comparative Advantage

Managers of sovereign wealth funds potentially have to pursue very different investment goals in the best interests of their sponsoring public. Stability funds manage, through cycles of government surplus and deficit, savings funds toward maximizing national wealth across generations, currency reserve funds against demands of foreign exchange policy with pension, and infrastructure funds focused on specific liabilities. Each form of sovereign wealth fund has potential competitive advantage:

- Scale, cost, and compensation
- Leverage
- Funding terms
- Hedging
- Quality and cost of capital
- Information
- Access to assets
- Tax and accounting rules
- Political and regulatory environment

Scale, Cost, and Compensation

The size of most sovereign wealth funds is sufficient to reduce most of the cost drag on performance and get the tools and expertise needed to manage assets efficiently. Central banks, which often oversee sovereign wealth funds, may have systems and staff able to manage certain assets, such as sovereign bonds or money markets, efficiently, but other investments can require external managers who offer efficient exposure to foreign assets. On scale and marginal cost, sovereign wealth funds should match most money managers of similar size.

For funds of similar size, sovereign wealth funds potentially have advantage in a more efficient investment decision process. A sovereign fund ultimately serves a single client, whereas most funds of similar size serve many. To the extent the sovereign fund has clear investment guidelines and authority to act, it should be able to review new, large, or complex investments and make investment decisions faster than rival portfolios. Rivals often have to educate and get approval from clients for investments outside the norm. This puts sovereign wealth funds in a good position to see the newest, most complex, and largest investments before other investors, especially when the firm looking for investment wants to move quickly. If these investments fit the fund's targeted risk and return, the fund can get good terms from firms that need a quick response.

Compensation at sovereign wealth funds is likely to parallel mutual funds, with similar benefits and limits for fund performance. In cost and compensation, sovereign wealth funds stand on par with the largest US mutual funds.

Leverage

Sovereign wealth funds vary in their use of leverage. Unlike banks or insurers, sovereign funds do not have deposits or premiums or similar sources of funds for leverage. Sovereign funds would have to borrow against the value of securities or issue debt either directly or through another government entity.

Currency reserve funds are most likely to have some leverage if the fund issues debt to help it sterilize local currency used to purchase foreign exchange. Other sovereign funds focused on savings, such as Norway (Chambers, Dimson, and Ilmanen, 2012), use little or no leverage, and others invest in hedge funds and at least take on leverage indirectly. Policy on leverage may be flexible enough to allow use, but the political consequences of losses from leverage likely discourage it.

Some sovereign reserve funds can use futures and other derivatives, which potentially add leverage (Goldberg, Hull, and Stein, 2013). The Swiss National Bank, for instance, can use equity futures. The United Kingdom's Equity Equalisation Account and the Bank of England can use foreign exchange forwards, interest rate and currency swaps, overnight indexed swaps, bond and interest rate futures, swap notes and futures, and forward rate agreements. The Bank of Canada can use foreign exchange and cross-currency swaps to manage reserves. Use of currency swaps grew during the 2008 crisis after the US Federal Reserve did swaps with a number of central banks.

Sovereign wealth funds consequently are at a disadvantage to mutual and hedge funds, banks, insurers, and others with more latitude to use leverage. However, sovereign wealth funds can invest in mutual and hedge funds, banks, insurers, and other portfolios with latitude to use leverage. The sovereign fund consequently can benefit indirectly. This could put sovereign funds back on par with competing investors.

Funding Terms

Funding for sovereign wealth funds, which arguably is indistinguishable from their capital, flows from commodity surpluses, government budgets, and inflows of foreign exchange or similar sources. To the extent the funding is stable, which is likely the case for savings funds and some stability funds, it enables the fund to plan long investment programs with limited risk of withdrawal. That caters to owning illiquid assets and collecting the return premium that goes with illiquidity.

To the extent funding flows in from commodity surplus and out from commodity deficits, the fund that would have advantage is buying negatively correlated assets because those assets have a valuable portfolio effect for the fund.

The cost of funds for a savings fund and some stability funds ultimately is the cost of meeting liabilities. The spread between assets and liabilities is whatever is left over, assuming the sovereign fund can earn any excess.

Hedging

Sovereign wealth funds have no intrinsic reason to limit hedging and usually report results based on fair market value, avoiding the limits put on hedging by bank and insurer accounting. Funds benchmarked against market indexes nevertheless might have limited incentives to hedge unless manager compensation is tied to generating alpha. Because few sovereign wealth fund managers get compensated for alpha, hedging in stability and savings funds usually plays a limited role.

Reserve funds may have good reasons to hedge if using derivatives proves more efficient than selling positions. Several reserve funds use interest rate and foreign exchange hedges (Goldberg, Hull, and Stein, 2013).

Quality and Cost of Capital

Similar to its funding, sovereign wealth fund capital comes from the government and can be patient and deep. That is only true to the extent a savings or stability fund is protected from calls to fund deficits. That gives the fund advantage in holding illiquid assets with longer cash flows and potentially volatile pricing. The public beneficiaries of sovereign wealth funds react to falling market values like any set of investors but do not have the ability to cut off or withdraw funding without going through a political process. The fund is buffered from these risks, unlike many private portfolios.

A sovereign fund also should know its sponsoring government's nonfinancial assets and liabilities better than any other party and should be able to create a more efficient overall portfolio. Here, the fund has an important advantage.

Information and Access to Assets

A sovereign wealth fund might have proprietary flow of information from the industry or other resources generating the country's core economic exposures. That information could be valuable for investing in assets that move with or counter to local economic growth.

15

Investing for Individuals

Imagine printing the market's list of all possible investments and watching it fill up the room, spill into the hallway, out the front door, and down the street. Follow it again to the ocean and watch it again start to fill up the deepest parts. The list of endless investments returns. But imagine, too, all the mutual funds and hedge funds, banks and insurers, brokers, and other portfolios poring over the same list for investment and opportunity. Imagine your ability to compete.

To that list of investments, the institutional portfolios would bring time, effort, experience, and the incentives of people with no other job to distract them. They would bring the lower costs of large organizations, greater access to funds at lower rates of interest, the ability to hedge some risks and take others, the flow of information that comes from multiple people and data suppliers, and trading counterparties.

With the global market of investment opportunities split into local markets, each combed over and often dominated by institutions with compelling advantages, most individuals will have limited room to compete. Some of the best fundamental work on financial intermediaries argues in fact that institutional portfolios develop to make up for the inefficiencies of individual investors (Diamond and Dybvig, 1983; Diamond, 1984, 1996). Institutions provide scale, leverage, hedging, access to assets, and specialized information and expertise that individuals find hard-pressed if not impossible to match. For these things, individuals need institutional managers. Individuals can do far better by joining forces with institutional teams than by competing directly.

Each individual nevertheless does bring one thing essential to good investing that no institutional investment manager can match: knowledge of his or her own financial future. Individuals know their own potential job prospects and potential earnings. They know their potential expenses from the mundane costs of daily life to the aspirational ones of homeownership or travel or philanthropy. They know the support they might expect from family or the support they might need to provide. An individual investor's full set of financial and nonfinancial assets and liabilities combine with traditional investments into a portfolio far more efficiently than almost any portfolio an institutional manager could offer. Individuals may not have competitive advantage in producing excess return from financial markets, but individuals do have advantage in producing excess return from their own unique private portfolios.

The Structure of Individual Investing

Most individuals do surprisingly little investing at all, at least in the publicly traded financial assets that seem to get so much attention. The financial press devotes exuberant money, time, and energy to stocks and bonds and all the influences on them, but most individuals are spectators to all of this. US household wealth is predominately tied up in bank accounts, cars and trucks, homes, and retirement accounts—although retirement accounts, of course, can hold stocks, bonds, and mutual funds (figure 15.1). Less than one in five households owns stocks or mutual funds outside of retirement accounts, and less than one in 10 owns bonds. Cash value in life insurance, ownership in a business or profession, real estate, annuities and trusts, and educational savings accounts are other assets important to individuals. But the share of households that have these things is small.

When it does come to investing, most individuals prefer their own counsel. A survey of households by the Office of the Investor Advocate for the SEC and the RAND Corporation found that less than half used professional financial advice at any point (Scholl and Hung, 2018). Of those that did use advice, a minority seemed to understand the difference between advice from a broker/dealer, legally only required to recommend suitable investments, and from an investment advisor, legally required to act as a fiduciary in the best interests of the investor.[1] Apparently the marketplace for investment ideas is noisy, confusing, and largely ignored.

Trust may be far more important than skill to individuals' choice of investment professionals. Investors who trust their financial advisors seem most likely to delegate investment decisions regardless of the individual's financial savvy (Calcagno, Giofré, and Urzi-Brancatì, 2017). Of course, skill may be critical to the calculus of trust, but it seems far from the only part. Investors almost certainly value trustworthy professionals who help investors take risk. As Nicola Gennaioli

---

1 A broker/dealer recommendation of an equity mutual fund, for example, might be suitable even if managed by the broker/dealer's own investment team. But the same fund would be in the best interest of the investor only if it offered the lowest fees among comparable funds.

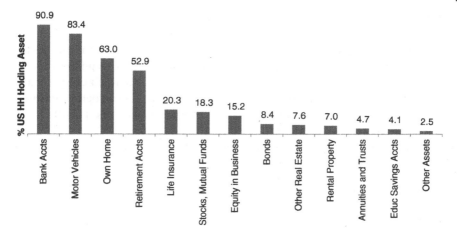

Figure 15.1 Most US household wealth is tied up in bank accounts, vehicles, homes, and retirement accounts.
Source: US Census Bureau (2015).

and his colleagues write in their work on *Money Doctors* (Gennaioli, Shleifer, and Vishny, 2015):

> In our view, financial advice is a service, similar to medicine. We believe, contrary to what is presumed in the standard finance model, that many investors have very little idea of how to invest, just as patients have a very limited idea of how to be treated. And just as doctors guide patients toward treatment, and are trusted by patients even when providing routine advice identical to that of other doctors, in our model money doctors help investors make risky investments and are trusted to do so even when their advice is costly, generic, and occasionally self-serving. And just as many patients trust their doctor, and do not want to go to a random doctor even if equally qualified, investors trust their financial advisors and managers. (p. 92)

Individual investors persistently invest in mutual funds that underperform passive benchmarks, and they pay fees to brokers and investment advisors that recommend these funds. Something other than performance clearly matters. Despite the competitive disadvantage of investing as an individual, whether professionally advised or not, investing in risky assets often leaves the individual better off than not investing at all. Money sitting in a bank is truly safe only as long as interest paid keeps up with price inflation, and that is often not the case. The main contribution of professional managers is to give individuals the confidence to take risk.

Sources of Comparative Advantage

On almost every dimension of competitive advantage in investing, individuals fall short against institutional investors. But there are important exceptions. Individuals know their own nonfinancial assets and liabilities—their job prospects and earnings, their stakes in real estate and private businesses, their expenses and aspirations, their pensions, and other benefits. These are all essential to building an efficient portfolio.

The potential sources of investment advantage apply as much to individuals as to institutions:

- Scale, cost, and compensation
- Leverage
- Funding terms
- Hedging
- Quality and cost of capital
- Information
- Access to assets
- Tax and accounting rules
- Political and regulatory environment

Scale, Cost, and Compensation

Individuals usually have none of the scale available to institutional investors. Institutions can subscribe to specialized news and data services, buy analytic software, and hire researchers and traders at a cost that few individuals can bear. Institutions can set up trading relationships with a wider range of broker/dealers and get a better flow of information. Institutions can hire lawyers, accountants, and consultants more efficiently. Institutions can assemble the hundreds or thousands of stocks or bonds in diversified market portfolios more efficiently than individuals. Institutions can usually trade securities in larger sizes and at much lower cost than individuals. In corporate bonds, for instance, transaction costs for amounts under $100,000—amounts typically traded by individuals—often run between three and four times the cost of trading $10 million positions (figure 15.2). When it comes to scale, individuals are at significant disadvantage.

When it comes to compensation, individuals have a nominal advantage over any institution. Individuals' incentives, after all, should be perfectly aligned with their own best interests. Individuals investing on their own behalf have clear incentive to draw out the performance best suited to their own goals. Institutions, meanwhile, have to weigh both clients' goals and the goals of the business. Client and institutional goals may conflict. An individual may have uncomplicated

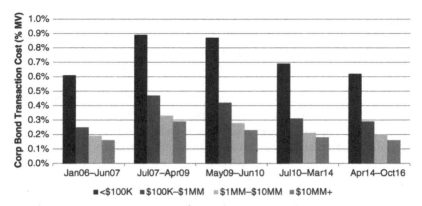

Figure 15.2 Transactions costs for retail run up to four times the cost of block trades. *Source:* Bessembinder, Jacobsen, Maxwell, and Venkataraman (2018), Table III.

incentives, but the disadvantages of limited scale nevertheless put a drag on individuals' ability to perform.

Leverage

Individuals can get investment leverage by posting their assets as collateral against brokerage or bank loans, but the amount of leverage is usually less and the cost of funds higher than institutional costs. The Federal Reserve's Regulation T allows investors to borrow up to 50% of the market value of stocks, and the SEC and Commodity Futures Trading Commission require investors to put up 15% to 20% of the notional value of futures contracts. But banks, insurers, and other institutions that effectively can borrow in their own name can use those funds to apply higher leverage to investments. These institutions, along with hedge funds and broker/dealers, can also use the repurchase market to leverage investments. And institutions with large portfolios can use a competitive market in lending to get better rates and other terms on funds than individuals might.

Individuals can borrow on terms comparable to institutions for investing in residential or commercial real estate. Individual investors can put down as little as 3.5% and borrow 96.5% of the value of homes that qualify for US Federal Housing Administration guarantees. Fannie Mae and Freddie Mac offer similar programs. Fannie Mae and Freddie Mac will also make loans to investors who put down 15% to 25% of the value of small commercial properties. If residential or commercial property values rise, individuals can borrow against the appreciation to fund investment either in the property or other assets. And US law allows income tax deductions for some portion of mortgage interest, lowering the after-tax cost of borrowing. Real estate puts individuals on par with institutions for leverage, but elsewhere individuals are at a disadvantage.

Futures and options also give leverage to individual investors, but on terms again no better and often worse than institutions. Futures contracts create leverage on individual stocks, global equity indices, currencies, interest rates, and commodities, and put or call options create leverage on most publicly traded individual stocks and exchange-traded funds. The leverage comes from a small investment controlling a large amount of the asset. The margin or initial investment in a futures contract is similar for individuals or institutions, and the margin often is more than the repurchase or repo market requires for taking the same risk. The repo market ultimately gives institutions the upper hand.

Funding Terms

The cost of funds is usually lower and the flexibility in maturity and other terms is usually greater for institutions than for individuals. Banks, for instance, can draw from funds that include deposits, commercial paper, repurchase agreements, fed funds, corporate debt, and loans from the Federal Home Loan Bank system or, in emergencies, the Federal Reserve. Insurers can draw on premiums from a broad range of product lines, also raise funds from repurchase agreements, issue corporate debt, or borrow from the Federal Home Loan Bank system. Hedge funds and mutual funds, too, can use repurchase agreements. Except for the wealthiest individuals or investors who can borrow against real estate or other collateral, rates for investment loans to individuals are relatively high and terms limited. On funding costs and terms, most individuals are at considerable disadvantage.

Hedging

Individual investors can hedge positions. Individuals can short-sell some securities in the equity market, for instance, and can use futures and options across a wide range of assets. But the costs for these instruments are usually relatively high and other terms usually more restrictive than for institutions. Individuals generally have no access to interest rate swaps or swaptions, which are used heavily by institutions to hedge risk. Hedging also usually requires frequent adjustment or rebalancing as markets move and risks change. Individuals may not have the time or expertise to actively manage hedges.

Quality and Cost of Capital

Here individuals have clear competitive advantage. This is where the individual's proprietary knowledge of their financial and nonfinancial assets and liabilities plays out. The quality and cost of capital for an individual is entirely aligned—or certainly can be—with the investor's own interests and investment strategy. Here the investor sets the terms.

The individual has proprietary knowledge about their own likely earnings, future expenses, investment horizon, return targets, and tolerance for volatility. No institution has similar knowledge. If an individual buys assets designed to match liabilities with acceptable return and risk, the value of the asset to the individual should be higher than the value of the asset in the general market.

Individual investors should be able to calculate a personal cost of capital. It is effectively the return and risk on capital needed to cover future expenses. The capital can be held in financial assets, such as savings and investments, or in non-financial assets, such as the education, skills, experience, and relationships that generate career earnings. The capital can be current or projected. And expenses can be the cost of food, housing, transportation, medical care, and other daily items. Or the expenses can be aspirational, such as education for children, weddings, vacations, charitable contributions, or inheritances.

The calculation starts with expenses. A simple approach takes current expenses and projects them forward assuming expenses rise at the rate of inflation. The investor might add the cost of future business ventures, education for children, weddings, significant travel, and so on. The projections might assume expenses fall as children leave the home or rise with medical expenses in later years. The estimate might assume charitable contributions or gifts to family. Some expenses will be basic and essential, others flexible and aspirational.

The assets needed to cover expenses largely depend on current investments, future earnings, and savings. For younger workers, earnings or return to human capital is by far the most valuable asset, dwarfing financial capital. By the end of a career, the relative value of human and financial capital often has reversed. The stream of future earnings is shorter, and more financial capital typically is available. The individual can make simple projections of earnings, assuming they rise with inflation, and assume certain rates of savings. But there are more realistic and valuable ways to imagine the future.

Career earnings have the same properties as any asset. They have expected return, risk, and, importantly, correlation. Fatih Guvenen at the University of Minnesota and his colleagues have done valuable work on the career pattern of individual earnings across industries (Guvenen, Schulhofer-Wohl, Song, and Yogo, 2017). Using records from the US Social Security Administration on individual earnings from 1978 to 2013, Guvenen shows that earnings clearly vary with GDP and stock market returns, and the sensitivity for each individual depends in surprising ways on gender, age, on where the individual sits in the earnings distribution, and on the individual's industry. In other words, every individual has a different level of investment in future economic growth.

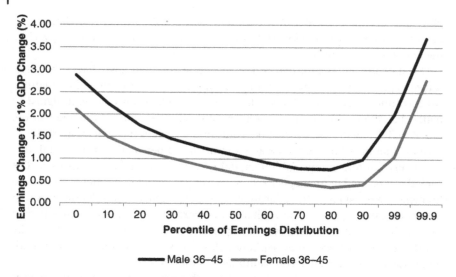

Figure 15.3 Earnings vary with GDP especially for very high or low earners.
Source: Guvenen, Schulhofer-Wohl, Song, and Yogo (2017).

Workers at the highest and lowest ends of the earning distribution have the most sensitivity to changes in GDP. For a 1% change in GDP, for example, a male between the ages of 36 and 45 with earnings in the bottom 10% will see earnings change by 2.88%; a similar female will see a change of 2.11% (figure 15.3). A male in the same age group with earnings in the top 0.01% will see earnings change by 3.70%; a similar female, 3.09%. A male in that age group with earnings at the 50% level, however, will see earnings change by only 1.09%; a female, by 0.69%. Workers at the highest and lowest end of the earnings distribution are most at risk from changes in economic growth. And males are more at risk than females.

Younger workers bear more of the risk of economic growth than older workers. For a 1% shift in GDP, a male between the ages of 26 and 35 at the 50% mark in the earnings distribution sees earnings move 1.55%. A male aged 36 to 45 at the same mark sees earnings move 1.09%, a male aged 46 to 55 sees a move of 0.86%, and a male aged 56 to 65 sees a move by 0.30% (figure 15.4). As a worker ages, the volatility of earnings steadily drops.

Earnings also depend on a worker's industry. For a male at the 50% mark in the earnings distribution for construction, for example, a 1% shift in GDP moves earnings by 2.31% (figure 15.5). In durable manufacturing, it's 1.97%. And in health and education, it's 0.23%. Construction looks relatively sensitive to the fortunes of the broader economy, whereas health and education do not.

The size of a company matters, too, according to Guvenen and colleagues, with workers at larger companies less sensitive to the changing economy than workers

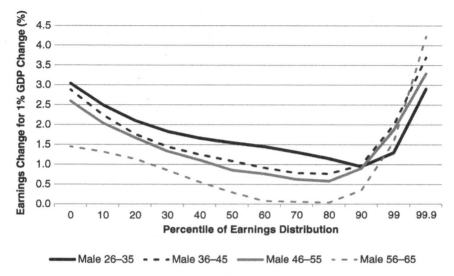

Figure 15.4 Younger workers bear more GDP risk than older workers.
Source: Guvenen, Schulhofer-Wohl, Song, and Yogo (2017).

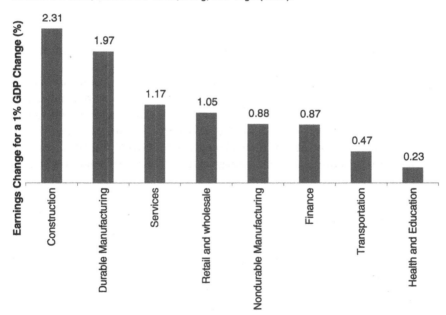

Figure 15.5 The impact of GDP on earnings varies across industries.
Source: Guvenen, Schulhofer-Wohl, Song, and Yogo (2017).

Note: Data shows the effect on earnings for a 1% change in GDP for a male aged 36 to 45 at the 50% mark of the earnings distribution for each industry.

at smaller companies. And Guvenen also finds that the patterns of sensitivity to the broader economy roughly parallel sensitivity to returns in the stock market.

The combination of education, skills, experience, and relationships that create a stream of career earnings plays out differently across gender, age, industry, and employer and represents a portfolio asset like any other. The return, risk, and correlation of this asset to others should play a central role in any portfolio designed to fit an individual and his or her projected expenses. David Blanchett and Philip Straehl show that adding earnings, homeownership, and pensions to portfolio construction changes optimal investment weightings over time and across industries (Blanchett and Straehl, 2015). In other words, the best portfolio depends on an individual's financial and nonfinancial assets.

Once an individual sets projected expenses and estimates future financial and nonfinancial assets, the investor can figure out the rate of return that covers expenses. If an individual projects a $1 expense in the future but holds $1 today, for instance, the individual can just keep holding the $1, take no risk, and eventually cover the future expense. If the individual instead holds only $0.95 today, the individual will need an investment that takes some risk, earns $0.05, and returns $1 by the time the expense is due. And if the individual holds only $0.75 today, the investment will need to earn $0.25—five times the earning of the first risky investment and presumably five times the risk. The required return and risk will point to an asset mix most likely to deliver targeted results. The investor can always adjust expenses, build in a margin of safety, and recalculate targeted return and risk. This becomes the investor's implied cost of capital.

Over time, circumstances change. Expenses move above or below projections. Earnings come in higher or lower. Financial assets perform above or below expectations. At any point, the individual can reset targeted risk and return and adjust the portfolio. Frameworks developed for other portfolios that balance financial and nonfinancial assets apply to individuals, too (Brown, Papaioannou, and Petrova, 2010). No institution can manage an individual's portfolio as efficiently as the individual who depends on it.

Information and Access to Assets

The falling cost and widening availability of data and computing have made individual investors more competitive with institutions than ever in getting and using this kind of information. And regulations that require public companies to share material information without preference have leveled the ground, too. This might eliminate some competitive disadvantage for individual investors, but it does not add up to competitive advantage. With rare exceptions, institutions have more scale, specialization, and focus for regularly gathering and analyzing information. When it comes to information costly in time or effort to get or simply hard to access, institutional advantages grow. Certain electronic or in-person surveys can be expensive. Access to leading experts in law, government, medicine, engineering, technology, and other fields may be finite and hard to come by. By the time this kind of information hits public or even professional media, a large part of the return to the information is likely already reflected in asset prices. For broadly available, traded assets, institutions should have clear information advantage. Individuals may have proprietary information about very local assets such as businesses or real estate. Individual investors should always try to assess whether they are early, late, or on par with other investors in the information flow.

Individuals may assume they stand on par with institutions in access to assets, but institutions have clear advantage. Banks and insurers, for example, hold trillions of dollars in loans that do not trade in public markets. Private equity funds hold ownership stakes in millions of companies that do not issue public equity. Almost all institutions can invest in hedge funds, private equity funds, and a steady flow of unregistered securities not available to individuals. Even with publicly traded debt and equity, over-the-counter markets give access to institutions that individuals cannot match. Although in theory individuals have access to the full investable set of assets, in practice they do not.

Tax and Accounting Rules

Individuals in the US have some advantages here in investment accounts that accumulate returns without getting taxed. Individual retirement accounts, or IRAs, come in a couple of varieties that let portfolio returns compound over time without annual tax. Many companies offer 401(k) plans that also allow returns to compound without annual tax. Individuals can invest funds intended for education in 529 plans that also compound without annual tax. Individuals can also put funds in insurance accounts that compound without annual tax. And individuals can invest directly in tax-exempt debt from federal, state, and local governments. These accounts and investments could give individual investors advantage in securities that generate significant amounts of return through income.

As for accounting, individuals have some advantage only because they do not need to bear the cost and complexity of accounting required for institutions. Individuals can track their investment results in as much or as little detail as they want.

Political and Regulatory Environment

Individual investors get much less political and regulatory scrutiny than any institutional investor, but this hardly outweighs any of the other comparative disadvantages. Individuals in the US usually are encouraged to invest, and regulatory limits on individuals investing on their own behalf are limited to the income and net worth requirements for investing in hedge funds and other alternative assets.

Predictions of Local CAPM

Individual investors have modest competitive advantage in investment incentives, quality and cost of capital, accounting, and taxation and clear disadvantage in scale, leverage, funding, hedging, information, and access to assets. Under these circumstances, local CAPM makes some broad predictions:

- *Individuals who manage for absolute asset performance portfolios will underperform institutions.* Individuals trying to extract excess return from asset portfolios will run up against institutions with significant advantages.
- *Individual investors will cede investment management of most asset classes to institutions but keep the job of asset allocation and liability management.* Ceding the management of asset return acknowledges the comparative advantage institutions have in extracting excess return from asset portfolios, but retaining asset allocation and liability management plays to individuals' better incentives and knowledge of their own cost of capital and liabilities.

Informal Results

Although a large body of work looks at different aspects of individual investing, little of it views the individual as just another competitor in the market for investment returns. Still, some of the work on individual investing is telling.

Individuals Underperform Institutions

Brad Barber at the University of California–Davis and Terrance Odean at the University of California–Berkeley wrap up their review of individual investing with this portrait (Barber and Odean, 2011):

> (Individuals) trade frequently and have perverse stock selection ability, incurring unnecessary investment costs and return losses. They tend to sell their winners and hold their losers, generating unnecessary tax liabilities. Many hold poorly diversified portfolios, resulting in unnecessarily high levels of diversifiable risk, and many are unduly influenced by media and past experience. Individual investors who ignore the prescriptive advice to buy and hold low-fee, well-diversified portfolios, generally do so to their detriment. (p. 37)

It is not a pretty picture.

After subtracting transaction costs, individuals underperform market benchmarks by much more than institutions (Barber and Odean, 2000). Gross returns on individuals' stock portfolios roughly match market benchmarks but with no signs of significant alpha or excess return. Individuals' returns after trading expenses, however, lag benchmarks by 110 bp annually. The lag would be worse, but individuals tilt toward value stocks, and smaller ones at that, which tend to outperform the rest of the market. After accounting for the tilt toward value investing, underperformance against the broad market rises to 370 bp annually, far worse than found with most studies of mutual fund returns after expenses. Individual investors would be better off by buying and holding. Trading hurts returns.

The beta of the average stock held by an individual is high, greater than 1.0. This mirrors the behavior of some mutual funds with limits to leverage (Frazzini and Pedersen, 2011). Individuals, too, have limited access to leverage. But stocks with a high beta tend to provide a poorer return for risk taken than stocks with low beta. Individuals tend to invest in more expensive assets.

Individual investors also tend to sell investments that have gone up in value and hold investments that have gone down, a pattern repeated in a wide range of work across different markets and dubbed the disposition effect (Barber and Odean, 2011). Individuals sell winners and hold losers in Australia, China, Finland, Israel, Korea, Taiwan, Sweden, and the US, among other places. Selling winners and holding losers creates a tax bill that any investor could avoid simply by selling offsetting winners and losers at the same time. But that's not what individual investors do. Individual investors learn to avoid the disposition effect as they get more experience. But individuals sell winners and hold losers more often than institutions.

Individuals also hold undiversified portfolios, investing too much in the stock of their own company. Enron employees held 62% of their retirement plan in company stock and lost both their job and accumulated wealth when the company failed in 2000. Global Crossing, Kmart, Lucent, and Polaroid employees could tell similar stories. A 2003 study of the 20 largest retirement programs managed by employers found 44% of assets in company stock (Poterba, 2003). Later studies have found lower concentration. Concentrated investments could be part of efficient portfolios considering individual nonfinancial assets. But because the most important individual nonfinancial asset likely is the stream of earnings from the employer, owning the employer's stock, too, is too much concentrated risk.

Individuals also miss opportunities to diversify by overinvesting in the stock of companies located nearby. Familiarity, easier monitoring, and possibly proprietary information could justify the concentration. But although not as obvious as investing in company stock, a downturn in the local economy is likely correlated with job prospects and earnings.

In occasional studies of both individual and institutional investing in the same markets, individuals trail. A study of stocks bought and sold over two years in Finland found individuals were net buyers of weak performers at the same time that financial firms and foreigners were net buyers of strong performers (Grinblatt and Keloharju, 2000). In Taiwan, stocks bought by institutions performed well while stocks bought by individuals performed poorly (Barber, Lee, Liu, and Odean, 2009).

With some exceptions, Barber and Odean (2011) note, "the evidence indicates that individual investors are subpar investors."

Individuals will Cede Asset Management

It is hard to know whether individual investors have ceded management of asset class returns to professionals and held onto asset allocation and liability management. Individuals would have to see their own shortcomings and find knowledgeable, trustworthy professionals. Neither would be easy. Even then, most individuals likely do not have access to professionals able to extract reliable excess return.

The steady growth of passively managed mutual funds and exchange-traded funds suggests individual investors have started ceding the job of assembling broad market exposure. Passive funds and ETFs held 8% of global investment funds in 2007 and 20% by 2017, and a large part of the growth came from displacing active managers, especially in equities (Sushko and Turner, 2018). Institutional managers can create broad exposure much more efficiently than an individual.

As to whether individuals actively manage asset allocation and invest with their own liabilities in mind, the evidence is sparse. Individuals clearly hold different portfolios, and the availability of mutual funds with target maturity dates suggests some eye toward covering liabilities. Individuals also buy annuities, wisely or not, which also points to liability management. But surveys showing limited use of financial professionals suggest anything beyond an occasional look at bank or brokerage statements is the norm. If that is true, then the art and science of individual investing has a long way to go.

Conclusion

The best individual investors ultimately create the most local of markets: a collection of financial and nonfinancial assets with expected return and risk uniquely suited to the individual's expenses and aspirations. On the margin, the individual investor drives pricing in those assets. They offer value no other portfolio can match, making the portfolio more efficient than any other. That is the most sustainable form of excess return available to individual investors. For all other aspects of efficient investing, individuals can turn to institutions far better equipped to extract return.

Part III

Markets

16

Turning the Tables: Investor Impact on Asset Values

Investors come with relative strengths and weaknesses that determine how they engage with the infinite set of investible assets. Some investors are large, and some are small. Some come with ample and flexible funding at low cost, and others do not. All come with different costs and terms of capital, with different amounts and quality of information, and with different benefits and drawbacks from tax, accounting, regulation, and politics. These things interact with the attributes of investible assets to determine both the behavior of the investment portfolios and the value of the assets themselves. A gardener shapes a field one way and a farmer another, and so investors shape markets.

Classic finance abstracts away from these relative strengths and weaknesses. They become just the underpinnings of so many investors' preferences with none having decisive influence on markets. But Merton (1973a) recognized that investors' strengths and weaknesses change over time, and their portfolios only benefit if they have a chance to hold investments and extract return long enough. As CAPM anticipates, investors do want to get the highest return for the lowest possible risk. But investors can hold this combination only within the constraints they face. Investors have to build portfolios that get them targeted risk, return, and correlation considering all possible future states of the world, including changes to major factors governing their ability to invest. Continual shifts in the factors governing investing—the things that create competitive advantage in investing—can be just as systemically important as shifting states of the economy.

The market of investible assets is better described as a series of neighborhoods, each one governed by local CAPM. The boundaries of the neighborhoods get set by major institutional features that set mutual funds apart from hedge funds, banks from insurers, and brokers from REITs, sovereign wealth funds, individuals, and others. Most of these institutions vary on a handful of factors that largely determine competitive advantage. Assets can trade in more than one local market, but each market puts a unique value on the asset, and, if large enough, can dominate asset valuation. The constraints on institutional capital create systemic risk in asset markets, and investors need compensation. The history of markets is full of episodes of major investors dominating the value of often broad and deep markets.

The Yield Curve Conundrum

On February 16, 2005, Fed Chairman Alan Greenspan appeared before the Senate Committee on Banking, Housing and Urban Affairs to describe in part a puzzle in the US yield curve. It was showing behavior Greenspan had not seen before. The Fed had lowered fed funds rates from 6.5% in 2000 to 1.0% by 2003 to ward off recession and had recently decided to reverse course. In June 2004, the Fed announced the first of what would become 17 hikes of 25 basis points each. By the time Greenspan sat down in February, the Fed had raised fed funds 150 basis points. But 10-year Treasury yields over the same time had dropped from around 4.50% to below 4.20%. That was the puzzle.

"Increasing short-term interest rates are normally accompanied by a rise in longer-term yields," Greenspan explained to the senators (Greenspan, 2005). The 10-year yield could be thought of as 10 consecutive one-year forward rates. Those rates usually rise with fed funds, but that was not happening. Greenspan could not attribute lower 10-year yields to a drop in inflation expectations. And rising stock prices and narrowing credit spreads made it hard to attribute it to lower growth expectations.

Then, among a litany of possible explanations for the puzzle, he offered one that would prove prescient. "Heavy purchases of longer-term Treasury securities by foreign central banks have often been cited as a factor boosting bond prices and pulling down longer-term yields." That was just a theory, however. Fed funds would reach 5.25% by June 2006 with 10-year yields at 5.15%. Lower yields on longer Treasury debt, he concluded, "remains a conundrum."

The conundrum Greenspan described that day likely had its roots in events nearly a decade before in Asia. The 1997 currency crisis had nearly bankrupted Thailand and other countries. Foreign investors had balked at rolling over old dollar debt into new and forced Asian countries to repay in heavily depreciated local currency. To insure against future crisis, Asian central banks had started building sizable foreign currency reserves, especially China. China's reserves accelerated after its 2001 entry into the World Trade Organization and subsequent expanding global trade. Foreign central bank holdings of US Treasury debt between January 2004 and June 2010 would rise from $400 billion to $3 trillion.

Less than two months after Greenspan's conundrum, his eventual successor, Ben Bernanke, would describe "the emergence of a global savings glut" (Bernanke, 2005). Bernanke again noted rising foreign exchange reserves and their investment in US Treasury debt. He laid out tables of numbers for the Virginia Association of Economists and described balance-of-payments deficits as many in the audience likely wondered whether even a global savings glut could distort the largest and most liquid bond market in the world.

A number of analysts have since sifted through the behavior of the yield curve in the 2000s to gauge the impact, if any, of foreign central bank investments (Rudebusch, Swanson, and Wu, 2006; Warnock and Warnock, 2009; Bertaut, DeMarco, Kamin, and Tryon, 2011; Beltran, Kretchmer, Marquez, and Thomas, 2012). Daniel Beltran and his colleagues looked at foreign central bank investment from January 1994 to June 2007. After accounting for a list of other possible influences on Treasury yields—the expected path of fed funds, interest rate volatility, liquidity premiums, signals of flight-to-safety, industrial production, oil shocks, budget deficits, risk appetite, and others—Beltran found a sizable impact. A flow of $100 billion into Treasury notes and bonds from foreign central banks tended to lower five-year yields by roughly 50 basis points. That estimate falls roughly in line with other studies.

"Between 1995 and 2010," Beltran and his colleagues write,

> China acquired roughly $1.1 trillion in US Treasury notes and bonds. A literal interpretation of our long-run estimates suggests that if China had not accumulated any foreign exchange reserves during this period, and therefore had not acquired these $1.1 trillion in Treasuries, all else equal, the 5-year Treasury yield would have been roughly 2 percentage points higher by 2010. (p. 16)

Greenspan's yield curve conundrum highlights the impact of a single class of investors on one of the world's largest markets. In this case, the prerogatives of foreign currency reserve managers, who typically attach the highest value to the safest and most liquid assets in a target currency, revalued the longer US Treasury market. Traditional analysis of Treasury value using a long list of plausible influences did not sufficiently explain longer yields. Foreign exchange reserve portfolios in China, Japan, Korea, Taiwan, Hong Kong, Malaysia, and elsewhere also invested in US agency mortgage–backed securities but little else. Treasury debt and mortgage-backed securities constituted almost the entire local asset market for the US dollar reserves of those central banks. Reserve portfolios competed against one another to extract value from these assets and collectively drove pricing to levels that investors in other local markets found puzzling to explain.

European Demand for Highly Rated Assets

While central banks in Asia poured capital into the US Treasury market, commercial banks in Europe had their eye on riskier US assets. European banks between 2003 and 2007 invested sizable amounts in US corporate debt and private asset- and mortgage-backed securities. Countries at the center of Bernanke's global savings glut led the way in accumulating US Treasury and agency debt and MBS, but Europe became the best bid for highly rated corporate debt and structured products (table 16.1). Total outstanding Treasury debt from 2003 to

Table 16.1 Europe invested heavily in corporate debt and structured products from 2003 to 2007 ($ billion)

		2003	2007	Pct Change
Treasury Debt	Outstanding	$3,342	$4,113	23%
	Held in Eur	$345	$399	16%
	Held in GSG	$449	$905	102%
	Held in US	$1,864	$1,729	−7%
Agency Debt	Outstanding	$5,969	$6,786	14%
	Held in Eur	$192	$308	60%
	Held in GSG	$198	$656	231%
	Held in US	$5,398	$5,402	0%
Corp AAA	Outstanding	$393	$425	8%
	Held in Eur	$74	$126	70%
	Held in GSG	$5	$9	80%
	Held in US	$236	$210	−11%
ABS/MBS AAA	Outstanding	$1,439	$3,154	119%
	Held in Eur	$86	$487	466%
	Held in GSG	$11	$44	300%
	Held in US	$1,277	$2,366	85%
Corp non-AAA	Outstanding	$4,093	$5,286	29%
	Held in Eur	$496	$993	100%
	Held in GSG	$33	$72	118%
	Held in US	$3,090	$3,607	17%
ABS/MBS non-AAA	Outstanding	$254	$458	80%
	Held in Eur	$15	$71	373%
	Held in GSG	$2	$6	200%
	Held in US	$225	$344	53%

Note: GSG stands for global savings glut countries, which includes Asia ex-Japan and the Middle East. MBS stands for mortgage-backed securities. ABS stands for asset-backed securities ex-MBS. *Source:* Bernanke, Bertaut, DeMarco, and Kamin (2011), Table 1; author calculations.

2007 grew 23%, for instance, and holdings in countries with rising reserves grew between 100% and 200%, with Europe and the US lagging. At the other extreme, outstanding AAA private asset- and mortgage-backed securities grew 119%, holdings in Europe grew by 466%, holdings in reserve countries grew 300% off a small base, and holdings in the US rose a comparatively modest 85%.

The reasons for aggressive European bank investment in highly rated US structured products are hard to pin down. Many European banks had access only to relatively short-term funding in US dollars and either had to invest in floating-rate assets or use interest rate swaps to convert fixed-rate assets into floating. The majority of private MBS issued in the mid-2000s had floating-rate coupons because most subprime mortgages had adjustable rates, so private MBS fit European dollar funding well. McCauley (2018) argued that aggressive expansion by European banks into the US during the decade meant many ended up helping produce the private MBS and consequently keeping large parts on their balance sheet. Others argue that low regulatory capital charges made private MBS look extremely profitable for shareholders (Acharya and Schnabl, 2010).

Whether European banks directed capital into US structured products for one or multiple reasons, it had all the signs of a structural flow. The particular funding and capital conditions for European banks made US structured products valuable for those investors, potentially more valuable for their portfolios than for others. European banks invested in a much wider range of securities and loans, so private US structured product was just part of European banks' structurally local asset market. The flow almost certainly shaped pricing and arguably encouraged production of more structured products to meet clear demand.

The Effects of Quantitative Easing

The US Federal Reserve's programs of quantitative easing, or QE, may be the most striking example of a systemic shift in asset markets at the hands of a single class of investors. In the case of QE, it was even narrower than a single class of investors; it was a single investor: the Fed itself.

The Fed launched three waves of QE designed to ease US financial conditions in the aftermath of the 2008 financial crisis. In QE1, from November 2008 to March 2010, the Fed bought $200 billion of Fannie Mae and Freddie Mac debt, $300 billion of Treasury debt, and $1.25 trillion of agency mortgage-backed securities. In QE2, from November 2010 to June 2012, the Fed bought another $600 billion in Treasury debt. And in QE3, from September 2012 to October 2014, the Fed added a further $1.7 trillion in Treasury debt and mortgage-backed securities. The Fed bought these securities without explicit regard to their risk, return, or correlation, as CAPM would highlight. The Fed instead bought these securities because it had legal authority and because the purchases met Fed policy goals. Policy, not portfolio, drove QE.

A number of analysts have found QE reduced interest rates through segmented or local markets. Joseph Gagnon and his colleagues at the New York Fed looked at eight major Fed announcements or speeches from November 2008 through November 2009 for signs that rates dropped as Fed policy expanded (Gagnon, Raskin, Remache, and Sack, 2010). They reasoned the market would see the Fed's intent to take longer Treasury debt and mortgage-backed securities out of the market and put more cash in. If the market treated the securities and cash as imperfect substitutes for each other, the anticipated lower supply of securities would trigger higher prices and lower yields. In other words, Fed policy hung on the assumption that investors operated in segmented markets even along the US Treasury yield curve. Looking at closing securities prices the day before and the day of each announcement, that is exactly what Gagnon and colleagues found. Beyond any changes in market expectations of future Fed funds, the announcements reduced 10-year rates by 50 to 100 basis points.

Arvind Krishnamurthy and Annette Vissing-Jorgensen also have done groundbreaking work on ways QE flowed through segmented or local markets (Krishnamurthy and Vissing-Jorgensen, 2011). Krishnamurthy and Vissing-Jorgensen argued that QE works through different channels. A signaling channel amplifies the Fed's commitment to keep Fed funds rates low for longer than usual policy rules might expect, lowering all interest rates. A duration channel uses investor preferences for bonds of specific duration and, by taking duration out of the market, raises prices and lowers yields. A liquidity channel reprices assets of different liquidity as QE shifts liquidity in the market. A safety premium channel uses some investors' preference for the safest assets and, by taking the safest assets out of the market, raises prices and lowers yields for the remaining supply. A prepayment risk channel takes advantage of investors who specialize in prepayment risk and, by taking prepayable mortgage-backed securities out of the market, raises prices and lowers yields. A default risk channel prices the impact of QE on the health of the economy and resulting corporate risk of default. And an inflation channel prices the impact of QE on expected inflation. Several of these channels anticipate investors who specialize in local markets.

Krishnamurthy and Vissing-Jorgensen ingeniously use differences between QE1, which included Treasury and agency debt and mortgage-backed securities, and QE2, which included Treasury debt only, to test channels of influence. Signaling, safety, and inflation channels drove down rates broadly through Treasury purchases in both QE1 and QE2. Prepayment, default, and liquidity channels brought down mortgage and some corporate rates, too, only in QE1, where the

Fed bought agency debt and mortgage-backed securities. Fed policy relied in part on some investors specializing in safe assets of specific maturities and on others specializing in prepayment and lower-grade credit risk. In other words, QE focusing only on Treasury debt would likely leave mortgage and lower-grade corporate markets behind.

The Fed's programs of QE took a massive portfolio operating in a narrow policy market and systematically repriced Treasury, mortgage, and corporate markets. Fed QE by design had influence on asset value as systemic as any other factor, and investors were well advised to view Fed policy as a risk they could not diversify away and for which their portfolio needed compensation.

Bank Liquidity Rules Shift Investment Portfolio Holdings

The value of liquidity has also seen systemic shifts. The 2008 financial crisis reminded bank regulators worldwide about the critical importance of being able to turn assets quickly into cash. Bear Stearns failed after its lenders doubted the value of the firm's mortgage investments and pulled their cash. Lehman Brothers fell for similar reasons. US regulators raised the value of bank deposits covered by government insurance from $100,000 to $250,000 to stop withdrawals by any customers worried about the safety of their bank. US regulators also guaranteed the value of money market funds after customers there looked set to run. Bank runs had happened routinely before the US set up the Federal Reserve System in 1913. The 2008 crisis refreshed that institutional memory.

The Basel Committee on Banking Supervision in 2010 and again in 2013 drafted rules requiring larger banks worldwide to hold more liquid assets, and US regulators posted a final rule on September 3, 2014. The most stringent US rules applied to banks with more than $250 billion in assets or more than $10 billion in foreign exposures, and a less stringent set applied to any bank with more than $50 billion in assets. Banks had to partially meet the new liquidity standards by January 1, 2015, and fully by various dates in 2018, depending on bank size and complexity. The rules set in motion a change in bank investing.

The rules required banks to hold a certain amount of high-quality liquid assets, or HQLA, and defined the types of securities that met that standard. Banks had to hold enough HQLA to cover a potential 30-day period when funding markets froze and depositors ran. Regulators wanted banks to be able to sell HQLA and meet depositors' and other lenders' demand for cash.

US Treasury and agency debt and mortgage-backed securities fell into the highest categories of HQLA, so it should come as no surprise that bank investing in those markets surged. From the end of 2013, when US banks likely first knew the outlines of pending liquidity rules, to the first implementation date in January 2015, absolute holdings in US Treasury and agency debt at large banks rose 63%, and holdings as a share of total bank assets rose 51%. Because Treasury debt especially is liquid, it seems reasonable banks would reach for that market first to meet initial deadlines. Absolute holdings in agency mortgage–backed securities rose 19% and as a share of total assets rose 10%. Banks continued to add these assets as full implementation continued. Between January 2015 and December 2018, absolute holdings in Treasury and agency debt rose another 18% and as a share of total assets another 6%. Absolute holdings of agency mortgage–backed securities rose another 32% and as a share of total assets another 19%. (See figure 16.1.)

Considerations other than meeting regulators' rules surely affected banks' mix of loans and securities—the relative value of different investments, changes in funding and capital, and so on—but regulation had given HQLA a new and special status. HQLA alone had the ability to meet regulators' requirements, giving them unique value to banks that other investors might not be able to realize. For regulators, HQLA had become collateral securing the most dangerous form of funding on a bank balance sheet (Gorton and Muir, 2015). Large banks would have to compete with one another to extract value from HQLA, and bank portfolios in general would compete with other investors by paying more for the unique regulatory value of the asset.

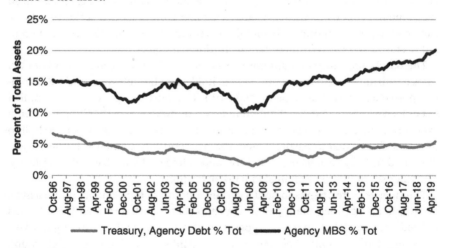

Figure 16.1 Liquidity rules have shaped bank appetite for liquid assets.
Note: Large domestically chartered commercial banks, non-seasonally adjusted.
Source: Federal Reserve Board (2019); author calculations.

Other Cases

Changes in policy and regulation have systemic effects on portfolios and asset values that perhaps become easy to detect because they offer a before and an after. But the other factors that add up to different configurations of competitive advantage drive asset values, too. Their effects may add up more slowly and be more diffuse.

Systemic differences in leverage available to equity investors and others sit behind the work on betting-against-beta. Investors with broad access to leverage can buy and leverage assets with low beta and relatively high rates of return for each unit of risk, whereas investors with limited or no access have to buy assets with high beta and less return for each unit of risk. This creates the flat capital markets line that Fama and French and others have pointed out as a persistent flaw in CAPM. It also creates opportunities for investors to bet against beta and capture persistent excess returns.

Among insurers, the lumping together of investments with AAA, AA, and A ratings by the National Association of Insurance Commissioners into one category requiring the lowest level of capital has led to disproportionate investment in A assets. Because A investments, all else being equal, will trade with the highest yields, they will offer the most net interest income and the highest return on equity. Insurers have clear incentives to tilt their portfolios toward A. In local CAPM, insurers operate in a market where A assets have value that other portfolios outside of insurance companies cannot realize.

In the late 1990s, when Fannie Mae and Freddie Mac operated freely as private companies with unique lines of credit from the US Treasury, they had powerful competitive advantages for investing in mortgage-backed securities. Their congressional charters, among other things, only allowed them to invest in agency mortgage–backed securities, creating a clear and narrow local market for their portfolios. Their regulator set capital requirements that allowed them to leverage mortgage-backed securities 40 times, much higher than most competing portfolios in the mortgage market. And Fannie Mae and Freddie Mac systematically created an extraordinarily flexible market in their own debt that provided funding at unusually low cost. When the US ran federal budget surpluses in the late 1990s and some investors thought supply of US Treasury debt might fall, Fannie Mae and Freddie Mac offered their own debt as possible substitutes and started funding at levels 20 basis points or more below other highly rated companies. The combination of focus, leverage, and funding made the Fannie Mae and Freddie Mac investment portfolios unusually profitable. The combined portfolios grew from around $100 million in 1990 to around $1.5 trillion by 2003, extracting returns beyond the reach of most competing portfolios.

On a daily basis, large investors or groups of investors respond not just to the changing risk and reward in available assets but also to systemic changes in their own ability to compete for and hold assets. The practical business of investing is an ongoing balance between competitive advantage and investment opportunity.

The Competitive Portfolio Response

Good investment portfolios continually try to raise return and reduce risk within a set of boundaries. Some boundaries are set by providers of portfolio equity and debt, some by accounting and tax rules, and some by regulation and politics. Others are set by organizational or operational factors where the portfolio often has more discretion such as size and scale, ability to hedge, quality of available information, and assets. Portfolios can sometimes move these boundaries by design and sometimes by opportunity. This is the stuff of competitive advantage in investing.

Good investment portfolios also have to continually monitor the impact of other platforms, some that compete in the same local market and others that compete in separate markets. Flows of capital into and out of these markets along with changes in likely fundamental risk and return determine which investments will best suit a portfolio's own targeted performance.

The ultimate benchmark of portfolio performance is not an abstract measure of excess return over a broad index of market returns. It is the concrete measure of excess return over the performance of portfolios bound by similar rules. It is the measure of investing that ultimately separates the winners from the rest of the pack.

References

Acharya, Viral V., and Philipp Schnabl. (2010). "Do Global Banks Spread Global Imbalances? Asset-Backed Commercial Paper during the Financial Crisis of 2007–09," *IMF Economic Review* 58, no. 1: 37–73.

Ackermann, C., R. McEnally, and D. Ravenscraft. (1999). "The Performance of Hedge Funds: Risk, Return and Incentives," *The Journal of Finance* 54, no. 3: 833–74.

Admati, Anat R., and Paul Pfleiderer. (1988). "Selling and Trading on Information in Financial Markets," *The American Economic Review* 78, no. 2: 96–103.

Agarwal, V., and Narayan Y. Naik. (2004). "Risks and Portfolio Decisions Involving Hedge Funds," *Review of Financial Studies* 17, no. 1: 63–98.

Agarwal, V., Naveen D. Daniel, and Narayan Y. Naik. (2005). "Role of Managerial Incentives, Flexibility, and Ability: Evidence from Performance and Money Flows in Hedge Funds," Working Paper, Georgia State University and London Business School.

Agarwal, V., and Narayan Y. Naik. (2005). "Hedge Funds," *Foundations and Trends in Finance* 1, no. 2: 103–69.

American Council of Life Insurers. (2018). *Life Insurers Fact Book 2018*. Washington, DC: Author.

Amihud, Yakov, Haim Mendelson, and Lasse Heje Pedersen. (2005). "Liquidity and Asset Prices," *Foundations and Trends in Finance* 1, no. 4: 269–364.

Anadu, Kenechukwu, Mathias Kruttli, Patrick McCabe, Emilio Osambela, and Chae Hee Shin. (2018). "The Shift from Active to Passive Investing: Potential Risks to Financial Stability?" Federal Reserve Bank of Boston, Working Paper RPA 18–04 (August 27).

Ang, A., and N.P.B. Bollen. (2010). "Locked Up by a Lockup: Valuing Liquidity as a Real Option," *Financial Management* 39, no. 3: 1069–95.

Ang, A., S. Gorovyy, and G. B. van Inwegen. (2011). "Hedge Fund Leverage," *Journal of Financial Economics* 102: 102–26.

Anson, M.J.P. (2001). "Hedge Fund Incentive Fees and the 'Free Option,'" *Journal of Alternative Investments* 4: 43–48.

Aragon, G. O. (2007). "Share Restrictions and Asset Pricing: Evidence from the Hedge Fund Industry," *Journal of Financial Economics* 83: 33–58.

Arrow, Kenneth J. (1963). "Uncertainty and the Welfare Economics of Medical Care," *American Economic Review* 53: 941–73.

Asness, Clifford S., Tobias J. Moscowitz, and Lasse H. Pedersen. (2013). "Value and Momentum Everywhere," *The Journal of Finance* 68, no. 3: 929–85.

Banz, Rolf W. (1981). "The Relationship between Return and Market Value of Common Stocks," *Journal of Financial Economics* 9, no. 1: 3–18.

Barber, B. M., Y. Lee, Y. Liu, and T. Odean. (2009). "Just How Much Do Individual Investors Lose by Trading?" *Review of Financial Studies* 22: 609–32.

Barber, Brad M., and Terrance Odean. (2000). "Trading Is Hazardous to Your Wealth: The Common Stock Investment Performance of Individual Investors," *The Journal of Finance* LV, no. 2: 773–806.

Barber, Brad M., and Terrance Odean. (2013). "The Behavior of Individual Investors," in *Handbook of the Economic of Finance 2B,* George M. Constantinides, Milton Harris, and Rene M. Stulz, eds. (Oxford, UK: Elsevier), 1533–70.

Basel Committee on Banking Supervision. (2010). "Basel III: International Framework for Liquidity Risk Measurement, Standards and Monitoring," http://www.bis.org/publ/bcbs188.htm.

Basu, Sanjay. (1977). "Investment Performance of Common Stocks in Relation to Their Price-to-Earnings Ratios: A Test of the Efficient Market Hypothesis," *The Journal of Finance* 12, no. 3: 129–56.

Beltran, Daniel O., Maxwell Kretchmer, Jaime Marquez, and Charles P. Thomas. (2012). "Foreign Holdings of US Treasuries and US Treasury Yields," Board of Governors of the Federal Reserve System, International Finance Discussion Papers, no. 1041.

Berk, Jonathan B., and Richard C. Green. (2004). "Mutual Fund Flows and Performance in Rational Markets, *Journal of Political Economy* 112, no. 6: 1269–95.

Bernanke, B. S. (2005). "The Global Savings Glut and the U.S. Current Account Deficit," Homer Jones Lecture (April 14), http://www.federalreserve.gov/boarddocs/speeches/2005/20050414/default.htm.

Bernanke, Ben S. (2012). "Monetary Policy since the Onset of the Crisis," Speech at the Federal Reserve Bank of Kansas City Economic Symposium, Jackson Hole, Wyoming (Aug. 31).

Bernanke, Ben S., Carol Bertaut, Laurie Pounder DeMarco, and Steven Kamin. (2011). "International Capital Flows and the Returns to Safe Assets in the United States, 2003–2007." International Finance Discussion Papers, no. 1014. https://www.federalreserve.gov/pubs/ifdp/2011/1014/ifdp1014.pdf

Bertaut, C., L. P. DeMarco, S. Kamin, and R. Tryon. (2011). "ABS Inflows to the United States and the Global Financial Crisis," International Finance Discussion Papers 1028, Board of Governors of the Federal Reserve System.

Bessembinder, Hendrik, Stacey Jacobsen, William Maxwell, and Kumar Venkataraman. (2018). "Capital Commitment and Illiquidity in Corporate Bonds," *The Journal of Finance* 73, no. 4: 1615–61.

Bhandari, Laxmi Chand. (1988). "Debt/Equity Ratio and Expected Common Stock Returns: Empirical Evidence," *The Journal of Finance* 43, no. 2: 507–28.

Black, Fischer. (1972). "Capital Market Equilibrium with Restricted Borrowing," *The Journal of Business* 45, no. 3: 444–55.

Black, Fischer. (1993). "Estimating Expected Return," *Financial Analysts Journal* (September–October): 36–38.

Black, Fischer, and Myron Scholes. (1973). "The Pricing of Options and Corporate Liabilities," *The Journal of Political Economy* 81, no. 3: 637–54.

Black, Fischer, Emanuel Derman, and William Toy. (1990). "A One-Factor Model of Interest Rates and Its Application to Treasury Bond Options," *Financial Analysts Journal* 46, no. 1: 33–39.

Black, Fischer, Michael C. Jensen, and Myron Scholes. (1972). "The Capital Asset Pricing Model: Some Empirical Tests," in *Studies in the Theory of Capital Markets*, Michael C. Jensen, ed. (New York: Praeger), 79–121.

Black, Fischer, and Robert Litterman. (1991). "Asset Allocation: Combining Investor Views with Market Equilibrium," *Journal of Fixed Income* (September): 7–18.

Blanchett, David M., and Philip U. Straehl. (2015). "No Portfolio is an Island," *Financial Analysts Journal* 71, no. 3: 15–33.

Bloomberg. (2017). "Bloomberg Barclays US Aggregate Fact Sheet," https://www .bbhub.io/indices/sites/2/2016/08/2017–02–08-Factsheet-US-Aggregate.pdf.

Blume, Marshall, and Irwin Friend. (1973), "A New Look at the Capital Asset Pricing Model," *The Journal of Finance* 28, no. 1: 19–33.

Bondarenko, O. (2004). "Market Price of Variance Risk and Performance of Hedge Funds," Working Paper, University of Illinois, Chicago.

Brown, Aaron, Michael Papaioannou, and Iva Petrova. (2010). "Macrofinancial Linkages of the Strategic Asset Allocation of Commodity-Based Sovereign Wealth Funds," IMF Working Paper WP/10/9.

Calcagno, Riccardo, Maela Giofré, and Maria Cesira Urzì-Brancati. (2017). "To Trust Is Good, but To Control Is Better: How Investors Discipline Financial Advisors' Activity," *Journal of Economic Behavior and Organization* 140: 287–316.

Cao, C., Y. Chen, B. Liang, and A. Lo. (2013). "Can Hedge Funds Time Market Liquidity?" *Journal of Financial Economics* 109, no. 2: 493–516.

Carhart, Mark M. (1997). "On Persistence in Mutual Fund Performance," *The Journal of Finance* 52, no. 1: 57–82.

Chambers, David, Elroy Dimson, and Antti Ilmanen. (2012). "The Norway Model," *The Journal of Portfolio Management* (Winter): 67–81.

Craig, Ben R., and Valeriya Dinger. (2011). "The Duration of Bank Retail Interest Rates," Federal Reserve Bank of Cleveland Working Paper 10–01R.

Cremers, K. J. Martijn, and Antti Petajisto. (2009). "How Active is Your Fund Manager? A New Measure That Predicts Performance," *Review of Financial Studies* 22, no. 9: 3329–65.

D'Amico, Stefania, and Thomas B. King. (2012). "Flow and Stock Effects of Large-Scale Asset Purchases: Evidence on the Importance of Local Supply," Finance and Economic Discussion Series 2012–44, Federal Reserve Board.

Damodaran, Aswath. "Annual Returns on Stock, T. Bonds and T. Bills: 1928–Current," pages.stern.nyu.edu/~adamodar/New_Home_Page/datafile/histretSP.html, accessed July 30, 2019.

DavisPolk. (2013). "US Basel III Final Rule: Visual Memorandum," July 8.

Diamond, Douglas W. (1984). "Financial Intermediation and Delegated Monitoring," *Review of Economic Studies* LI: 393–414.

Diamond, Douglas W. (1996), "Financial Intermediation as Delegated Monitoring: A Simple Example," *Federal Reserve Bank of Richmond Economic Quarterly* 82, no. 3: 51–66.

Diamond, Douglas W., and Philip H. Dybvig. (1983). "Bank Runs, Deposit Insurance, and Liquidity," *Journal of Political Economy* 91, no. 3: 401–19.

Douglas, George W. (1968). *Risk in the Equity Markets: An Empirical Appraisal of Market Efficiency* (Ann Arbor, MI: University Microfilms, Inc.).

Driscoll, John C., and Ruth A. Judson. (2013). "Sticky Deposit Rates," Federal Reserve Board Finance and Economics Discussion Series 2013–80.

Duffie, Darrell. (2012). "Market Making under the Proposed Volcker Rule," Rock Center for Corporate Governance at Stanford University Working Paper No. 106.

Durham, J. Benson. (2015). "Betting against Beta (and Gamma) Using Government Bonds," Federal Reserve Bank of New York Staff Report No. 708.

Ebrahimzadeh, Christine. (2018). "Dutch Disease: Wealth Managed Unwisely," Finance & Development, International Monetary Fund, https://www.imf.org/external/pubs/ft/fandd/basics/dutch.htm.

Elton, Edwin J., Martin J. Gruber, and Christopher R. Blake. (1995). "Fundamental Economic Variables, Expected Returns, and Bond Fund Performance," *The Journal of Finance* 50, no. 4: 1229–56.

Fama, Eugene F., and Kenneth R. French. (1992). "The Cross-Section of Expected Stock Returns," *The Journal of Finance* 47, no. 2: 427–65.

Fama, Eugene F., and Kenneth R. French. (1993). "Common Risk Factors in the Returns on Stocks and Bonds," *Journal of Financial Economics* 33, no. 1: 3–56.

Fama, Eugene F., and Kenneth R. French. (1996). "Multifactor Explanations of Asset Pricing Anomalies," *The Journal of Finance* 51, no. 1: 55–84.

Fama, Eugene F., and Kenneth R. French. (2004). "The Capital Asset Pricing Model: Theory and Evidence," *Journal of Economic Perspectives* 18, no. 3: 25–46.

Fama, Eugene F., and James D. MacBeth. (1973). "Risk, Return, and Equilibrium: Empirical Tests," *Journal of Political Economy* 81, no. 3: 607–36.

Federal Deposit Insurance Corporation. (2015). "Risk Management Manual of Examination Policies," Section 2.1, Capital, https://www.fdic.gov/regulations/safety/manual/section2-1.pdf.

Federal Insurance Office. (2014). "Annual Report on the Insurance Industry," US Department of the Treasury, (September).

Federal Insurance Office. (2018). "Annual Report on the Insurance Industry," US Department of the Treasury, (September).

Federal Reserve Bank of New York, Primary Dealers, Current Data, Quarterly Market Share Data of Primary Dealer Transactions, www.newyorkfed.org/markets/primarydealers.html.

Federal Reserve Bank of New York. Primary Dealer Statistics Historical Search, www.newyorkfed.org/markets/gsds/search.

Federal Reserve Board. (2013). "Federal Reserve Board Issues Final Rule Aligning Market Risk Capital Rule with Basel III," *press release (December 6).*

Federal Reserve Board. (2019). Financial Accounts of the United States, March, www.federalreserve.gov/releases/z1/current/default.htm, accessed June 6, 2019.

Feffer, S., and C. Kundro. (2003). "Understanding and Mitigating Operational Risk in Hedge Fund Investments," Working Paper, The Capital Markets Company Ltd.

Felice, Lou. (2002). "Comparison of the NAIC Life, P&C and Health RBC Formulas, memo, American Academy of Actuaries (Feb. 12).

Feng, Z., S. M. Price, and C. F. Sirmans. (2011). "An Overview of Equity Real Estate Investment Trusts (REITs): 1993–2009," *Journal of Real Estate Literature* 19, no. 2: 307–43.

Frazzini, Andrea, David Kabiller, and Lasse H. Pedersen. (2018). "Buffet's Alpha," *Financial Analysts Journal* 74, no. 4: 35–55.

Frazzini, Andrea, and Lasse H. Pedersen. (2012). "Embedded Leverage," AQR Working Paper, November 1.

Frazzini, Andrea, and Lasse H. Pedersen. (2014). "Betting against Beta," *Journal of Financial Economics* 111: 1–25.

Friedman, Milton, and L. J. Savage. (1948). "The Utility Analysis of Choices Involving Risk," *Journal of Political Economy* 56: 279–304.

Fung, W., and D. A. Hsieh. (2004). "Hedge Fund Benchmarks: A Risk Based Approach," *Financial Analysts Journal* 60, no. 5: 65–80.

Fung, W., D. Hsieh, N. Naik, and T. Ramadorai. (2005). "Lessons from a Decade of Hedge Fund Performance: Is the Party Over or the Beginning of a New Paradigm," Working Paper, Duke University and London Business School.

Gagnon, Joseph, Matthew Raskin, Julie Remache, and Brian Sack. (2010). "Large-Scale Asset Purchases by the Federal Reserve: Did They Work?" *Federal Reserve Bank of New York Staff Report* No. 441 (March).

Garcia, Diego, and Joel M. Vanden. (2009). "Information Acquisition and Mutual Funds," *Journal of Economic Theory* 144: 1965–95.

Garleanu, Nicolae B., and Lasse H. Pedersen. (2015). "Efficiently Inefficient Markets for Assets," NBER Working Paper Series, Working Paper 21563 (September 2015).

Gennaioli, Nicola, Andrei Shleifer, and Robert Vishny. (2015). "Money Doctors," *The Journal of Finance* 70, no. 1: 91–114.

Getmansky, Mila, Peter A. Lee, and Andrew W. Lo. (2015). "Hedge Funds: A Dynamic Industry in Transition," Working Paper, NBER (July 28).

Getmansky, M., A. W. Lo, and I. Makarov. (2004). "An Econometric Model of Serial Correlation and Illiquidity of Hedge Fund Returns," *Journal of Financial Economics* 74: 529–610.

Goetzmann, W. N., J. E. Ingersoll, and S. A. Ross. (2003). "High-Water Marks and Hedge Fund Management Contracts," *The Journal of Finance* 58, no. 4: 1685–1717.

Goldberg, Linda, Cindy E. Hull, and Sarah Stein. (2013). "Do Industrialized Countries Hold the Right Foreign Exchange Reserves?" *Federal Reserve Bank of New York Current Issues in Economics and Finance* 19, no. 1.

Gorton, Gary B., and Tyler Muir. (2015). "Mobile Collateral versus Immobile Collateral" (July 29), https://ssrn.com/abstract=2638886 or http://dx.doi.org/10.2139/ssrn.2638886.

Gorton, Gary, and George Pennacchi. (1990). "Financial Intermediaries and Liquidity Creation," *The Journal of Finance* 45, no. 1: 49–71.

Greenspan, Alan. (2005). "Testimony before the Committee on Banking, Housing and Urban Affairs," U.S. Senate (February 16), http://www.federalreserve.gov/boarddocs/hh/2005/february/testimony.htm.

Grinblatt, M., and M. Keloharju. (2000). "The Investment Behavior and Performance of Various Investor Types: A Study of Finland's Unique Data Set," *Journal of Financial Economics* 55: 43–67.

Grinold, Richard C., and Ronald N. Kahn. (1999). *Active Portfolio Management,* 2nd ed. (New York: McGraw-Hill).

Grossman, Sanford J., and Joseph E. Stiglitz. (1980). "On the Impossibility of Informationally Efficient Markets," *American Economic Review* 70: 393–408.

Grossman, Sanford J. (1981). "An Introduction to the Theory of Rational Expectations under Asymmetric Information," *Review of Economic Studies* 48: 541–59.

Gundikunst, Arthur, and Joseph McCarthy. (1992). "Determinants of Bond Mutual Fund Performance," *The Journal of Fixed Income* (June): 95–101.

Guvenen, Fatih, Sam Schulhofer-Wohl, Jae Song, and Motohiro Yogo. (2017). "Worker Betas: Five Facts about Systematic Earnings Risk," Federal Reserve Bank of Minneapolis, Staff Report 546.

Hanson, Samuel G., Andrei Schleifer, Jeremy C. Stein, and Robert W. Vishny. (2014). "Banks as Patient Fixed-Income Investors," *Journal of Financial Economics* 117: 449–69.

He, Guangliang, and Robert Litterman. (1999). "The Intuition behind Black-Litterman Model Portfolios," Goldman Sachs Investment Management Research (December).

Heath, David, Robert Jarrow, and Andrew Morton. (1990). "Bond Pricing and the Term Structure of Interest Rates: A Discrete Time Approximation," *Journal of Financial and Quantitative Analysis* 25, no. 4: 419–40.

Ibbotson, Roger G., Peng Chen, and Kevin X. Zhu. (2011). "The ABCs of Hedge Funds: Alphas, Betas and Costs," *Financial Analysts Journal* (January/February).

Idzorek, Thomas M. (2005). "A Step-by-Step Guide to the Black-Litterman Model: Incorporating User-Specified Confidence Levels," Ibbotson Associates.

International Monetary Fund. (2013). "Global Financial Stability Report," *Changes in bank funding patterns and financial stability risks.* Washington, DC: Author, pp. 105–48.

Jegadeesh, Narasimhan, and Sheridan Titman. (1993). "Returns to Buying Winners and Selling Losers: Implications for Stock Market Efficiency," *The Journal of Finance* 48, no. 1: 65–91.

Jensen, Michael C. (1968). "The Performance of Mutual Funds in the Period 1945–1964," *The Journal of Finance* 23, no. 2: 389–416.

Johnson, J. Walker, and Jean Male Baxley. (2004). "*Taxation of Property and Casualty Insurance Companies,*" Steptoe & Johnson, LLP.

Johnson, J. Walker, and Alexis MacIvor. (2012). "Taxation of Life Insurance Companies," Steptoe & Johnson, LLP.

Jurek, Jakub W., and Erik Stafford. (2011). "The Cost of Capital for Alternative Investments," Working Paper, Harvard Business School (September 8).

Jylhä, Petri. (2018). "Margin Requirements and the Security Market Line," *The Journal of Finance* 73: 1281–321.

Kahneman, Daniel, and Amos Tversky. (1979). "Prospect Theory: An Analysis of Decision under Risk," *Econometrica* 47, no. 2: 263–92.

KPMG. (2018). *Hedging as Amended by ASU 2017–12: Handbook,* https://frv.kpmg .us/content/dam/frv/en/pdfs/2018/hedging-handbook.pdf.

Kramer Levin Naftalis & Frankel. (2013). "Overview of Key Mutual Fund Regulations" (April 26).

Krishnamurthy, Arvind, and Annette Vissing-Jorgensen. (2007). "The Demand for Treasury Debt," Working Paper, Northwestern University.

Krishnamurthy, Arvind, and Annette Vissing-Jorgensen. (2011). "The Effects of Quantitative Easing on Interest Rates: Channels and Implications for Policy," *Brookings Papers on Economic Activity* (Fall): 215–65.

Kruttli, M., A. Patton, and T. Ramadorai. (2014). "The Impact of Hedge Funds on Asset Markets," Working Paper, Oxford University.

Kunzel, Peter, and Yinqiu Lu, Iva Petrova, and Jukka Pihlman. (2011). "Investment Objectives of Sovereign Wealth Funds—A Shifting Paradigm," IMF Working Paper WP/11/19.

Laws, Stephen. (2015). "Mortgage Finance, BDC and Specialty Finance Quarterly," Deutsche Bank (May).

Liang, B. (1999). "On the Performance of Hedge Funds," *Financial Analysts Journal* 55, no. 4: 72–85.

Lintner, John. (1965). "The Valuation of Risk Assets and the Selection of Risky Investments in Stock Portfolios and Capital Budgets," *Review of Economics and Statistics* 47, no. 1: 13–37.

Lintner, John. (1969). "The Aggregation of Investor's Diverse Judgments and Preferences in Perfectly Competitive Security Markets," *The Journal of Financial and Quantitative Analysis* 4, no. 4: 347–400.

Lo, A. (2001). "The Statistics of Sharpe Ratios," *Financial Analysts Journal* 58, no. 4: 36–52.

Loughran, Tim, and Jay R. Ritter. (1995). "The New Issues Puzzle," *The Journal of Finance* 50, no. 1: 23–51.

Malkiel, Burton G. (1973). *A Random Walk down Wall Street: The Time-Tested Strategy for Successful Investing* (New York: W. W. Norton & Company).

Markowitz, Harry. (1952). "Portfolio Selection," *The Journal of Finance* 7, no. 1: 77–91.

McCauley, Robert. (2018). "The 2008 Crisis: Transpacific or Transatlantic," *BIS Quarterly Review* (December): 39–58.

Merton, Robert C. (1973a). "An Intertemporal Capital Asset Pricing Model," *Econometrica* 41, no. 5: 867–87.

Merton, Robert C. (1973b). "Theory of Rational Option Pricing," *The Bell Journal of Economics and Management Science* 4, no. 1: 141–83.

Merton, Robert C. (2008). "A New Generation of Pension Fund Management" in *Innovations in Investment Management,* H. Gifford Fong (New York: Bloomberg Press), 1–18.

Mitchell, M., and T. Pulvino. (2001). "Characteristics of Risk in Risk Arbitrage," *The Journal of Finance* 56, no. 6: 2135–175.

Mitchell, Mark L., and Erik Stafford. (2000). "Managerial Decisions and Long-Term Stock Price Performance," *Journal of Business* 73, no. 3: 287–329.

Miller, Merton, and Myron Scholes (1972). "Rates of Return in Relation to Risk: A Reexamination of Some Recent Findings," in *Studies in the Theory of Capital Markets*, Michael C. Jensen, ed. (New York: Praeger), pp. 47–78.

National Association of Insurance Commissioners [NAIC]. (2017). U.S. Property and Casualty Insurance Industry 2017 First Half Results.

National Association of Insurance Commissioners [NAIC]. (2019). "NAIC Releases 2018 Market Share Data."

National Association of Insurance Commissioners [NAIC] and The Center for Insurance Policy Research. (2011). "Capital Markets Special Report: The Insurance Industry and Hedging with Derivative Instruments."

National Association of Real Estate Investment Trusts. (2019). NAREITWatch, August.

Nissim, Doron. (2010). "Analysis and Valuation of Insurance Companies," Columbia Business School, Center for Excellence in Accounting and Security Analysis.

Office of Thrift Supervision. (2001). "The OTS Net Portfolio Value Model," Department of the Treasury, http://www.ots.treas.gov/?p=NetPortfolioValueModel.

Pastor, Lubos, Robert F. Stambaugh, and Lucian A. Taylor. (2015). "Scale and Skill in Active Management," *Journal of Financial Economics* 116, no. 1: 23–45.

Petajisto, Antti. (2013). "Active Share and Mutual Fund Performance," *Financial Analysts Journal* 69, no. 4: 73–93.

Poterba, J. M. (2003). "Employer Stock and 401(k) Plans," *American Economic Review* 93: 398–404.

Prequin. (2018). "Sovereign Wealth Funds," Prequin Special Report (August).

Rosenberg, Barr, Kenneth Reid, and Ronald Lanstein. (1985). "Persuasive Evidence of Market Inefficiency," *Journal of Portfolio Management* Spring, no. 11: 9–17.

Ross, Stephen A. (2005). "Markets for Agents: Fund Management," in *The Legacy of Fischer Black,* Bruce N. Lehmann, eds. (New York: Oxford University Press).

Rothschild, Michael, and Joseph Stiglitz. (1976). "Equilibrium in Competitive Insurance Markets: An Essay on the Economics of Imperfect Information," *Quarterly Journal of Economics* 90, no. 4: 629–49.

Rudebusch, G. D., E. T. Swanson, and T. Wu. (2006). "The Bond Yield 'Conundrum' from a Macro- Finance Perspective," *Monetary and Economic Studies* 24, no. S1: 83–109.

Scholl, Brian, and Angela A. Hung. (2018). "The Retail Market for Investment Advice," Report to the US Securities and Exchange Commission from the Office of Investor Advocate and the RAND Corporation.

Sensoy, Berk A. (2009). "Performance Evaluation and Self-Designated Benchmark Indexes in the Mutual Fund Industry," *Journal of Financial Economics* 92: 25–39.

Sharpe, William F. (1964). "Capital Asset Prices: A Theory of Market Equilibrium under Conditions of Risk," *The Journal of Finance* 19, no. 3: 425–42.

Sheehan, Richard G. (2013). "Valuing Core Deposits," *Journal of Financial Services Research* 43: 197–220.

SIFMA. (2015). *SIFMA fact book 2015.* www.sifma.org.

SIFMA. (2018). *SIFMA fact book 2018.* www.sifma.org.

Sovereign Investor Institute, Sovereign Wealth Center, Fund Profiles, August 30, 2019, www.sovereignwealthcenter.com/fund-profiles.html.

Stattman, Dennis. (1980). "Book Values and Stock Returns," *The Chicago MBA: A Journal of Selected Papers* 4: 25–45.

Stein, Jeremy C. (2014). "Banks as Patient Investors," Speech at the American Economic Association/American Finance Association, Philadelphia, PA.

Sun, Lin, and Melvyn Teo. (2019). "Public Hedge Funds," *Journal of Financial Economics* 131, no. 1: 44–60.

Sushko, Vladyslav, and Grant Turner. (2018). "The Implications of Passive Investing for Securities Markets," *BIS Quarterly Review (March)*: 113–31.

Tobin, James. (1958). "Liquidity Preference as Behavior toward Risk," *Review of Economic Studies* 25, no. 2: 65–86.

Toevs, Alden L., and William C. Haney. (1986). "Measuring and Managing Interest Rate Risk: A Guide to Asset/Liability Models Used in Banks and Thrifts," in *Controlling Interest Rate Risk,* Robert B. Platt, ed. (New York: John Wiley & Sons), 256–351.

US Census Bureau, Wealth and Asset Ownership, 2015 Detailed Tables, www.census.gov/data/tables/2015/demo/wealth/wealth-asset-ownership.html.

US Treasury Office of Financial Research. *Asset Management and Financial Stability* (September 2013).

US Treasury, Treasury International Capital System, www.treasury.gov/resource-center/data-chart-center/tic/Pages/index.aspx, accessed August 2019.

Warnock, F. E., and V. C. Warnock. (2009). "International Capital Flows and U.S. Interest Rates," *Journal of International Money and Finance* 28, no. 6: 903–19.

WillisTowersWatson. (2018). "The World's Largest 500 Asset Managers," Looking Ahead Institute.

Wiltbank, Laurel J. (1989). "The Financial Theory of Pricing Property-Liability Insurance Contracts by Stephen P. D'Arcy, Neil A. Doherty," *Journal of Risk and Insurance* 56, no. 2: 366–68.

Yankov, Vladimir. (2012). "In Search of a Risk-Free Asset," Working Paper, Federal Reserve Bank of Boston.

Yin, Chengdong. (2016). "The Optimal Size of Hedge Funds: Conflict between Investors and Fund Managers," *The Journal of Finance* 121, no. 4: 1857–94.

Yu, Marc. (2013)."RBC U L8TR," Paper presented at Session 146 of the Society of Actuaries Annual Meeting, October 23.

About the Author

Steven Abrahams has covered US capital markets since 1991 and has advised investment teams at banks and insurers, mutual and hedge funds, and other portfolios worldwide. He started his career at Morgan Stanley, served as senior managing director in investment research at Bear Stearns, managing director and head of mortgage- and asset-backed research at Deutsche Bank, and currently is senior managing director and head of investment strategy at Amherst Pierpont Securities. He also served as a director of MTGE Investment Corp., a publicly traded REIT. He continues to write and speak extensively on markets and investing. He holds a BS from Northwestern University and a PhD from Columbia University, and he has taught as an adjunct professor of finance and economics at Columbia Business School. He lives with his family in New York.

Index

Page references in *italics* refer to figures and tables.